JOURNEYS OF PAUL

from Tarsus 'to the ends of the earth'

Fatih Cimok

A TURİZM YAYINLARI

FRONT COVER
A stretch of the Roman road Via Tauri leading
from Tarsus to the Cilician Gates. This was possibly a very
ancient route paved or repaired by Marcus Aurelius (161-80 CE).

BACK COVER
Detail from the long face of a sarcophagus very probably belonging
to a captain. First to second centuries CE. Sinop Museum. The inscription on
the short face of the casket in Greek (p 41) reads 'Cornelius Arrianus, lived 60 years'.

HALF-TITLE PAGE
View of the Akdağ from Anahşa Castle (medieval Rodendos/Butrentrum) near ancient Podandos (Pozantı).

SUBTITLE
"For so the Lord commanded us, 'I have made you a light to the Gentiles, that you may be
an instrument of salvation to the ends of the earth' " (Acts 13.47 quoted from Is 49.6; also Acts 1.8). The
expression is regarded as Paul's own way of referring to the boundaries of the earth. For the Romans, normally,
it referred to the north of Britain and the region of Iceland and/or Norway about which they had no definite idea.

EDITOR
Takeko Harada

PICTURES
Archives of A Turizm Yayınları

LAYOUT
Güzin Sancaklı

First printing 2004
Second printing 2007

ISBN 975-7199-96-6

PUBLISHERS
A Turizm Yayınları Ltd Şti
Şifa Hamamı Sokak 18/2
34122 Sultanahmet, İstanbul, Turkey
Tel: (0212) 516 24 97 Fax: (0212) 516 41 65
info@aturizm.com

Contents

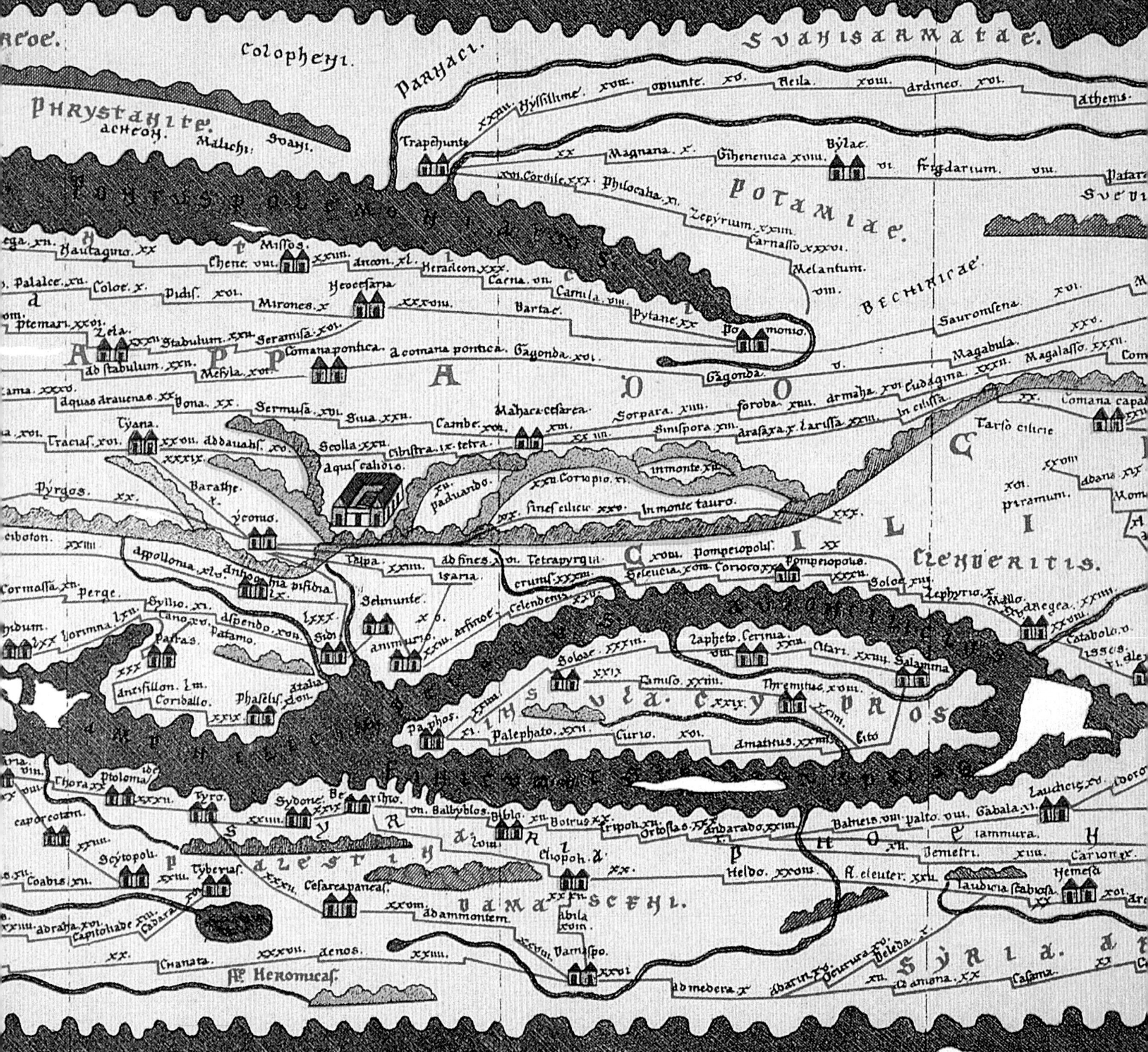

Colopheni
Parhaci
Svahisarmatae
Phrystanite
Trapezunte
Magnana
Frigdarium
Potamiae
Philocalia
Zepyrium
Carnasso
Melantum
Bechiricae
Sauromena
Missos
Nautagino
Chene
Ancon
Heracleon
Caena
Camila
Pytane
Bartae
Polemonio
Neocesaria
Mirones
Pidis
Coloe
Zela
Stabulum
Seramisa
Comana pontica
a comana pontica
Gagonda
ad stabulum
Mesyla
Magabula
Magalasso
Comana capadocie
Aquas drauenas
Sermusa
Siua
Cambe
Mahaca cesarea
Sorpara
Foroba
Armaha
Sinispora
Arasaxa
Larissa
Tyana
Scolla
Cibistra
Aquis calidis
Tarso cilicie
Adana
Piramum
Padiando
Coriopio
Inmonte
Fines cilicie
Inmonte tauro
Barathe
Pyrgos
Icomo
Apollonia
Antiochia pisidia
Perge
Syllio
Aspendo
Patara
Phaselis
Atalia
Sidi
Selinunte
Isaria
Anemurio
Arsinoe
Celendenis
Tetrapyrgia
Ad fines
Pompeiopolis
Seleucia
Corico
Soloe
Zephyrio
Mallo
Clenderitis
Catabolo
Issos
Lapetho
Ceriniа
Citari
Salamina
Soloe
Tamiso
Tremitus
Insula Cypros
Paphos
Palephato
Curio
Amathus
Cito
Ptolomaide
Tyro
Sydone
Berytho
Balbyblos
Biblo
Botrus
Tripoli
Orthosias
Antarado
Balneis
Palto
Gabala
Laudicia
Scytopoli
Tyberias
Capitoliade
Gadara
Coabis
Cesareapaneas
Ad ammontem
Abila
Damasco
Aenos
Chanata
Heromicas
Damasceni
Palestina
Syria
Laudicia scabiosa
Hemesa
Casama

Preface

This book is intended primarily as a companion for Paul's complete journeys, but mainly for the three missionary journeys and his voyage to Rome, all mentioned in the *Acts of the Apostles*. It has been prepared by a former tour guide with a traveller of Pauline places in mind. Almost all of the countries, routes and sites mentioned in the book have been visited by its author and editor, often more than once. Effort has been spent to keep the information which is not directly related to Paul's journeys and to the first century CE to a minimum. Plenty of interesting sites which are not yet within the easy reach of common travellers, in other words, within the paths of commercial tour itineraries, have been left out. The reader will notice that special effort has been spent to inform him about the routes Paul may have taken during his journeys, what the possibilities were of tracks and what Paul would have seen in the cities where he proclaimed the Gospel, with emphasis on Ephesus where he stayed longest. In addition, Ephesus is the only site whose ruins can give us the atmosphere of a Pauline metropolis.

From Paul's letters only the sections which make up the compressed text of Acts and thus help us to understand the social world of the time and Paul's journeys better are included. Biblical scholarship differs on points such as which of the letters bearing Paul's authorship were really written by him, and where and when they were recorded. Such discussions are beyond the scope of this volume and qualifications of its author.

In spelling ancient names of places and persons, their most popular English forms among non-academics have been used. The dates are often approximate. The repetitive appearance of c (circa) or 'about' is avoided. The Turkish equivalent of names and the reign of rulers are usually mentioned in parentheses when it is thought this will help to understand the text better. The dates of rulers, as in Claudius (41-54), indicate their reigns. All biblical quotations are from the New American Bible, 1987 edition, Nashville, USA. The dates which are not marked as BCE (BC) or Before the Common Era, are Common Era, CE (AD). When there is no danger of confusion the suffix BCE or BC is omitted

All of the pictures in this volume are from the archives of the publishers, almost all of them taken by the author himself.

(opposite) A section of the eastern Mediterranean, central Anatolia, Cyprus and the Holy Land from the Peutinger Map (*Tabula Peutingeriana*). The map is thought to have been a twelfth-century copy of fifth-century original which may have been based on an earlier map.

Wall painting from the Grotto of St Paul at the skirt of Mount Coressus (Bülbül Dağı). Sixth century. Ephesus. The apostle is dressed in a long-sleeved blue-white tunic with a vertical decorative stripe (*clavus*). Over this a himation is worn. He is bearded and shown with little hair. He is shown seated holding an open book of his letters probably with his left hand. His other hand is raised in a gesture of address. Courtesy of Österreichisches Archäologisches Institut.

Approximate chronology

Conversion on the Damascus road	34
Sojourn in Arabia	34-36
First visit to Jerusalem	36
Sojourn in Syria and Cilicia	36-46
Journey to Antioch	46
Second visit to Jerusalem	46/47
First journey	46/47-48
Third visit to Jerusalem (Jerusalem Council)	49
Second journey	49/50-52
Third journey	53/54-57
Imprisonment at Caesarea	57-59
Journey to Rome	59/60
Martyrdom	62-64

Introduction

Antioch on Orontes, Ephesus, and Corinth, cities second in wealth and importance in the Roman Empire only to Alexandria in Egypt and to Rome, are inseparably linked with the early history of Christianity. According to the information supplied by Acts it was in Antioch that the word 'Christians' was first used to refer to the adherents to the new religion. Yet it was not only in these great cities that Christianity found adherents, for it gathered them also in far distant towns and communities of Anatolia, Macedonia and Greece. From the Levant through the uplands of the Taurus and to the well-settled valleys of western Anatolia, cities to the other side of the Aegean, to all these places, on foot or riding or by slow moving ships, Paul, the tireless apostle, carried the Gospel. At each place he gathered into fellowships of churches men and women, Jews and Gentiles, rich and poor, who had accepted the message and he nurtured the faithful, both by his presence and his letters. Although born as a movement within Judaism, it was in Anatolia and the immediate lands on the other side of the Aegean that the Gospel first took root, largely as a result of Paul's missionary work in about the middle of the first century. It was in these countries that Christianity developed away from its origins in Palestine to become a religion of the Greco-Roman world, and ultimately of the present.

Paul's journeys through Anatolia, Macedonia and Greece are recorded in the second and longer part of the *Acts of the Apostles*, written in Greek by the evangelist Luke, author of the Third Gospel perhaps a few decades after the martyrdom of Paul. A sequel to his Gospel, Acts continues Luke's history of Christian origins and tells us the story of the early church and how it spread from Jews to Gentiles, largely through the efforts of Paul. In regard to the subject matter of this book the absolute chronology of these journeys and their length are circumstantial.

The works of various Greek, Roman and Jewish authors and other contemporary sources, as well as discoveries in archaeology, help to shed light on this period and on the world in which Paul travelled. Paul's journeys fall into the history of the Greco-Roman world when the spark of the Hellenistic period had come to an end. The Roman overtake of Macedonia, Greece, Anatolia and the eastern Mediterranean was followed by the economic collapse of these countries because of the exploitation of Roman tax farmers

A humped ox (Indian) and a cross. Decoration on a door jamb after which the first- or second-century-CE Roman monument near the Magnesian gate of Ephesus was named the 'tomb of St Luke,' author of the Third Gospel and the *Acts of the Apostles*. The original ox relief, symbol of Luke, may have been the cause of the choice of this ruin as his grave; the cross was added later, when the building was turned into a church, perhaps around the sixth century. A much smaller cross was also chiselled above the animal's hump.

(Mt 11.19 and others) and the harshness of Roman laws of debt. In these countries the first century BCE is marked by other disasters brought by the Mithradatic wars, the feud between Pompey and Julius Caesar, the wars between the latter's murderers Brutus and Cassius and his avengers Octavian (later Augustus) and Mark Antony, and finally between the avengers themselves. Big earthquakes may be added to these conflicts. Still, beginning with Julius Caesar the economic conditions of the Roman provinces saw a relative rehabilitation which was best reflected in the architecture of big cities. Thus Paul could see what had been left from the Hellenistic age and what was built at the time of the early Roman rulers: Caesar, Augustus, Tiberius, Claudius and Nero, and by Herod the Great in the East.

Paul's letters do not give any hint about the routes that he followed during his journeys. Apart from Acts 17.1 where two stations on the Via Egnatia, and 28:15 two more on the Via Appia are mentioned we are not informed about the roads the apostle travelled. At some sites that Paul should have visited there has been little or no excavation, and in towns and cities that have been continuously inhabited there is sometimes virtually nothing to be seen, as the remains of earlier ages have either disappeared or lie beneath the existing structures.

Nevertheless, in one form or another, be it a stretch of Roman road and a milestone, or the remains of a synagogue, a bridge still in use after some two millennia, or a dedication to Artemis or Hermes, such evidence can help us to understand something of the Greco-Roman world in which Paul travelled and make so-called educated guesses about Paul's routes. Ultimately Anatolia, Macedonia and Greece became the most Christianized region in the Roman Empire and it was at the middle point of these countries, on the Bosphorus, at Byzantium that the victory of Paul's missions was officially acknowledged by Constantine the Great, who would found his new and Christian capital as New Rome and dedicate it in 330.

PAUL THE APOSTLE

Fragments of a two-leaf bronze military *diploma* (discharge certificate) from Jebel Ires (Laertes) in Pamphylia. Alanya Museum. From the inscription in Latin on both its sides we learn that it belonged to Galba from Cyrrhus (Nebi Uri) near Turkish-Syrian border. He joined the Roman army in Syria in 113 CE and when

he was discharged in 138 after 25 years he was serving in Lycia-Pamphylia. Thus he received the right of Roman citizenship and his marriage to a Pamphylian woman was recognized by Roman law. He had two sons. Originally, a wire which went through the three diagonally-placed holes held the two leaves together.

Paul is thought to have been born in the Cilician city of Tarsus about the same time, perhaps a few years after Jesus was born. His family was Jewish and from them he inherited Roman citizenship. Paul was privileged to have been born a Roman citizen at a time when it was not yet a universal right for people in the Empire. Initially confined to freeborn natives of Rome itself, as Roman control was extended throughout Italy and then to the lands bordering the Mediterranean and beyond, certain individuals and communities were given this right.

At the time of Paul's ancestors, one way of attaining Roman citizenship was by serving in the Roman army (auxiliary forces recruited from foreigners). When he was discharged a veteran was awarded a diploma of Roman citizenship for himself, his wife and children. The eastern Roman legions were mostly made up of foreigners recruited in this manner. A Roman citizen's responsibilities included the performance of military service. However, because of the sabbath and the Mosaic food prescriptions, and the imperial cult's being a common ritual of the whole Roman army, this profession, although the existence of Jewish mercenaries is known, would not have been normally possible for a Jew. According to Josephus the Jews were given some privileges by the Romans as early as the time of Julius Caesar and these privileges were confirmed by subsequent Roman rulers, along with the right to observe their own rites after they were released from military service.

The second way by which Roman citizenship could be gained was manumission. It is known that during the two centuries preceding Paul's time, thousands of people were deported from the Levant to Rome and made slaves. In time some of these were able to distinguish themselves by their skill and profession and were either manumitted by their masters or they bought their freedom and thus were given Roman citizenship. It has been speculated that a remote ancestor of Paul, after obtaining his citizenship in this manner, may have returned to his native city Tarsus. It is also known that early Roman rulers like Pompey, Caesar, Mark Antony or Augustus gave Roman citizenship to the elite of some cities. It has been claimed that Tarsus may have been one of these with Paul's parents included among those who were granted this right. Whatever the cause for gaining Roman citizenship in Paul's time, it was not yet frequently encountered in the eastern provinces of the Empire.

The most important privilege that Roman citizenship conferred on a subject was that he enjoyed legal protection and could not be scourged, although surviving evidence shows that Roman governors could disregard such restrictions, and had the right of appeal to a higher authority, such as to the emperor in person, hence Paul's journey to Rome to appeal to Nero. Even if they were condemned to death, Roman citizens could not be crucified. Pliny the Younger, who was born about the time that Paul journeyed to Rome, writing to Trajan from perhaps Amasia (Amasya) in Pontus says that he ordered the Christians to be executed but those 'who are Roman citizens I have entered them on the list of persons to be sent to Rome for trial' and thus shows that even when they did not claim their right for trial by the emperor, a Roman governor was hesitant to punish Roman citizens. We are informed by the inscription at the Temple of Augustus in Ankara that according to the last census (14 CE) this right was possessed by 4,937,000, perhaps about one out of ten people in the whole Roman Empire. In 212 CE Caracalla extending it to almost all the free men in the Empire — probably including the Jews who were free — made the privileges of being a Roman citizen meaningless.

According to two Roman laws dating from 4 CE and 9 CE, children born as Roman citizens were registered at the record office. It was possible to obtain a copy of the birth certificate — perhaps in papyrus or parchment — for identification purposes. The certificate contained the child's sex and name, date of birth, birthplace and names of his parents, etc and declared that he was a Roman citizen. However, if Paul was born before the above dates it would not be possible for him to have possessed such a certificate. The fact that the apostle mentions and makes use of his Roman citizenship rarely has led to speculation such as that he may have regarded it as a symbol of Roman rule, a privilege provided by a power which he challenged and which would soon be replaced by that of the one he proclaimed. Thus for him his Roman citizenship came after his status as a Christian, and a Jew. Yet to have been 'born' as a Roman citizen was still a matter of pride and at the time of Claudius it seems that some government officials began giving this right for bribes as admitted by the Cohort commander Claudius Lysias, whose *praenomen* is same as the ruling emperor, to Paul in Acts 22.28: 'I acquired this citizenship for a large sum of money'.

A Roman citizen carried a three-fold name: a given personal name or first name (*praenomen*), a family name (*nomen*), which was that of the clan or gens to which he belonged, and in addition, usually, a second individual or surname (*cognomen*): thus Gaius Julius Caesar. A new Roman citizen would

Nomads in tents of black goat-hair cloth, or *cilicium* in Smooth Cilicia.

(opposite) Inscription from the necropolis of Rhosus (Arsus). Archaeological Museum. Antakya. The inscription (139 x 58 cm) in Greek is a collection of letters written by Octavian (later Augustus) to Rhosus between 42-30 BCE. In the oldest letter he grants Roman citizenship to his naval commander Seleucus who is already a citizen of Rhosus, his parents, children, wife, and descendants, along with a series of exemptions ranging from taxation to military service for his naval aid to Rome. The inscribed marble piece may have been a leaf of the door of Seleucus' tomb. The wars referred to were probably fought along the coasts of Italy or Sicily after the battle of Philippi (42 BCE). The inscription is an example of double-citizenship which Paul is claimed to have possessed.

keep his own name as the *cognomen* and take the forename (*praenomen*) and name (*nomen*) of his owner who granted his freedom, added to his own name at the end; such that following their manumission Theopompus of Cnidus, who was granted Roman citizenship by Caesar, would be known as Gaius Julius Theopompus, or Celsus Polemaenus of Ephesus by Tiberius, as Tiberius Julius Celsus Polemaenus. Although after the manumission the patron would, legally, lose his power over his slave, the attachment of his *praenomen* and *nomen* to the slave's name symbolized his former command. Thus, Paul's name may have lingered in the family from the time of his ancestor who was first granted Roman citizenship.

Apart from this there are several theories about why the apostle chose the name by which he is known today. Paul's *cognomen* in Latin (paulus) means the 'little' or 'short' one and it has been suggested that the word might also have been an allusion to his size. It has been speculated that it may have been chosen because of its similarity to Saul in Hebrew, his unofficial name by which he was called in the family and Jewish community. This was the name of the first king of Jews, traditionally, about a millennium earlier. By the time of the early Empire era, when Paul was born, the use of two names, a Gentile name along with a Jewish name, seems to have been acceptable, at any rate in the NT, thus Joseph/ Barsabbas, John/Mark, Symeon/Niger, etc. The apostle must have had a second name which is not mentioned. The use of a single name was a common Greek tradition and this is the reason why the NT lacks the complete names of the persons it mentions. Whatever the reason for choosing it, Paul was a rare name even among Gentiles. Paul is mentioned in Acts for the first time after the events in Cyprus. It has also been suggested that Luke may have decided to bring forward this name of the apostle after his first Gentile convert known by name, Sergius Paulus, in Cyprus. If Paul's trial at the court in Rome had been recounted in Acts we would have learned the apostle's full name.

Acts and his letters make it clear that Paul worked to support himself during his missionary journeys. He was born in a land where and at a time when boys usually learned and carried on their fathers' occupation. Paul's profession was common trade and practiced everywhere in the Middle East and Paul may even have learned it elsewhere than his hometown. The nature of his work is clearly stated as tentmaking in Acts 18.3 when he stayed with Priscilla and Aquila.

It has been speculated that Paul's family was running some sort of tentmaking establishment because if Paul were just a common worker he would not find working with his hands worthy of remarking. Although working with one's hands — to support themselves as they taught — was a principal of Pharisees in the Greco-Roman world of the first century CE manual labour was not something worth mentioning, and one could normally make enough money just for sustenance by Paul's profession. Literally *skenopoios,* the Greek word used for Paul's profession, means tentmaking. The profession would require looms and material for weaving which would not have been convenient to carry for a person like Paul who was usually on the move. It is thus commented that in the case of Paul the word may mean just tent-manufacture, comprising all kinds of leatherwork, where the material was supplied by the client and thus requiring no more than a set of awls on Paul's part. It has been suggested that Paul's family may have made their money equipping the Roman legions, who used large tents, eight men sharing one, made of leather panels sewn together, in the shape of a camping tent. Scholars have calculated that a tent of this type required 70 goatskins which would make the number of goats required for a single legion some 50,000 and it has been suggested that Paul's unknown ancestor may have been granted Roman citizenship for his cooperation in providing Roman legions with such tents. These were, however, not the goat-hair tents that are still being produced in Cilicia for nomads. Such tents are made of the rough material manufactured from goat's hair, which in the past was known as *cilicium* ('çul') and took its name from the region. Tentmaking might well have embraced not only the manufacture and the repair of large military tents, but also a range of related leather and woven goods. Since there were many Roman camps in Syria tentmaking was perhaps a profitable profession, considering the flourishing animal husbandry in the region since early antiquity. Apart from military tents, there would have been considerable demand for awnings, canopies, rope and even shoes from vendors at market places and elsewhere. In theatres rich people were seated under retractable awnings which were sometimes woven from valuable material. There must have been a big demand for them during festivals held in cities like Tarsus, Antioch on Orontes, Ephesus or Corinth.

St Paul. Mosaic. 1315-21. Kariye Museum (former Church of Saint-Saviour-in Chora). İstanbul.

In his address to the elders of Ephesus at Miletus the apostle reminds them of his work, saying 'these very hands have served my needs and my companions' (Acts 20.34); also when he says 'we toil, working with our hands' (1 Cor 4.12) or 'nor did we eat food received free from anyone. On the contrary in toil and drudgery, night and day we worked so as not to burden any of you' (2 Thes 3.8). In fact, at the time, there was nothing unusual for a preacher (a sophist or an orator) in accepting help from the community or individual patrons. Paul seems to have been at pains to inform his readers that he should not be confused with one of these. In addition to the hospitality and gifts he seems to have received from Christian communities for which he expresses his gratitude, he relied on his own resources, a fact which is often hinted at in his letters and clearly expressed in the one addressed to the Philippians: 'for I have learned, in whatever situation I find myself, to be self-sufficient...Still, it was kind of you to share in my distress' (4.11,14); 'For even when I was at Thessalonica you sent me something for my needs' (4.16), and in other cases. We learn from the later Christian tradition that hospitality to travellers was limited to a few days, and if they stayed longer they should contribute to their support by working, the real prophets excepted. Paul's profession also helped him to mix with the people of the places, such as Antioch on Orontes, Corinth and Ephesus, where he stayed long and shared the daily life of common people. It is generally thought that Christianity

Basalt altar from Suweida, Syria. First century CE. İstanbul Archaeological Museums. It is decorated with bulls' figures

and votive inscriptions in Aramaic script. On the top it carries two shallow and circular indentations to place offerings.

did not become a world religion by preaching to crowds in agoras but by patient personal conversations with individuals or small groups in private meetings.

Neither Acts nor his letters give information about Paul's ancestors or parents. Family relations in Jerusalem, where he is said to have had a married sister and a nephew, are mentioned in Acts 23.16. From Acts we learn that he spent his early years in Jerusalem studying with Gamaliel, the foremost Pharisee teacher of the time. His education would have normally begun around the age of five or six and lasted until about eighteen. Pharisees (Aramaic 'separated ones') were a sect which first appeared in the 160s BCE, the Maccabean era. Its members thought that they alone could interpret the Torah (first five books of the OT) correctly and felt their responsibility to teach other Jews the correct way of living. They observed strict ritual purity and adherence to the law of Moses. They also believed in resurrection and rewards and punishments of the future. The difficulty of leading a Pharisaic life in the Gentile surroundings of Tarsus has caught the attention of scholars and it has been commented that Paul's parents may have adhered to the sect after the birth of Paul in one of their pilgrimages to Jerusalem, a suggestion also compatible with Paul's Tarsian citizenship. The 'son' in Acts 23.6 is interpreted by some as in 'a pupil of Pharisees', not an actual son. Although the number of Jews living in the Roman Empire at this time is not known, more than one-third of them are thought to have been living in Judea, and Jerusalem was the centre of Hebrew learning and education. If Paul spoke Hebrew and knew the Torah in this language this would, normally, have been the result of his synagogue education in Jerusalem. In Acts 21.37-40 Luke says that after talking to the Cohort commander in Greek, Paul switched into *Hebrais dialektos* when he addressed the Jews. It is, however, not clear if Luke means Hebrew or Aramaic. The latter was the spoken language of most of the Jews in Judea. This was a tongue related to Hebrew and widely used in Palestine and the rest of the Near East. It was almost impossible to come across a Jew who knew Hebrew but no Aramaic. For one who could speak the language travelling in Arabia would have been easy. There is no information as to whether Paul knew Latin. Owing to his surroundings in Tarsus and/or Jerusalem he may have been familiar with the language.

The diaspora Jews and some other Jews in Jerusalem could speak Greek. In Acts they are referred to as the 'Hellenists', Greek-speaking Jews. These used the Septuagint (Torah in Greek). Paul could speak Greek fluently (Acts

21.37). It is impossible to know how much of his learning in Greek comes from Jerusalem and how much from Tarsus or from where he was until the first time he appears in Acts 7.58 as 'a young man', a term which was normally used for a single man perhaps below the age of thirty. Jerusalem had been a Hellenistic city since the 160s BCE, the time of Antiochus IV, Epiphanes and the Jews of Paul's time were more open to the influence of Greco-Roman culture than they had been in the past. Apart from this, Paul may have made use of the opportunities that his hometown offered both for Jewish and Greco-Roman education. Paul's letters show that he was well-educated in the scriptures, and familiar with Greco-Roman culture.

There is no information about the life of the apostle after he began studying in Jerusalem until he appears as a zealous persecutor of Christians and witness to the death of Stephen, the first Christian martyr around the year 33. It is not known if Paul returned to Tarsus or married as any Jewish youth would normally have done at about the age of twenty, after he finished his studies. From his words 'Indeed, I wish everyone to be as I am...Now, to the unmarried and to the widows, I say: it is a good thing for them to remain as they are, as I do' in 1 Cor 7.7-8 it is assumed that he was not married at the time of writing this letter. He may have been celibate throughout his life. The speculation that his words 'If the unbeliever separates, however, let him separate' (1 Cor 7.15) may refer to the fact that he was married, and upon his return to Tarsus as a Christian (Acts 9.30) his wife may have deserted him is, generally, not accepted by scholars.

Relief of St Stephen from the former Church of the Holy Cross on the island of Ahtamar in Lake Van. 915-21 CE. The inscription in Armenian identifies him as the first (*proto*) martyr.

The Greco-Roman world and period in which Paul lived gave much importance to physical appearance and the lack of information about the physique of Paul in ancient literature has caught the attention of many scholars. The only available early information about the apostle's appearance comes from the apocryphal *Acts of Paul,* thought to have been recorded in the late second century. Here, Onesiphorus, a man of Iconium (Konya), who wants to receive Paul in his house, with his wife and two children, waits on the 'king's highway' leading to Lystra, for 'a man of little stature, thin-haired upon the head, crooked in the legs, of good state of body, with eyebrows joining, and nose somewhat hooked, full of grace: for sometimes he appeared like a man, and sometimes he had the face of an angel', his description by Titus whom Paul had sent before him to the city to announce his arrival. With the prevailing values of Paul's time these adjectives describe a healthy, agile and an impressive figure, if not handsome. Also, the fact that this is not a flattering description is regarded by some as reflecting Paul's actual physique.

Some scholars believe that it is not by accident that this description avoided Paul's eyes which at the time were regarded among the parts of body that revealed one's character. Paul's own words in Gal 4.12-20 show that he suffered a kind of repulsive disease so obvious that he was surprised when he was received by the natives of Galatia. The latter however, may culturally have paid less attention to such deformities because they believed that the gods could visit them in many forms.

St Paul. Detail from the Dormition. Nineteenth-century icon. Sinop Museum.

The literal meaning of the word used in Greek for Paul's baldness refers to absence of hair by 'plucking or shaving', to his shaven head, in accordance with his vow (Acts 18.18). The apostle himself seems to have been conscious of his insignificant physical looks because he admits that this could be used against him by his enemies so that in 2 Cor10.10 he says it is believed in Corinth that his 'bodily presence is weak, and his speech contemptible'. It is not known how much of Paul's weak physique was the result of the persecutions he suffered at the hands of the Jews or Romans although in Gal 6.17 he admits that he bears marks of Jesus on his body, unless he used the expression in a metaphorical sense. Paul also admits that he is 'untrained in speaking' (2 Cor 11.6) something which means that he lacked the eloquence of a sophist or preacher, something accorded to him by Luke. According to Greco-Roman values such a defect was a normal result of a weak physique.

The early information about Paul's physique was supplemented by later traditions and in time the 'short dark hair, domed brow and black, pointed beard' became the distinct features of his physiognomy in Byzantine art. Motioning 'with his hands' may have been not only a characteristic gesture of Paul but of his time. The details of this gesture are not known. In Greco-Roman art, figures in address are usually shown extending the thumb, sometime together with the second finger, toward the listeners. The gesture is first mentioned when he talks at the synagogue at Pisidian Antioch in Acts 13.16 and repeated a few times.

Paul admits that he did not know any of the apostles, and Peter with whom he stayed for fifteen days seems to have been the only one he met (Gal 1.18). His subsequent words show that he also regarded 'James the brother[1]

[1] In Semitic usage the term is also used for nephews or cousins; a fact which resulted in speculations about the relationship of James to Jesus.

of the Lord' an apostle. Thus Paul accepts the apostolate of the Twelve, James and himself. Except for two cases (14.4 and14) where it is used to mean 'envoy' Acts does not use the term apostle for Paul. For Luke apostleship came from being companion in Jesus' ministry and witnessing his resurrection. Paul's letters show that the title 'apostle' carried great weight for him. In addition to what he says in Rom 1.1 and 1 Cor 15.8-10, writing to the Galatians (1.1) he refers to himself as 'an apostle not from human beings nor through a human being but through Jesus Christ and God the Father who raised him from the dead' and in 1 Cor 9.2 he says 'Although I may not be an apostle for the other, certainly I am for you, for you are the seal of my apostleship in the Lord'. Paul believed and claimed that his status came from God, his witnessing of the risen Lord and the commission given to him, and having God as his teacher his apostleship was higher than that of the Twelve. In the Christian church it was, however, not Paul's own claim but his missions which he repeatedly carried out with endless vigour in all dangers of the time to the places where the Gospel had not yet been heard and the persecutions he suffered which would move him to apostleship. In another tradition, by the sixth century Paul replaces Matthias, who had taken the place of the traitor Judas Iscariot after the latter's death (Acts 1.26) among the Twelve or is regarded as the thirteenth apostle. Byzantine iconography usually depicts the apostle looking to his right, with the book of his letters in his left hand, his other hand in a gesture of address, or blessing, garbed in a dark green or dark blue tunic (chiton) on which he wears a dark red mantle (himation).

St Paul Vision Patriarchal Abbey near Damascus. To the right is the hill of Kaukab where, according to a tradition from the time of the Crusaders, Paul's conversion took place.

As is well known, Paul was converted to Christianity after a vision of the risen Christ appeared to this 'man from Tarsus named Saul' on the Damascus road, generally thought to have taken place in about 34 or close to it. At this time Damascus had a large Jewish community to which according to Acts 9.1 Saul carried letters from the high priest in Jerusalem with orders to persecute the 'disciples of the Lord' who had fled to the city perhaps after the martyrdom of Stephen. Blinded, he was led to Damascus and there, after three days of fasting and praying, Paul recovered his sight, was filled with the Holy Spirit and then baptized.

There have been innumerable attempts by theologians and others to understand and explain precisely what happened at this turning point in Paul's life. Paul claimed to have received his Gospel 'through a revelation of Jesus Christ' (Gal 1.12); this in turn led to his proclamation of salvation

Roman triple gate of the Sun (Bab Sharqi, 'gate of east') of 'the street which is called straight', or Darb al-Mustaqim ('straight street'), the *decumanus maximus* of Roman Damascus where Paul is said to have stayed (Acts 9.11). Turn of the third century CE.

It maintains its original form of a triple entrance with the one at the centre reserved for wheeled traffic. A house traditionally identified as that of Judas is located at the western end of the street.

through the reconciling grace of God; thus the death of Christ for the atonement of sins was God's reconciling the world to himself through Christ.

In whichever way Paul's vision and conversion are understood, it is clear that, like the prophets of the OT, he saw himself as chosen by God, a witness of resurrected Jesus for a specific task, namely, to be an apostle, a messenger of the church to Gentiles. For him the Christian message that Christ died to atone for the sins of man and for the salvation of man, was resurrected and ascended to heaven, was both the fullfilment of Jewish Messianic hopes and the basis for a united humanity and salvation by faith that were the central theme of his theology.

Damascus was an ancient and prosperous city situated in Syria, some 250 km from Jerusalem. The Bronze Age archives of the mid-third millennium BCE from Mari and Ebla refer to the city as Dimashqa and Dimaski, respectively. From the OT we learn that Damascus was the most important Aramaic kingdom in the region and the early relations between the city and the United Monarchy and later the divided monarchies of Israel and Judah were not friendly. Still in 1 Kgs 20.34 Ben-Hadad addressing King Ahab of Israel says 'I will restore the cities which my father took from your father, and you may make yourself bazaars in Damascus as my father did in Samaria'. Thus there was perhaps a Jewish minority in the city as early as the ninth century BCE. During the following era both Syria and Judea were under Assyrian, Babylonian and Persian rules successively. After Alexander's death when the city became a part of the Seleucid Kingdom along with the Greek language and culture the institutions of a *polis* were introduced. In accordance with the Seleucid policy the minorities in the local population may have continued to protect their ethnic identity. The origins of the Hippodamian plan (streets meeting at right angle) that survive in the city to the present probably went back to this period. The appearance of the Nabateans in ancient literature also corresponds to the Seleucid period. When the Romans arrived on the scene in the mid-60s BCE, like Cilicia and Antioch, Damascus was in the hands of Tigranes I of Armenia. In about 64 BCE it became a free city under the protection of the Roman rule.

The history of the antecedent of the Straight Street mentioned in Acts may have gone back to the Seleucid era. Research has shown that it was some 1,350 m long and 26 m wide, four times wider than its present-day namesake and flanked by a line of columns on each side with the roof of its colonnades, however, of canvas. It seems to have served as the principal west-east thoroughfare. Today, there is no trace of the theatre, which was according to ancient literature built by Herod the Great and stood to the south of the street. To the north stood the Temple of Jupiter (Zeus) whose premises may have at Paul's time contained a shrine dedicated to Augustus and the goddess Roma, and the agora. In the reign of Theodosius I (379-95) the temple would become a church dedicated to St John the Baptist and later in 708, the Umayyad Mosque. The latter still, at the lowest parts of some of its walls, incorporates architectural material going back to the Roman period or earlier.

Acts 9.2 by using the plural 'synagogues' implies the existence of a large Jewish population in Damascus and Josephus says that in the city there were many Gentile women 'addicted to the Jewish religion'. In the world in

Paul being lowered in a basket over the walls of Damascus. Late twelfth-century mosaic. Cathedral of Monreale. Palermo.

Deir ('monastery'). First century BCE. Petra. The low benches in the interior show that the structure may have served as a meeting

place for the cultic meals for the dead king Obodas III (Ubdat; 30-9 BCE) whose name was found in a nearby inscription.

which Paul lived — despite the belief in miracles — a sudden change of personality was not a normal phenomenon and the Damascene Jews were probably shocked at the news of a converted Paul. The zealous Pharisee whom they were waiting for and with whom they would have punished this new sect had shown up as one of the latter. They may have even punished the apostate Paul with one or more of the synagogue beatings that he mentions in 2 Cor 11.24. On the other hand the 'disciples of the lord' themselves, whether Gentile or Jewish, may not have believed in Paul's conversion, for he was already notorious among them because of his persecutions in Jerusalem. It has been suggested that for such and similar reasons returning to Jerusalem would have been more dangerous than staying in Damascus and Paul had to leave for Arabia (Gal 1.17).

In Paul's time Arabia referred to the Kingdom of the Nabateans whose territory extended to the east and south of Damascus. For Jews the Nabateans and Arabs were their kin as being the — illegitimate — descendants of Abraham by Ishmael, son of Abraham by the slave woman Hagar. Some of them practiced circumcision because Ishmael was also circumcised by his father (at the age of thirteen; not like Isaac on the eigth day). The practice, however, unlike with the Jews, was not an obligation; nor was it despised as by the Romans. It is not known if meeting circumcised people who did not believe in the God of Israel made the operation meaningless in Paul's eyes. The Nabateans led a partly nomadic partly settled life. They spoke a dialect of Aramaic and used a similar script. Strabo informs us that their capital Petra (Wadi Musa) was a city 'fortified all around by a rock' and that his friend the Stoic philosopher Athenodorus (of Tarsus) described the government here with admiration, mentioning the existence of many Romans and other foreigners in the city. Gerasa (Jerash), Philadelphia (Amman) and Bostra (Busra esh-Shara) were among the important cities. Including the capital most of the cities were probably settled also by Jews and in addition to Aramaic, the surviving epigraphic evidence shows that Greek was spoken by some of them. Paul's Arabian sojourn falls into a period of territorial conflicts between the Jewish tetrarch Herod Antipas and King Aretas of Nabateans and a Jewish missionary was not perhaps welcome in Nabatean lands. Both of them wanted to incorporate the lands of Philip who had died in 34 and recently there had been fights between the forces of the two. The defeat of Herod Antipas in about 36 CE would have been regarded by the later Christian tradition as a punishment for Antipas' murder of John the

Baptist.[2] It has been speculated that the feud between the two nations was rather unfavourable for a Jewish missionary and this may have been the reason why Paul was compelled to return to Damascus. The Nabateans believed in their local tribal deities but often held a 'highest god' (Greek *theos hypsistos*) as the god of heaven and thus were not strangers to the conception of monotheism. This was originally an epithet of Zeus popularly used in Macedonia and to a less extent in Anatolia and Arabia, and was chosen for the one and only God (Yahweh) by the translators of the OT into Greek. It is not known if Paul travelled to distant regions of Arabia or lived near Damascus and how long he stayed there. The expression in Acts that Paul 'went into Arabia' but was not 'called into the desert' in the fashion of John the Baptist or Jesus is regarded by some scholars as being against the idea that Paul lived by himself in solitude and contemplation. His identification of Hagar, the concubine of Abraham, with Mount Sinai (Gal 4.25) is sometimes regarded as a sign that he was familiar with the southmost regions where his journeys took him, unless it was just an answer to the claim of his opponents in Galatia, in which case no geographical familiarity with this region would have been necessary. In the geography of the time Sinai was put to the south of the Kingdom of Nabatea near the city of Hagra (Hegra/Medain Saleh in Saudi Arabia).

Bab ('Gate') Kaysan at St Paul's Chapel. The traditional spot where Paul is said to have been lowered in a basket. Damascus.

Whether Damascus was under Nabatean rule in this period is still an issue of discussion among scholars. It has been suggested that the title 'governor' (Greek *ethnarches*) which normally implies a ruler may have been used by Paul in 2 Cor 11.32 to refer to the chief of the Nabatean quarter, where he may have taken refuge, something which may have called for the interference of the Jewish enemies of Paul mentioned in Acts 9.23. Otherwise, in this period Damascus was outside the dominion of the Nabatean King Aretus (Aretas IV; 9 BCE-40 CE). Later Arabic literature mentions the existence of a quarter named after the Nabateans in the northeast quarter of the city between the East Gate (Bab Sharqi) and St Thomas Gate (Bab Tuma). Today's Ananias Chapel which incorporates the remains of a church from the fifth-sixth centuries is thought to have been located in this quarter. The traditional spot where 'his disciples took him one night and let him down through an opening in the wall, lowering

[2] Herod Antipas' wife was a daughter of King Aretas. She was sent back home when Herod fell in love with Herodias, his niece and the ex-wife of his half-brother. Herodias later demanded the head of John the Baptist.

him in a basket' (Acts 9.25), however, falls to the west of the East Gate. Although it does not agree with the account of Acts 9.27-29 in detail Paul's own words in Gal 1.18 inform us that he returned to Jerusalem to see Peter but also met James staying with the former for fifteen days. It is usually believed that Paul's orientation with some apostolic views took place during this short stay. Except for these two the 'apostles' of Acts 9.27 seem to have avoided him. Despite the secrecy, his arrival in the city was probably heard of by others and may have created serious unrest. The non-Christian Jews were angry with him for his conversion. The Aramaic-speaking Jewish-Christians ('Hebrews') were angry with him for his radical views, and his activities in Damascus and/or Arabia of which they may have already heard. The Greek-speaking Jewish-Christians ('Hellenists') doubted his conversion and did not trust him. The fact that his brethen decided that the safest place for Paul was Tarsus reconfirms Paul's occasional remarks about his being from the city. Although scholars still argue whether he was born there or not, it is evident that he had very close connections, which may have included relatives and patrimony in Tarsus. Thus he was taken to Caesarea (Maritime) and was sent home. The conditions which compelled Paul to leave all of a sudden were probably very serious because the apostle was to stay away from Jerusalem for over a decade. This Cilician sojourn in Acts is confirmed by Paul's own words in Gal1.21 when he says that he 'went into the regions of Syria and Cilicia' and is usually placed between the years 36-46. Sometime toward the end of this long period he was fetched and brought to Antioch on Orontes by Barnabas to help him there. According to Luke sometime in this period Paul and Barnabas took the famine aid collected in Antioch to Jerusalem. Some scholars believe that it was during this visit that Paul explained his evangelistic activities to the church at Jerusalem. Others, however, suggest that Paul stayed away from Jerusalem during this visit and this is the reason why he does not count it when he says he went to Jerusalem again 'after fourteen years' (Gal 2.2).

From Antioch on Orontes, in about 46/47, Paul and Barnabas set out on their first main missionary journey to Cyprus and then to Pamphylia and Pisidia and southern Galatia, returning to Antioch after one or two years, by sea from the Pamphylian city of Attalia.

In Antioch, the adherents to the new religion included many Gentiles, a situation which ultimately led to a crisis from which Paul emerged as the advocate of Gentile conversion. The controversy had at its heart circumcision and Jewish purity observances which made Jewish-Christians reluctant to eat with non-Jewish Christians. The latter, being uncircumcised or not bound by the obligations of Mosaic dietary observances, were regarded as impure. According to Luke the church of Antioch sent Paul and Barnabas to Jerusalem to discuss the problem. The resolution of this at the so-called Jerusalem Council probably in about 49 and Paul's decision to convert Gentiles, ensured that Christianity did not remain just another Jewish sect, but in time became a universal religion. Some scholars believe that this visit is the one that Paul refers to in his letter to the Galatians.

On a second journey, about 49/50, accompanied by Silas — and Timothy after Lystra — Paul travelled from Antioch through Cilicia to southern Galatia, then to Alexandria Troas by way of Phrygia and Mysia — Luke joining the party here — and onto Macedonia and Achaia, once again returning by sea this time by way of Ephesus to Caesarea and Jerusalem, and from there to Antioch, perhaps in 52.

On his third missionary journey, about 53/54, Paul again visited the southern Galatian churches on his way to Ephesus, where he remained for about three years. From there he went to Macedonia by way of Alexandria Troas, and perhaps Illyria, and Achaia. He returned again to Alexandria Troas by way of Macedonia. Finally left from Miletus for Phoenicia and onto Jerusalem about the year 57.

Obverse of a bronze sesterce (*sestertius*) of Claudius (41-54) who was the Roman Emperor at the time of most of Paul's journeys. İstanbul Archaeological Museums.

Most of Paul's journeys, although their exact years are difficult to establish, correspond to the reign of Claudius (41-54) whose rule was known to have been milder and more peaceful than that of his predecessor Gaius (Caligula; 37-41), and his successor Nero (54-68). When the latter sat on the Roman throne in 54 and soon after encountered troubles with the Parthians on his eastern frontier, Paul was on his third journey. The first few years of Nero's reign were very mild. Paul was lucky to embark on his missions during a period of Roman history when not just the lands in which he journeyed but even the frontiers were, relatively, untroubled.

Paul's third missionary journey ended at Jerusalem. There he was accused by the Jews who thought, mistakenly, that he had broken Jewish law by taking a Gentile, Trophimus of Ephesus, into the sacred ground of the Temple. His charges were given a political twist and he was arrested. After his defence before the Sanhedrin he was taken to Caesarea, where he was imprisoned until about 59/60. When the next governor tried to send him to Jerusalem for trial, Paul claimed his right as a Roman citizen to be put on trial in Rome. This journey also took him to Crete and Malta. Paul arrived in Rome around 60 and lived under house arrest for two years. The unfinished narrative of Acts closes with him awaiting trial.

The circumstances of Paul's death are not known and there are conflicting traditions. His martyrdom may have happened sometime in 62. According to one tradition he was acquitted and released and made a further missionary journey, which would have corresponded to the years 62-63. He was rearrested, imprisoned in Rome and sentenced to death. Whichever the case, it is sure that he was martyred at the latest sometime around 64 during the persecution of Christians in Nero's reign.

A section of the Via Sebaste which climbs the Taurus chain at Döşeme Pass, north of Antalya. The road is paved with unhewn stones and for the borders larger stones have been used. At this pass it probably overlaps the road built by Manius Aquillius.

TRAVEL AND TRANSPORT IN PAUL'S TIME

Over a period of some ten years in the middle of the first century, Paul made several journeys, travelling through Cyprus, Anatolia, Macedonia and Achaia and, traditionally, to Spain, spreading the Gospel. In the course of his journeys, he visited much of these countries probably walking a good deal of the way, accompanied by one or more companions.

The destination of Paul's missions, when it was not dictated by the Holy Spirit or unexpected events to unknown destinations, was the urban Greco-Roman settlements each with a Jewish population and one or more synagogues where the existence of godfearers, Gentiles attracted to Judaism, could be anticipated. It has been estimated that Paul may have travelled some 20,000 km on his missionary journeys. By land the easiest way to visit such cities was to follow the roads of the time. A considerable part of the distance Paul covered was through Anatolia and probably on Roman roads, which frequently followed the ancient routes. Research and surviving rock-cut reliefs by ravines or mountain passes show that some of these trails had been used for military transportation in remote antiquity when most of the peninsula was ruled by the Hittites. These ancient trails adapted themselves to the topography of land. Some of the ones in Anatolia have survived under names such as Kırk Geçitler ('forty crossings') or Doksan Dolaş ('ninety turns') and similar giving hints about the route. There is no reason not to think that some of the tracks that the apostle took were trodden in antiquity by the armies of mobile eastern potentates like Cyrus the Great, Darius I or Xerxes, and the Ten Thousand of Xenophon or Alexander the Great or later by Roman generals and troops.

Paul and his companions were able to make their missionary journeys with relative ease and safety largely because of the Roman presence. Under the *pax Romana*, the Roman peace, instituted 'by Augustus, the roads were by and large kept free of brigands and in good repair'. The Romans had begun to construct these roads immediately after they established the provinces of Macedonia, Achaia, and Asia (western Anatolia) in the second century BCE, and by the time of Paul had extended their network to western Anatolia, all the way from the Black Sea coast to the Mediterranean and southern Galatia and as far as northern Syria and Phoenicia. The oldest of these Roman roads in Anatolia began at Pergamum and ended at Side, crossing the province of Asia by way of Ephesus and the Meander route. It belonged to Manius Aquillius, the first Roman governor. The Roman network, which ran from the Pamphylian flats through Pisidia and Phrygia to Lycaonia was built by the orders of Augustus and known as the Via Sebaste and very familiar to Paul. In Macedonia he travelled on the Via Egnatia, another Roman highway which connected Byzantium, running across Macedonia and Illyria, to the Dalmatian coast. From Brundisium (Brindisi) on the opposite coast the Via Appia ran as far as Rome. The Appian Way was the most important of the Roman highways in Italy. As he was being taken to the Roman capital as a prisoner Paul also marched on this road.

The roads on which Paul travelled were built to carry the Roman armies, which at this date mostly consisted of troops, and imperial officials and couriers of many kinds, along the straightest route as swiftly as possible. The engineers who built these roads disregarded any obstacle and crossed rivers by bridges or paved fords and marshes by viaducts. As is the case of the Via Appia which crossed the Pomptine marshes, these roads, in addition to being instruments of transportation and communication, symbolized Rome's hegemony on the forces of nature. Still, in dry climates they would follow the water sources and in winter snow would have made even some of best roads impassable.

Rock-cut road at the Late Bronze Age city of Puranda mentioned in the 'Annals' of the Hittite King Mursili II (1321-1295 BCE) between Smyrna (İzmir) and Apasa (Ephesus). It may have been the road which was, according to a late local tradition, opened by St Paul using his sword to cut the rock.

Although some of them were repaved after Paul's time what has survived to the present gives us an idea about the roads on which Paul journeyed. The size and type of a Roman road changed in accordance to expected traffic, terrain and materials available, but the general principles of its construction were those described by the Greek author Plutarch, born about a decade before Paul's martyrdom: 'The roads were carried straight across the countryside. They were paved with hewn stones and bolstered underneath with masses of tight packed gravel; hollows were filled in, and torrents or ravines that cut across the route were bridged'. To facilitate travelling sometimes pounded loam was spread on the surface. The earthen tracks which extended by some of the surviving roads served for carriage transportation.

Milestone on the Via Appia. It is only inscribed with the numeral III which stands for the third mile from Rome.

At the time of Paul's journeys there were no maps or itineraries available to travellers. One moved from one place to the other by asking directions. The milestones placed along the main roads and of which some four thousand have survived (with over six hundred from Anatolia) usually showed the distance in Roman miles (Latin *mille*, 1,478 m) but sometimes carried more detailed information, such as the name of the person who built or repaired the road and the number of available cisterns or garrisons on the way. Plutarch mentions stone columns serving as distance markers and some others which enabled 'riders to mount their horses without the need of further assistance'. In Anatolia, along with other Roman building material, some of them in their later history served as tombstones. There were also stone markers on the borders of the territory belonging to different provinces, cities, communities or individuals. These milestones and road inscriptions were also the visible signs of the Roman presence and served as imperial propaganda.

At the time Paul travelled, although the regular posting stages belonging to the Roman government post were known, the system was not available for civilians. The Roman courier-service (*cursus publicus*) was established by Augustus, and based on obligations placed by the Roman state on private persons to keep the system running smoothly. A bilingual edict dating from the time of Paul — in Latin and in Greek (Burdur Archaeological Museum) — fixes the number of animals that the people of Sagalassus (Ağlasun) in Pisidia were obliged to provide for different types of officials and the cost of such services, and the priority of the various kinds of officials who might require them. Thus it also shows the burden that the system put on the

Milestone at the foot of a Moslem grave. Cemetery of İğdecik village near Isparta. From the worn out inscription in Latin we learn that it was put to use three different times: the first is undecipherable, the second is under Licinius/Constantine in 313-17 CE, and the last under Constantine in 333-35 CE.

locals and how much the Roman governor of the time cared for orderly transportation in his realm. Roman troops are known to have taken an active part in road construction. The task was perhaps not a cherished assignment. In a papyrus letter from the time of Trajan (98-117 CE) a soldier writing to his father states that by obtaining an office job at headquarters he was able to avoid it. Local people were also forced to build the roads and from Cicero we learn that sometimes Roman officials were accused of 'accepting bribes for exemption from the duty to construct or repair roads'.

The information about the inns or hostels of the period is not flattering. They were known to be dirty and dangerous or frequented by prostitutes. In the apocryphal *Acts of John*, the apostle, as he travelled from Laodicea on Lycus to Ephesus when bothered by bed bugs in the inn where he spent the night, banished them from his room. Nevertheless, next morning he found the insects waiting outside for his permission to return to their dwelling. In the apocryphal *Acts of Paul*, after he was scourged and expelled from Iconium the apostle finds Onesiphorus and his family 'in an open sepulchre', an unfinished tomb construction and stays with them. The only name which probably originally belonged to an inn mentioned during Paul's journeys is the Three Taverns (Acts 28.15). Still, until he found accommodation with a Jew or Christian convert Paul would have had to stay at an inn. Writing about a century after Paul's time Aelius Aristides informs us how he journeyed from Smyrna to the Asclepium at Pergamum: the first two inns he found (one by the Hermus River and the other at Larissa) were very dirty and the next two (at Cyme and Myrina) were closed.

At the time of Paul's travels in the Mediterranean world ethnic groups or people of the same profession lived in their own quarter. Ancient literature gives the impression that hospitality was common and travellers preferred, when or where this was possible, to stay at other people's houses. If they had no acquaintances, arriving in an unknown city, they probably walked to the sanctuary of their cult, in the case of Jews to the synagogue, or Egyptians to the temple of Serapis or Isis, or to the market place with the members of their profession and introducing themselves expected an offer of hospitality. Being of the same race, same city, same religion or profession increased one's chance of receiving an invitation. In Acts 16.13-15 Paul meets Lydia at the Jewish 'place of prayer' and accepts her invitation. In Acts 18.1-3 he probably met Aquila in the part of Corinth where tents were manufactured and later visited him and his wife Priscilla, and stayed with them. In a similar manner in Acts 21.4 at Tyre Paul's party 'sought out the disciples and stayed' with them. A synagogue was the first place a travelling Jew would look for accommodation in the diaspora, and some of the synagogues in the countries where Paul travelled probably had hostels. However, as the events showed,

Epitaph above the door of a tomb at the northern necropolis of Hierapolis. End of the first century CE. The inscription in Greek reads: 'Titus Flavius Zeuxis, merchant, having sailed on seventy-two voyages beyond Cape Maleus toward Italy, built a monument for himself and for his sons Flavius Theodoros and Flavius Theudas and for any others they may wish to grant permission to'. Although not indicated he may have traded in textiles for which his city was famous. He may have included the name of Cape Malea, the southernmost point of the Peloponnese on the Aegean side, where sailing was proverbially dangerous, as a matter of pride.

Bilingual (Latin and Greek) milestone erected by 'Manius Aquillius son of Manius, Roman consul' near Ephesus. It also reads 'From Ephesus 5 miles'; *m*(ilia) *p*(assuum)= in Roman miles. 129-126 BCE. The logic of a Roman milestone could be contrary to that of a modern road-sign,

so that it does not read 'Ephesus 5 miles'. This is one of the first milestones that the Romans set up with Ephesus as the terminal point of the road in western Anatolia after establishing the province of Asia. It is now in Ephesus and placed near the Arcadiane.

the hospitality Paul received from his own race did not last long, something which would be immediately amended by non-Jewish Christians. The information about Paul's overnights at friends' houses is confirmed by Paul's own words in his letters such as in Phlm 22 when Paul asks Philemon in Colossae to prepare a guest room for him.

Acts mentions two occasions when the apostle and his friends rented establishments; the hall of Tyrannus in Ephesus during the third missionary journey, and a private lodging in Rome while waiting for trial. Acts also shows that Paul did not like travelling alone. It is not known if his sickness may have played a part in this. His words in 1 Thes 3.1-2 show that (together with Silas) he regarded 'to remain alone in Athens' as an important gesture for the sake of his Thessalonian converts. The vanity of 'a solitary man with no companion' is elaborated in the OT (Eccl 4.7-12) and Jesus says that his disciples would travel in companion with another brother (Mk 6.7). Except during the Arabian, Syrian and Cilician sojourns whose details are not known Paul travelled with one or more companions.

During the hundred-year period before Paul's travels Anatolia had seen — after going through another hundred year of wars and devastations — a relative expansion of prosperity and the roads, in addition to the military, were increasingly used by merchants or other private travellers. The worn-out surfaces on the main roads indicate a busy traffic of pack animals, mainly donkeys or mules and wagons with heavy loads drawn by teams of oxen as well as an assortment of carts and carriages. The fact that Roman engineers preferred the straightest course is best displayed by long ramps without grades which, however, made the roads unsuitable for carts carrying heavy loads. Land transportation for long distances was expensive and the carts or wagons carried local products just to nearby markets. Few people other than the cavalry rode horses. It was tiring and uncomfortable. Saddles were fairly rudimentary and stirrups would not be invented until as late as the fourth century. Some rode on mules or donkeys. The mule was the most popular animal for travel and transportation because it could travel faster than an ox and make a longer journey than a horse and could easily carry some 70 kg, as much as a horse. Roman troops were accompanied with a high number of carts drawn by mules or donkeys which carried the soldiers' heavy equipment and siege machines.

In regard to the surviving Roman roads of Paul's time and later, Anatolia is the richest of the countries in which the apostle travelled. Such roads are

Bilingual (Latin and Greek) milestone erected by 'Manius Aquillius son of Manius, Roman consul' at Side where the road he built terminates. 129-126 BCE. It has been suggested that the 331 Roman miles mentioned on the milestone, which makes

494 km, is the distance from Pergamum to Side by way of possibly Thyatira, Sardis, Philadelphia, Hierapolis, Laodicea, Colossae, Climax (Döşeme Pass), Antalya and Perge.

now called by locals in Turkish Kral Yolu ('King's Road'), İpek Yolu ('Silk Road'), Bağdat Yolu ('Baghdad Road') or Gavur Yolu ('Infidel's Road'), the last adjective referring to anybody who is not Moslem. There are not many bridges surviving from Paul's time. They forded the big rivers at their shallowest spots and bridges were thus very long. On the brooks they were no more than a single arch. The remains of some of them can easily be distinguished at the bottom of the Seljuk or Ottoman bridges which were built over them or lie by their modern successors in concrete.

People travelled for many purposes: recreation, pilgrimage, health or business. Cicero writing in 51 BCE tells us that when he met P Vedius at Laodicea on Lycus, the latter was travelling 'with two gigs and a coach and horses and a litter and a crowd of servants...a baboon as well in one of the gigs, and some onagers'. Although the mobility reflected by the seventy-two voyages of the merchant Titus Flavius Zeuxis of Hierapolis to Italy may have been a rare experience it was not suprising to meet people like the woman Lydia, from Thyatira selling 'purple cloth' (Acts 16.14) at Philippi across the Aegean, or Priscilla and Aquila, tentmakers originally from Pontus on the Black Sea, who had left Rome and migrated to Corinth (Acts 18.2-3) and were about to move to Ephesus and would later return to Rome, or Apollos, a Christian missionary from Alexandria in Egypt travelling between Ephesus and Corinth. Still most of the travellers whom Paul saw on the Roman roads were peasants who normally, did not travel beyond the nearest market place. From the remark in Acts 21.15 that before departing from Caesarea Paul's party 'made preparations' for the journey to Jerusalem one may conclude that some kind of transportation, animals or vehicles were sought, an arrangement which the apostle may have made at other times as well.

Although there were many traders' vehicles or carriages bearing magistrates to the cities of their new assignments, most travellers would have walked. An early estimate about travel on foot comes from Herodotus. Writing about the Royal Road of the Persians which ran between Sardis and Susa, the historian says travelling 'at the rate of 150 furlongs [about 30 km] a day, a man will take just ninety days to make the journey'. Paul probably covered a similar actual distance a day on foot, sleeping at the homes of friends or in the open when the weather was good along the way or in any shelter. The distance he would walk would depend on the weather and the road and the length of the daylight hours. Jesus' advice (Mt 10.5-15 and others) that his apostles should depend on God for food and shelter is regarded to have applied to Palestine or its hinterland, where a fertile soil of evangelization was ready for them, but not to unknown foreign lands where the Gospel had not been heard.

Most of the world in which Paul travelled has the Mediterranean climate, dry hot summers and rainy warm winters, and this has not changed from Paul's time to the present. Old or sick people preferred not to travel during the hottest part of the day. Pliny the Younger writing to Trajan says that — on his way to his new post of governorship of Bithynia Pontus — after travelling from Ephesus to Pergamum overland he switched to a coastal boat because of the extreme heat. To the north of the Taurus and in Macedonia, however, winter was long, bitter, rainy and snowy. From the words in I Cor 16.6: 'perhaps I shall stay even spend the winter with you' or Ti 3.12: 'try to join me at Nicopolis, where I have decided to spend the winter' we understand that Paul, unless it was indispensable, preferred not to travel in winter. A traveller of Paul's time would have worn light leather or felt shoes or sandals and a tunic and a travelling cloak. The last was a rectangular woollen cloth, which could be as large as 5 x 2 m, worn around the body encirling one shoulder and the head when required, and would have been the most important garment for the fact that it could be used as a cover in the cold. It is not surprising that in 2 Tm 4.13 Paul, in addition to his papyrus rolls and parchments, asks for 'the cloak' he left in Troas. Spare garments, which would include a rain-wrap, a pair of heavy shoes or half-boots, blankets or hammocks plus provisions and cooking and eating utensils would have been probably loaded on a pack animal which would also carry a tent. A traveller would have kept his money in a leather purse either on his belt or on a cord hung from the neck. He may have used a long staff to help him on rocky paths and against sheepdogs. In summer, on the paths that Paul followed, travellers on foot are still prone to attack by deadly adders. On the road a traveller's diet may have included some stuff like biscuits, salt, onions, olives, or dry fruits (carobs, figs, almonds, grapes and similar). Water and/or wine would normally be carried in a baked clay jar or a whole skin of a kid or goat. Such skins were also used to carry milk, which was thickened, sour and was drunk thus or eaten as curd. Water would not have been a problem because in the area of Paul's journeys it was possible to find a perennial spring or a well every 10 or 15 km. Ancient paths and Roman roads followed the low skirts of mountains where water was available. On the road, a meal of bread, herbs, salt and water such as Paul, Thecla and the Onesiphorus

Block incised with a menorah. Priene. The building to which it belonged very probably served as a synagogue.

family shared outside Iconium, was not regarded as uncommon. When necessary the only way of starting a fire was the fire drill, rubbing of two pieces of dried wood together, or banging a stone against a piece of pyrite. For light travellers carried small earthenware oil lamps in the shape of a saucer with a lip on which the wick stood. Normally, one tends to think that Paul, in his eating habits, followed the teaching of his own Gospel. He reveals his attitude in 1 Cor 9.22-23 saying 'To the weak I became weak, to win over the weak I have become all things to all, to save at least some. All this I do for the sake of the Gospel'. While behaving like a Gentile when he was among them he was expected to have shown consideration for the scruples of simple-minded or 'weak' believers to whom he also refers in 1 Cor 8.9 and Rom 14.1-3;20-21. There is no doubt that he followed the common Jewish food obligations when he was among his own race.

In the Greco-Roman world of the time if one wanted to keep his friends one was expected to visit them frequently or if this was not possible send letters, again frequently. For a person in the position of Paul writing letters would have been a serious occupation and among Paul's personal equipment which may have been most carefully guarded would have been his writing material. It is known that some ancient writers could make quick notes or even write or dictate letters on the way. This they usually did when they travelled in a carriage as was the case with Cicero. For making such notes or drafts wood or metal or ivory tablets with rims and covered with a layer of wax were used. The history of writing on wax went back as far as ancient Mesopotamia. These tablets also served as dictionaries to which the writer could refer for quotations or extracts. At the time of Paul such tablets had begun to have been replaced by parchments carried in the form of codex. This was carried easily and its pages could be washed and reused. It has

In the rocky heights of Anatolia the donkey is still the most useful assistant of a peasant, serving for ploughing or transportation. A donkey costs only about $150. Its sustenance is cheap for the animal can eat anything. Caravans of donkeys and kings riding on them are mentioned in ancient history.

(opposite) Reused furniture leg from Philadelphia (Alaşehir). Manisa Archaeological Museum. It is decorated with a menorah and an inscription which in Greek reads: 'Jewish memoriam [tomb]'. The menorah is flanked by an ethrog, a citrus fruit (left) and a lulab, palm branch (right).

been suggested that since making notes would not have been easy for Paul as he was mobile most of the time his 'parchments' mentioned in 2 Tm 4.13 may have served a similar purpose. Writing letters constituted an important part of Paul's missionary work and Paul could only write his long letters when he stayed for a relatively long period, settled, rested and brought his thoughts together. Scholars believe that Paul's letters require some degree of familiarity with Greco-Roman rhetorical tradition and that Paul may have learned it in Jerusalem or Tarsus or acquired it during perhaps his long Cilician and Syrian sojourn. Paul was frequently accused by his opponents and without being oriented with general Hellenistic thought it would have been impossible to refute the charge of his enemies.

Paul's writing material would have included a set of reed pens and a sharpener, a knife or an abrasive stone, soot or ground carbon deposit compounded with glue and mixed with water for making ink which may have been kept dry or liquid, and papyrus rolls or parchment sheets and a writing board. The use of animal skins for writing is first mentioned by Herodotus who says that the Ionians called paper (papyrus) 'skins'. This however, being very expensive, was rarely used in Paul's time. The popular paper of the period was made from papyrus. Its cost, one roll about a worker's wage of several days, compared to the limited use of writing, could not be regarded as expensive. However, ready-made lined sheets were not available and it was necessary to smooth the surface or sheet-joints of the papyrus rolls with the help of a stone or lead disk and use a straight ruler to keep the lines even. The average length of a papyrus sheet was no more than 30 cm and Paul's long letters would have required a large number of these. The preparation of the paper, in addition to sharpening of his pens and preparation of the ink, would most probably have been the responsibily of one of Paul's companions. Since writing material may not have been always available, to save space paragraphs, grammatical divisions, punctuation marks and suchlike were avoided. Paul lived in an era when only two of every ten people could read. Paul's letters were written to be recited rather than to be read, often to make up for his absence in a church. Some of his letters carry the obvious signs of secretarial assistance of varying degrees, which was common for the time. Paul's secretaries were his fellow-workers, such as Sosthenes, Timothy, and Silvanus (Silas) and others. At the end of Paul's letter to the Romans (16.22) his co-worker adds 'I, Tertius, the writer of this letter greet you in the Lord'. In addition to their assistance in composing

and writing the letter they would have carried it to its destination and explained what was missing or difficult to understand in the text. Thus most of the time the apostle would choose his metaphors carefully and dwell on the oral value of the words or sounds imagining their impact on listeners. The latter would probably memorize or copy some sections of Paul's letters to repeat at other churches. In antiquity letters were read aloud. Forged letters were not unheard of and in 2 Thes 2.2 Paul warns his flock about 'a letter allegedly from' him. Authentication of the letter by a sign was common in the world of Paul and the apostle follows the tradition (Gal 6.11; 2 Thes 3.17). Although shorthand was known, Paul's assistants, not being professional scribes, may not have been familiar with it and each one may have followed his own method of taking notes. After writing it in longhand his secretary probably would read it to Paul and following the practice of the time would have made two copies. Paul would keep one, a tradition which would eventually help the survival of his letters. It has even been speculated that Luke may have inherited these copies after Paul's death, something that eventually helped their survival. Paul's saying in Gal 6.11 'See with what large letters I am writing to you in my own hand!' has been interpreted as being the result of an eye disease that he suffered. A finished letter would be rolled with the writing inside and sealed with wax. This was a time when people, unless they could afford a private courier, had no other way than relying on the travellers or merchants going in the direction of their sending them, because of the fact that the official post served just the state. Writing from Laodicea on Lycus to his friend Atticus in Rome Cicero says 'You will have plenty of opportunities to send letters, by the tax-farmers' couriers', but such state facilities would not have been a possibility for people like Paul.

Although he says that observing the Jewish customs was not necessary to become Christian, as a Jew, Paul would most probably have observed them. Like any other Jew he would have attended the synagogue regularly both for praying, and as a part of his missionary work also for proclaiming his Gospel. He would also have followed the Jewish calendar and when possible arranged his travel plans in accordance with Jewish festivals (1 Cor 16.8). This calendar was lunar, consisting of twelve months of twenty-nine days, with the remaining eleven days made up by inserting seven leap months over the course of a nineteen-year cycle. Otherwise, at the time of Paul, while some cities followed their own calendars, some used the luni-solar Macedonian calendar, which began in 312 BCE the date of their conquest of Seleucia on Tigris, and some had switched to more practical calendar based on the Julian system in which the year began on September 23, Augustus' birthday.

The ancient fauna and landscape of the world in which Paul travelled have not changed much. At present the greatest change is the lack of forests which most of the places he travelled possibly lined the roads he followed. By Paul's time, with the decline of the large fleets of the Hellenistic period, the deforestation of cedar mountains had slowed down. From today's landscape the cash crops such as tobacco and cotton should be removed and perhaps more grapevines and olives added. These two were the only fruit trees that the Roman administration found worth of taxation. Otherwise, figs, almonds, pears, plums, peaches which the Greeks called 'Persian apples' and other fruit trees, both wild and cultivated, were as common as they are today. Ancient literature considers over a dozen kinds of Anatolian wines worth of mentioning. According to Galen the wine produced in Paul's home Cilicia was both austere and sweet and thick and black. The most common feature of the landscape of Paul's time with the present was the abundance of olive trees since olive oil was an essential part of life in antiquity. It was used for cooking, for preserving food, for fuelling lamps and so on. Its high calorific value made it an indispensable part of travel diet. It could also be used in place of soap. At Salamiou near Palai Paphos on Cyprus some old olive trees are believed to have grown from the stones that Paul and his companions left after their meal.

Funerary relief from Isaura Vetus (Bozkır) in Lycaonia. Konya Archaeological Museum. It shows a peasant carrying a goad and ploughing with a team of two oxen.

Paul and his party would likely have carried a substantial amount of money with them because travel was an expensive venture. In addition to food and lodging there were tolls at ferry crossings or bridges or at provincial boundaries, ship fares to be paid and pack animals to be bought or changed. At the time, in addition to the Roman state, hundreds of cities issued their own coins and their usage was widespread especially in urban centres. The popular Roman bronze coins in circulation were 'as' and 'sestertius' (four asses). The 'denarius' was silver and worth sixteen asses. The gold piece, 'aureus', was worth 25 denarii. The Greek silver coin 'drachma' was mostly minted in the cities of eastern Roman provinces and by permission of the emperor. This was a unit of weight which varied from place to place but the word was used for the silver coin of the related weight. At the time of Paul the value of a drachma was about a denarius. The value of coins changed with time and place and one had to find a money-changer, who usually did money-testing as well, and pay a commission, which could be as high as 5 percent, to change money. Foreign

Stele in Seydişehir. Under a vine tree laden with bunches of grapes and a bird with open wings a man is leading two animals.

exchange was not known but also not indispensable because of the wide use of Roman currency. Long distance money transfer or cheques transmissible by endorsement was unknown. From Cicero we learn that he stopped in Laodicea on Lycus in 51 BCE for a few days to collect the sum due to him by the Roman treasury on his way to Tarsus. Later, he entrusted the amount he earned during his consulship in Cilicia to the tax-collectors here. Thus the governor avoided both the physical transfer and exchange of the funds involved. Such a facility, surely, would not have been available for Paul. Banks were rare and, normally, served for depositing money and other valuables rather than for loaning. When one ran out of money one had no other option than turning to friends or working. The monetized economy of cities did not reach the countryside. In rural life money was not indispensable because of the fact that peasants produced most of what they needed or obtained it by barter at the markets held near their farms. Donkeys or cows, plough and sickles or pruning knives, spinning equipment such as distaff or comb used in weaving, grapes or wheat sheaves or whips and dogs on the funeral monuments imply an agricultural way of life. What is known about the prices at Paul's time does not amount to much and is confusing. The peasants or herdsmen encountered travelling probably would have refused any payment for a jar of wine or milk because of the long-established traditions of hospitality. When receiving a coin from a traveller it would be put away as hoard or for paying taxes without its exact value known. Paul's early trips in Arabia and Cilicia and Syria would certainly have taught him how much cash he would need in the course of his long missionary journeys.

While most of Paul's missions were accomplished by walking, he travelled also by ship. In fact he was attracted by the sea which could take him faster to his fruitful evangelization fields, the crowded coastal urban settlements, each at least with one synagogue with Jews and hopefully with godfearing Gentiles. Although considerably faster than land travel, for a coaster sailing 4 to 6 knots per hour could easily make over 100 km under normal conditions in daytime and with suitable winds, it was also more dangerous, not just because of pirates who still roamed in some waters, but also because of the reefs and shallows, which were unmarked, and of the weather. The growing number of shipwrecks that underwater archaeology has been bringing to light from the waters in which Paul travelled shows the frequency of disasters. It is not surprising that Roman money-lenders charged some 30 percent interest (thrice the usual rate) for maritime loans and that ship-owners were not obliged to pay it back if the vessel and its cargo were lost because of forces beyond their control.

Dedication of Artemas Ammiados to Zeus Anpeleites. First half of the third century CE. Kütahya Museum. The epithet possibly identifies the god as the protector of vineyards and/or herds.

Even in summer, voyages across the open sea were unpredictable. This was an era when passenger ships were not known. One had to go to the port and ask for a merchant vessel scheduled to sail to one's destination, and finding one pay the price, for which one would be at the captain's mercy, and begin to wait. Writing some three hundred years after the time of the apostle, Libanius, the pagan Antiochene orator remarks, 'In Constantinople I went down to the Great Harbour and made the rounds asking about vessels sailing for Athens'. Having found a vessel that could take him the passenger would have to wait near the harbour, perhaps several days, for the right winds and omens fitting the pilot's cult. The apocryphal *Acts of Philip* informs us that at the port of Caesarea he found a vessel bound for Carthage which had been waiting 'for twenty days' for a favourable breeze.

Lifeboats were unknown. In case of danger, without the pilot there was no chance of survival. Paul, as an experienced traveller who claimed to have suffered three shipwrecks (2 Cor 11.25) knew this well because when the vessel carrying him faced shipwreck during his journey to Rome and some of the crew tried to sneak off using the dinghy to save their own lives, he got the

Short face of a casket. First to second centuries CE. Sinop Museum. The inscription in Greek reads 'Cornelius Arrianus who lived for 60 years'. In addition to the relief accompanying the

epitaph, the two sailing vessels displayed on one of the long faces (back cover picture) of the casket implies that the sarcophagus belonged to a captain/pilot or ship-owner.

officer and the soldiers and told them that unless those men stayed with the ship, they could not be saved (Acts 27.30-31). People also took passage on vessels carrying cargo. On the same ill-fated voyage, Paul's party embarked at Myra on one of the big grain vessels bound for Italy. We learn from Acts 27.37 that this ship had 276 people aboard, counting the crew. Josephus' words that on his way to Rome in 61 CE, about the time of Paul's sea accident, when his ship sank in the Adriatic Sea they were about six hundred in number or Pliny the Elder's ship of twelve hundred passengers would refer to vessels of unusual size for the period — unless the numbers are exaggerated — and have been viewed with suspicion by scholars.

By the first century CE the captains and pilots who navigated in the Mediterranean possessed information accumulated over the centuries since the time of the Phoenicians. Although in the Mediterranean the winds and currents are known not to have changed for the last two thousand years, in order to minimize the dangers of sailing in the open sea, at Paul's time captains sailed without losing the sight of the coastline, a practice which lasted as late as the sixteenth century. The Mediterranean was good for sailing in the open sea except in winter when storms and fog affected visibility. The compass was not known and the ability to tack was limited. In good weather vessels either followed the Pole star or any landmark. Except for the central part of the Mediterranean it was always possible to spot a landmark, the silhouette of a mountain such as the peaks of the Taurus, the African coastline or some islands. Since the winds along the length of the Mediterranean are westerly, the square-rigged sailing vessels of Paul's time could sail eastward with relative ease especially before the Etesians ('annual winds'), which blew for forty days after July 20 from the northwest. The journey in the opposite direction was more difficult. Forced to make use of the winds generated by the land the ships sailing west stayed near the coast even at the risk of being blown ashore during a storm.

The sailing season was short and limited to the period of good weather, beginning in the early spring and lasting until October. Ancient art and literature show that its opening day, March 5, *navigium Isidis* ('ship of Isis') was an important festival and celebrated all around the Mediterranean by the launching of a sacred ship to the goddess. Writing in the seventh century BCE, the Greek poet Hesiod shortens the navigable season in the Mediterranean to the period between 5 May and 25 October. The safe sea travel season in the rabbinical literature is between Pentecost (May) and the

Feast of Booths (end of October). In winter when the sky was cloudy, the stars and sun, by which sailors found their course, were often not visible. In such cases there was nothing that the pilot could do but to shelter in a port and wait for favourable weather. In Acts the dangers of winter weather and tempests are vividly described in the account of the voyage that ended in shipwreck off Melite (Malta), when Paul was being taken to Rome.

Acts does not give any information about the kind of ships in which the apostle embarked during his sea journeys. At the time, except the ships which carried grain from Alexandria to Rome, or Roman troops to the frontiers, most of the sea traffic consisted of small open deck ships that sailed along the coasts, coming into harbour each night. Such ships hopping from one port to the other collected any kind of available passenger or merchandise. This practice is evident in the schedule of the one on which Paul embarked on his journey to Rome as a prisoner; a boat 'bound for ports in the province of Asia' (Acts 27.2) which on the next day after its departure from Caesarea stopped at Sidon.

On such coastal ships merchants, exiles, entertainers or pilgrims and soldiers, all travelled together. Travelling by sea may have had risks similar to land journeys. Despite some optimistic claims that pirates had been cleared from the Mediterranean by the Romans, pilots did not neglect asking the vessels coming from the direction in which they were heading if pirates had been spotted. In a letter from Egypt and dating after Paul's time, a husband asks his wife to travel in the company of men she knows and says 'When you come, bring your gold ornaments, but do not wear them on the boat'. As they made zigzags between islands and mainland the travelling merchants, among other cargo, would be collecting timber from Phoenicia, copper from Cyprus, amphorae full of oil or wine from Rhodes or grain mills from Cos. Such coasters did not have an exact schedule and when the captain decided that his business was done and the wind was favourable he would send one of the crew to announce in the streets and taverns of the port that he was soon leaving. Once the sun set, in the absence of shore lights to mark the coast navigation would become difficult and by the time darkness fell, unless he put into a nearby port, he usually found a sheltered shallow bay and dropped anchor or beached his ship where hopefully he would find friendly people or no people at all rather than hostile inhabitants.

On ships small or large Paul would have sailed the eastern Mediterranean, to carry Christ's message to Cyprus, Anatolia, Macedonia and Achaia.

TARSUS

Column fragment with the name 'Tarsos'. Tarsus Museum.

At the time of Paul's birth and upbringing, Tarsus was the most important city in the Cilician plain (Çukurova) which was then known as Level or Smooth Cilicia.[1]

When Paul was born Tarsus was already very ancient. Excavations at Gözlükule tumulus in the present city have shown that the site has been occupied since the Neolithic period, from about the seventh millennium. Its location on the upper tip of the Fertile Crescent seems to have created a cosmopolitan population of Tarsians who in addition to agriculture lived on trade between east and west from the very beginning of their history. The earliest known Cilicians were of Luvian stock. During its later Bronze Age history the settlement is thought to have been a part of the Kingdom of Kizzuwadna. In the fifteenth century the territory of Kizzuwadna was included in the Hittite Kingdom and Tarsus came to be known as Tarsa. In the 1190s the so-called Sea Peoples swept the region. Some of these immigrants may have settled here and mixed with the native population. Toward the end of the eighth century BCE King Azitiwatas in the bilingual inscriptions of Karatepe, claims that he was descended from the 'House of Muksas ('Mopsus')' who was one of the supposed leaders of the immigrants. The major Greek elements in the settlement's culture date from the mid-eighth century BCE when Greeks appeared in the Levant as pirates and merchants establishing their own living and trading quarter in harbour cities like Tarsus. In this period the city's Eastern pantheon was supplemented by deities from the west. When choosing Greek ancestry became a fashion in the Common Era the Tarsians decided on an Argive descent and accepted Heracles whom the oriental inhabitants identified with their god Sandan, as the founder of their city.

In Assyrian annals the tumulus appears as 'Tarzi', capital of the kingdom of Que in the Cilician plain, also called Hilakku. The reference to Cilicia (Que) in 1 Kgs 10.28-29 is related approximately to this period in the city's history: 'Solomon's horses were imported from Cilicia, where the king's agents purchased them. A chariot imported from Egypt cost six hundred shekels, a horse one hundred and fifty shekels; they were exported at these rates to all the Hittite and Aramean kings'.

[1] Greek 'Cilicia Pedias'; Latin 'Cilicia Campestris'. To the west of the plain rose the heavily forested mountains of Rough Cilicia, Greek 'Cilicia Tracheia'; Latin 'Cilicia Asperas'.

A stretch of the Roman road network between Olba Ura and Corycus (Kız Kalesi) in Rough Cilicia.

Funerary stele from Seleucia Pieria. First century BCE. Tarsus Museum. The epigram in Greek informs us that it was raised by Andron to preserve the memory of his wife Hermione, his daughter Pamphile and his sons Pamphilos and Andromachos. They were not all buried Seleucia Pieria because the mother and daughter died in Seleucia Pieria, the first son at Delos and the other at Rhodes.

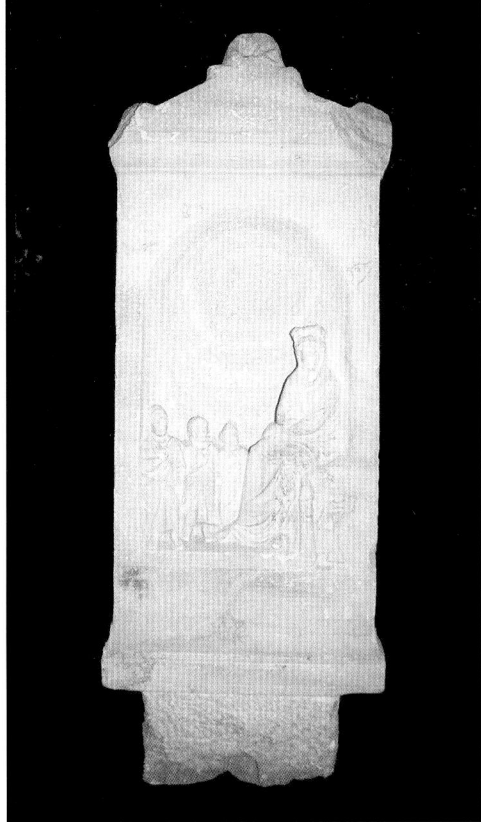

In the reign of Shalmanesser III (858-824 BCE) Cilicia became a vassal of Assyria. King Sennacherib[2] (704-681 BCE) is known to have destroyed and moved the city in 696 BCE from the tumulus to its present location on the Cydnus River (Tarsus Çayı). Before reaching the Mediterranean the Cydnus flowed into a large lagoon, which was known as the Lake of Rhegma in Roman times, and was navigable up to the city. At present the area where this lake existed is a fertile cotton field. In the OT, Tarshish, which frequently means large merchant ships, is used as a place name in the Mediterranean after the sixth-fifth centuries BCE, from which metals like silver, iron or lead came to Tyre in Phoenicia: 'Tarshish traded with you, so great was your wealth, exchanging silver, iron, tin, and lead for your wares' (Ez 27.12). Later Jewish literature regards this city as being Tarsus, the major port in Cilicia having connections with inland states of Anatolia rich in metals, horses and slaves. The more popular candidate, as a place name, is Tartessos in southern Spain. It is not known which one is meant when Jonah ran away from his mission and took a ship 'to Tarshish' (Jon 1.3). All of what was built in ancient Tarsus after its refoundation on the plain lies under the silt of the Cydnus River and the city's apartment houses, some 6 m deep.

Following the collapse of the Assyrian Kingdom, Cilicia seems to have survived as an independent state until Anatolia was captured by Cyrus the Great (555-530 BCE) of the Persian Empire which kept Cilicia as a vassal, ruled by the Syennesis, a local dynasty. Tarsus was the first urban centre with the amenities of civilization after passing the Cilician Gates to south, and thus an indispensable staging post to recover before travelling on to Syria and the countries beyond. According to Xenophon, Cyrus the Younger, and Arrian, Alexander the Great did not miss the chance of enjoying the opportunities the city offered. In *Anabasis*[3] Cyrus, after crossing the 'impassable' Cilician Gates (401 BCE) found himself in the large and well-watered Cilician plain 'full of all kinds of trees and of vines', which 'produces quantities of sesame and millet and wheat and barley', its capital 'a large

[2] Failed to enter Jerusalem (701 BCE) and was smitten by the angel of the Lord (Is 37.21-36; 2 Kgs 19.20-35).

[3] Cyrus the Younger marched from Sardis to Babylonia in order to dethrone his brother Artaxerxes II. He would eventually lose the battle of Cunaxa (401 BCE) and be killed. *Anabasis* ('march up-country') is the story of the journey of the ten thousand Greek mercenaries who had joined Cyrus in this expedition and travelled from Sardis to Mesopotamia and returned through eastern Anatolia and the Black Sea.

Uncovered section of the ancient street in Tarsus. It may have been first paved during the early rule of the Seleucids. The present-day remains are Roman and consists of black basalt blocks sloping on the sides toward the drainage channels. The road is also provided with a gutter. The ruins of a portico and halls flanking it are thought to date from a later period, third-fourth centuries CE.

and prosperous city' with a river called the Cydnus running 'through the middle of the city'. Strabo says that an immersion in the Cydnus was 'beneficial both to beasts and to men who suffer from sinews'. Vitruvius adds that 'In the Cilician city Tarsus there is a river, Cydnus by name, in which gouty persons bathe their legs to relieve the pain'. It is not known if Alexander knew any of the healing properties when he plunged into the river some three hundred years earlier ending up with instant acute pneumonia which almost cost him his life. The city's name as Antioch on Cydnus is first encountered in mid-third century BCE and may indicate a refoundation by Seleucus I, Nicator ('conqueror'; 321-281 BCE). This name is known to have survived until the mid-second century BCE when it was no more used. Although Tarsus is said to have been refounded as Antioch on Cydnus by Antiochus IV, Epiphanes ('god manifest'; 175-164 BCE), by this time the Seleucid vigour for colonization had been left in the past and Tarsus' refoundation was probably no more than another case of renaming. Even if there is no way of proving it, as was the case in the other Hellenistic cities, the cosmopolitan population of Tarsus may have included a substantial Jewish minority at the time of the early Seleucid rulers. Writing at the time of Paul, the Jewish philosopher Philo of Alexandria mentions Cilicia as one of the countries where Jews lived. In Acts 6.9 the Jews of Cilicia are mentioned attending 'the so-called Synagogue of Freedman'.

The city went through the tumultuous period of the First Mithradatic War (89-84 BCE), and the occupation of King Tigranes of Armenia from 83 to 69 BCE. In 67 BCE the Roman rule, following his subduing of the Cilician pirates, was reestablished by Pompey. Until this period the province that the Roman sources called Cilicia included Pamphylia and only a small portion of Rough Cilicia which was very different from Smooth Cilicia not only in its geography but also its social and economic life. For centuries the only commodity that the former could produce, apart from timber, was manpower. Until the time that Rome took over the region, with the decline of the Seleucids and the Ptolemies, unable to find employment anymore as mercenaries, the men had turned to brigandage and pirating. In 64 BCE Pompey, reshaping the political structure of Anatolia established the province of Cilicia extending from Cape Chelidonium to the Gulf of Issus. Smooth and Rough Cilicia were brought together with Tarsus as capital. In 51-50 BCE the Roman statesman Cicero is known to have served as the Roman governor of the province. Sometime around 44 BCE Cilicia was combined with Syria by Caesar as a single province and this situation lasted until it was divided by Vespasian in 72. Thus when in Acts 23.34 Felix asks for the 'province' of Paul and learns that he is from Cilicia, the word does not reflect the correct administrative situation of the time; either Paul had in mind the previous political status of the region or Luke is reflecting his time of relating the events.

One of the most memorable events of the city's early Roman history, which was later commemorated by Shakespeare, was the love story of Mark Antony (Marcus Antonius) and Cleopatra which began here in the autumn of 41 BCE. Some eight years before Cleopatra had had herself delivered to Caesar in Alexandria by a slave, wrapped in a carpet. This time she arranged a parade which may have been exaggerated by later writers, but still appropriate to the vulgar and ambitious character of her host Antony who had sent for the Queen to rebuke her for aiding Cassius. She had built for herself a barge with fittings in gold and silver and equipped with purple silk

Mosaic detail inscribed *kibotos Noah*, Noah's Chest ('Ark'). Misis (Mopsuestia) Mosaic Museum. End of the fourth-beginning of the fifth centuries CE. It has been claimed that the pavement it belonged to was the floor of a synagogue or a church.

sails. The vessel's crew, young boys and girls, were dressed as Erotes and Nereids. The sound of music and scent of rich perfumes reached across the water to the Tarsians who had flocked to the Cydnus' banks to watch Cleopatra 'reclined beneath a canopy of cloth of gold'. The couple moved to Daphne near Antioch to spend the winter. This was the beginning of a love story which lasted about a decade, with the well-known fatal end. Among many things which Antony would bestow on Cleopatra after a few years were the cedar-rich mountains of Rough Cilicia, a major timber resource of the ancient world for shipbuilding.

Recent excavations have shown that Tarsus of this period was a smaller flourishing copy of Antioch on Orontes. Rome had made it a 'free and independent city'. Although this privilege, in general, made a city think that it was still autonomous, but nothing more, it continued having a governing body of citizens — responsible to the Roman governor — and was exempted from some Roman taxes. At the time of Paul's travels Tarsus was the second important city of the province of Syria with Antioch as its capital. In the world of Paul it was very important to be not from the obscure countryside but from a prosperous and ancient city and Paul's pride in his home is evident when he says 'I am a Jew, of Tarsus in Cilicia, a citizen of no mean city' in Acts 21.39 to the Roman officer, and 'I am a Jew, born in Tarsus in Cilicia' in 22.3 during his defence before the Jerusalem Jews. Ancient literature tells us that the people of other Cilician cities did not like Tarsians and the patronage of Tarsus over them. Paul's words also imply that his family must have lived in Tarsus at least for a few generations, or more. Acts mentions Paul's Tarsian citizenship twice and does not give any information about it. Hellenistic ethics despised physical labour and normally a tentmaker would not have been given citizenship. Since obtaining this status cost a certain sum of money one may conclude that Paul's family was wealthy. Writing at the end of the century in which Paul lived Dio Chrysostom informs us that admission into the citizenship of Tarsus cost 500 drachmae, at the time a considerable amount. As was the case with his Roman citizenship Paul is thought to have inherited his Tarsian citizenship from his parents. Some scholars think that by Paul's Tarsian citizenship Acts may have referred to the local privileges the Jews held here although this did not give them the right of participating in the citizen body (*demos*) of the city. Citizenship was reserved for the wealthy aristocracy and involved both privileges and responsibilities. Some of the latter, such as the worship of local deities and the requirements of Greek education, which included athletic festivities, were not compatible with the religion of a Jew, especially for a Pharisee like Paul.

The ancient street which has recently been excavated in the city centre, the poor remains of the theatre on the Gözlükule Tumulus, the stretches of the Via Tauris connecting the city to the Cilician Gates and the large floor mosaic which was brought to light in the city (displayed at Archaeological Museum in Antakya), although all dating after Paul, give us an idea about the Tarsus of the Roman period.

It is impossible to know how much of his childhood Paul spent in Tarsus. Paul's command of the Septuagint, the Stoic traces of which some scholars find in his teaching, the method of argumentation in his letters — although such opportunities were also available at Jerusalem — are sometimes regarded as evidences of a diaspora Jewish setting, his hometown Tarsus. Learning Greek would indispensably bring a diaspora Jewish youth like Paul into contact with the culture that the language represented. Strabo compliments and perhaps exaggerates by saying that the 'people at Tarsus have devoted themselves so eagerly, not only to philosophy, but also to the whole round of education in general, that they have surpassed Athens, Alexandria, or any other place that can be named where there have been schools and lectures of philosophers'. Stoicism was a philosophical school founded by Zeno of Cyprus in about 300 BCE. It laid the greatest emphasis on ethics and so appealed particularly to the ethically-minded Romans and was very influential at the time of Paul. Among the Tarsian philosophers Strabo mentions Antipater, Archedemus, Zeno and Athenodorus. The last was one of the advisors of Augustus and appointed as the governor of Tarsus by the Emperor in about 15 BCE. Philostratus, however, writing in the first half of the third century CE in *Life of Apollonius* says the young Apollonius of Tyana left Tarsus soon — for its rival Aigai (Ayaş/Yumurtalık) — because the Tarsians 'attend more to their fine linen than the Alhenians did to wisdom; and a stream called the Cydnus runs through their city, along the banks of which they sit like so many water-fowl'. From Dio Chrysostom we learn that the Tarsians had a habit of making a peculiar unendurable sound, encountered both in adults and children, indoors or outside and day and night so that 'no one could walk even a short distance without encountering that ill-omened sound'. The literal translation of the Greek word used for this sound has a range of meanings from 'snorting' to 'snoring'.

St Paul's Well. Tarsus. In Anatolia, since the Christian traditions were superseded by Islam there is not much 'later Christian tradition' which has survived to the present. A rare case is the naming of a well in Tarsus as St Paul's Well, in Turkish Sümbül Kuyu ('well with hyacinth'). The first word being a corrupted form of the French 'San Pol' (Saint Paul) because 'sümbül' was also used as a man's name. Recent excavatians around the well have brought to light remains dating from the fourth century CE. The high number of churches known by Paul's name in Turkish — with or without his painting — shows how strong Paul's tradition was in Anatolia.

Epigram about Paul's contemporary Apollonius of Tyana. Adana Archaeological Museum. Third-fourth centuries CE. The fragment is thought to have come perhaps from Aigai (Ayaş/Yumurtalık) where the philosopher stayed after leaving Tarsus. In Greek it reads 'This man, named after Apollo, and shining forth from Tyana, extinguished the faults of men. The tomb in

Tyana [received] his body, but in truth heaven received him so that he might drive out the pains of men'. Apollonius of Tyana was a sage/philosopher/ascetic teacher contemporary with Paul. At the time of the latter's journeys he also travelled extensively through Antioch, Ephesus, Corinth, Athens, Rome and other cities of the Roman world.

It is not known if or how often the young Paul visited Tarsus while he was studying in Jerusalem. Or where he was for over a decade until he appeared in Acts as a persecutor of Christians. After his conversion and sojourn in Arabia, Paul returned to Damascus and had to flee to Jerusalem. Here perhaps around the year 36 his Christian brethren 'took him down to Caesarea and sent him on his way to Tarsus' (Acts 9.30). The Jewish tradition of the time identified Tarsus with the Tarshish of Is 66.19, the first of the countries which the eschatological mission of God covered. Since the choice of Tarsus, normally, would have been the apostle's own preference it has been suggested that he may have even imagined himself like a new Jonah. The city was, after all, his hometown and he may have also thought of sheltering under his Tarsian citizenship, with friends or family there. Paul, himself, knew that after his recent experiences at Damascus and Jerusalem, he could not expect a welcome from his own race in Cilicia. Although it has been suggested that he may have been disowned and disinherited by his family there is no evidence to support this. Acts mentions Cilician Jews among those who opposed Stephen and debated with him. Paul's conversion was most likely a shock for his family circle and friends and he may have been rejected by them. His kinsmen and neighbors were perhaps frightened to speak to him. Some of the five lashing incidents ('forty lashes minus one' cases) and other persecutions that the apostle mentions in 2 Cor 11 may have taken place during this stage of his life. His words in Phil 3.8 'More than that, I even consider everything as a loss because of the supreme good of knowing Christ Jesus my Lord' are sometimes interpreted to imply broken relations, both materially and spiritually, with his family. Some of his family may have later become Christians and helped him financially during his imprisonment.

Paul lived hereabouts until about 46 when Barnabas came and asked for his help in Antioch. The apostle's own words in Gal 1.21 that he 'went into the regions of Syria and Cilicia' are interpreted by some as indicating that Paul preferred to stay away from Tarsus. Paul's saying that the Christians in Judea heard that he 'was preaching the faith' also confirms his activity (Gal 1.23). Normally Smooth Cilicia extended from Rhosus (Arsus) to the Pyramus (Seyhan) and Rough Cilicia as far west as the Melas (Manavgat) River. At the time of Paul Rough Cilicia still kept much of its complicated pre-Roman political structure. Some of it was ruled by Archelaus II of Cappadocia. Sometime around 38 CE territory was given to Antiochus IV of Commagene who kept it until the time of Vespasian. The territory of Diocaesarea and Claudiopolis belong to a M Antonius Polemo, related to Polemo of Laodicea who was first a king in Cilicia and later in Pontus. The larger part of the region however belonged to native principalities, such as the temple state of Zeus at Olba, or the state of Seleucia on Calycadnus. Although there is no information about the activities of Paul some of the early churches which blossomed among the Jewish and Gentile population in places such as Soloi/ Pompeiopolis (Viranşehir), Elaiussa/Sebaste (Ayaş), Canytelis (Kanlıdivane), Olba (Ura), Diocaesarea (Uzuncaburç), Corycus (Kız Kalesi), Corasium (Susanoğlu), Seleucia on Calycadnus (Silifke), Claudiopolis/Ninica (Mut), Mopsuestia (Misis/Yakapınar), Anazarbus (Anavarza Kalesi), Castabala Hierapolis (Bodrum Kalesi), Mallus (Kızıltahta) or Epiphania (Gözneler) may have owed their origins to the apostle. Paul's words in Gal 1.22 that he 'was unknown personally to the churches in Judea' are interpreted as solitary missionary activity independent of the Jerusalem church. Though not explicitly stated in Acts it seems likely that he visited Tarsus and the churches he founded in Cilicia again when he travelled in the direction of southern Galatia and further during his second and third journeys.

Sarcophagus from the necropolis of Corycus (Kız Kalesi). Roman period. Its epitaph on the casket in Greek informs us that it belonged to Aurelius Eusambatios Menandros, citizen of Corycus, and his wife Matrona. He was a town-councillor. The inscription ends with the Jewish formula 'Do [not despai]r, for no one is immortal but one who has commanded that this should happen, and [who has also put us in the ci]rcle of the planets'. His name Eusambatios and the closing words of the epitaph, in addition to the worn-out menorah decorating the lid, show that he was a Jew.

ANTIOCH ON ORONTES

Antioch on Orontes (Antakya), once called the 'Queen of the East' and known as the third largest city of the Roman Empire after Rome and Alexandria, played a pivotal role in the spread of Christianity from Palestine to the rest of the world, and from Jews to Gentiles.

On the main trade routes from the east to the Mediterranean and from Syria to Anatolia this prosperous city was founded by Seleucus I, Nicator (321-281 BCE) in the 300s BCE. Seleucus I was Alexander's childhood friend in the class of Aristotle at Pella, and later became one of his generals and carved for himself the largest portion of Alexander's lands after the latter's death. The frontiers of the Seleucid Kingdom extended from the Hellespont to India. 'Orontes' (from Assyrian *arantu*) was attached to the city's name to distinguish it from the other fifteen Antiochs which this King is said to have founded,[1] naming all of them after his father who was a general in Philip II's army. Among Antioch's foundation stories the one which does justice to the character of the later Antiochenes, who seem in the course of time to have cultivated a great number of vanities, is probably the one told by the people of the city of the present day. According to this, a king who suffered from insomnia came to the slope of Mount Silpius in his search to find a place which would help him to fall asleep. Here, to the surprise of his family and retinue he descended from his horse, lay on the grass, put his head on a piece of stone and started snoring. After waking up he decided that this was the right spot for his new city.

Silver coin of Seleucus I, Nicator (321-281 BCE), founder of Antioch. İstanbul Archaeological Museums.

Limited excavation and fairly extensive ancient sources provide the evidence for our knowledge of the ancient Antioch. It was laid out on the flat area between the Orontes (Asi) River and Mount Silpius (Habib Neccar Dağı, 500 m) and surrounded by a wall. It was founded on the grid plan, which was the fashion of the period and possessed all the essential institutions of a *polis*; an assembly (*demos*), a council (*boule*) and temples and a gymnasium, although all operating under the Macedonian monarchy. Since the top of the Silpius carried a strategic importance for the settlement's defence there

[1] Research has shown that most of the Antiochs in Anatolia owed their existence to the Seleucids: Antioch on Cydnus (Tarsus), Antioch on Sarus (Adana), Antioch on Pyramus (both Mallus/Kızıltahta and Magarsus/Dört Direk), Pisidian Antioch (Yalvaç), Antioch on Meander (Başaran Köy), Antioch of the nation of Chrysaorians (Alabanda, near Çine), Antioch by Callirhoe (Edessa/Urfa) and Antioch in Mygdonia (Nizip).

was, probably, a citadel here at this early date. What is seen here today dates from Justinian's time, 527-65 CE. Ancient literature informs us about some of the monuments built by the Seleucid rulers. The agora that Seleucus I built probably stood by the bank of the river close to the docks and warehouses.

The turning point in the Seleucid history was the defeat of Antiochus III, the Great (223-187 BCE) by the Romans at the battle of Magnesia (190 BCE). With the treaty of Apamea (188 BCE) the Seleucids left all of their possessions to the north of the Taurus, Pamphylia and Pisidia to Rome who turned them over to its ally Pergamum. The Seleucid kings, however, still possessed a vast territory and seem to have continued their efforts to make their capital physically and culturally a rich city, trying hopelessly to imitate the Ptolemies of Egypt. The slope of Silpius beyond the Hellenistic city wall was settled during the reign of Antiochus IV, Epiphanes (175-164 BCE) and called Epiphania. There is, however, no trace of any of the monuments mentioned by ancient literary sources. Antiochus IV had spent fourteen years as a hostage in Rome and ancient literature informs us that it was he who introduced gladiatorial games to the east in 166 BCE.

Simplified plan of ancient Antioch.

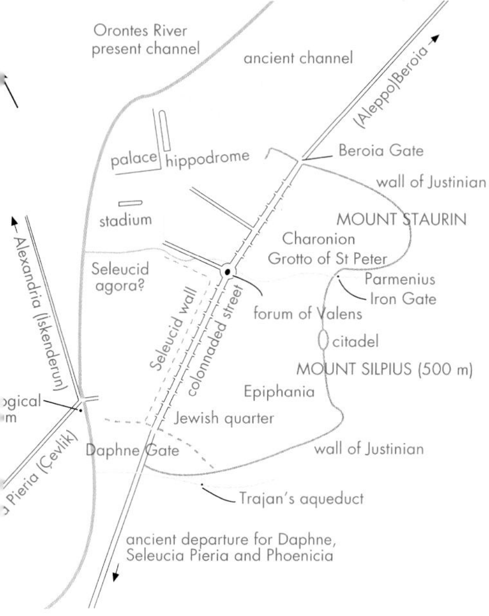

The earliest settlers of the city are said to have been the Greek and Macedonian veterans in the Seleucid army and other people like Syrians, Cretans and Cypriots, and Jews who may have been supplemented by immigrants from Palestine and Mesopotamia. The information about the Jews of Antioch mostly comes from Josephus. Writing several decades after the death of Paul, the Jewish historian says that the Jews were among the people that Seleucus I settled at Antioch to whom he gave privileges. The historian's remark about full citizenship granted to the Jews of Antioch may have been an exaggeration; like anywhere else the Jews of Antioch may have had the *politeuma*, a political body for self-government, headed by a *gerousia*, an association of elders and were allowed to follow their ancestral laws. The Antiochene Jews may have felt the tension created by the war Antiochus IV carried out against the Jews in Palestine. Ancient Christian, Jewish and Arabic literary sources, the earliest of which does not go back before the fifth century CE, mention synagogues built on the grave sites of the Maccabean martyrs and that in course of time these were turned into churches.

In general, the Jews of Antioch were wealthy and since Seleucid times had enjoyed most of the rights of citizenship to the chagrin of non-Jewish citizens, so that in about Paul's time they still received money to buy their own oil — instead of the (defiled) oil prepared by Gentiles — for exercises in the gymnasium. The information is interesting in showing the uncertain situation of some of the Antiochene Jews inasmuch as they were Hellenized enough to participate in the gymnasium yet kept their regulations of purity. Thus it is not a surprise that during the conflict between Paul and Peter the Antiochene Jewish Christians supported the latter. All of them probably could speak Greek and used the Septuagint. Judaism's monotheism and its ethical teachings about the conduct of life became attractive for non-Jews and according to Josephus 'They also made proselytes of a great many of the Greeks perpetually, and thereby after a sort brought them to be a portion of their own body'. Nicholas of Antioch, who is mentioned as one of the seven deacons in Jerusalem chosen at the church of Jerusalem for the daily distribution from the common fund (Acts 6.5), may have been one of such early proselytes.

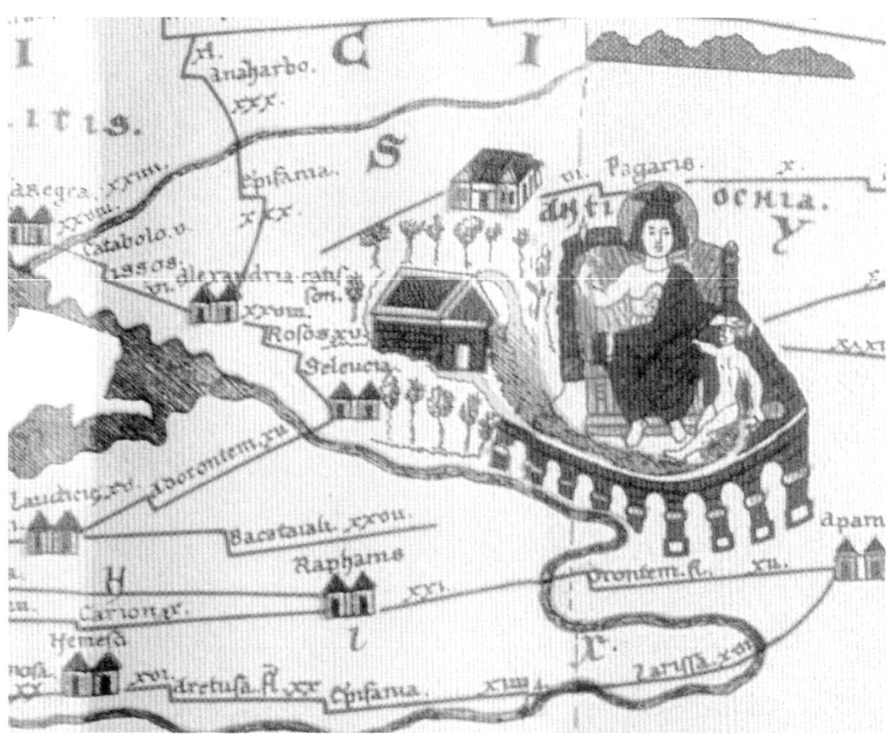

Personification of Antioch on Orontes in the Peutinger Map (*Tabula Peutingeriana*). The city is shown as a man seated on a throne holding a spear in his right hand. His nimbed head divides the name of the city, 'Antiochia' into two. His left hand rests on the head of the deity of the Orontes River, personified as a young nude boy. Water pours out of the vessel which he holds in his left hand and flows by an aqueduct toward a pool covered by a building in the grove of Daphne (Defne). In the map Seleucia Pieria (Çevlik), Rhosus (Arsus), Alexandria (İskenderun), Epiphania (Gözneler) and other familiar cities are mentioned.

In later history, with the decline of the Seleucid power, Syria and Antioch were occupied by Tigranes I of Armenia from 83 to 69 BCE, and then again in 64 BCE, following his defeat of Mithradates, Antioch was taken over by Pompey, to be made the capital of the province of Syria which would be established a few years later. Thus the city became the most important Roman civil and military post in the east against the Parthians. Almost all of the early Roman rulers are known to have visited Antioch as they occupied posts in the east, or after they became emperors, and showed interest in the public works of this eastern capital and donated various edifices. In the spring of 53 BCE the governor of the east Marcus Crassus began his fateful expedition, which ended with the loss of the legionary standards to the Parthians, from Antioch. In about 44 CE, when Cilicia was attached to the province of Syria, Antioch continued to be the capital. There is no trace of any of the monuments claimed to have been built by the early Roman rulers. Normally, by Paul's time the cult of the divine Julius (deified Caesar) and Dea Roma, goddess of Rome would have been introduced to the city. New aqueducts and cisterns were added to those built by the Seleucids to meet the need of the growing population which must have been getting close to some 200,000 inhabitants. With the establishment of Roman rule, in addition to Roman administrators the number of businessman from Italy who traded in the city had also increased. After the defeat of Brutus and Cassius at Philippi, Mark Antony visited Antioch in 41 BCE and restored the property that Cassius had previously seized from the local Jews. He is said to have rebuilt the pantheon and the theatre and added an amphitheatre for gladiatorial fights, on the slope of Mount Silpius. His wedding with Cleopatra in the winter of 37/36 BCE is said to have taken place at Antioch. Augustus was also known to have visited Antioch twice and showed interest in the development of the city. Some of the monuments which would be completed later would have been started by his initiation. The major event of this era was the foundation of the local games which would in time become the Olympic Games of Antioch.

Among its monuments Antioch's fame came from the great colonnaded street which ran from east to west. While the Beroia (Aleppo) Gate on the east led to Syria, at the opposite end the departure for Phoenicia was by the Daphne Gate. The street was begun by Herod the Great (37-4 BCE) who visited the city frequently and by the time it was completed, in the reign of Tiberius (14-37 CE) it was a 10 m wide marble-paved street, with double-storey colonnades on each side, making it possible to walk for 4 km under

Charonion on Mount Staurin. Antakya. The carving of this apotropaic image was commanded by a 'philosopher and wonder-worker' named Leios in the reign of the Antiochus IV, Epiphanes (175-164 BCE) to protect Antioch from a plague. This was a great mask with some special words on it, which have not survived, for the salvation of the city. The talisman was called by the people of Antioch 'Charonion', the name of a chthonic deity, who was appeased and ended the disaster which had already sent many souls to Charon. On its right shoulder there is a small standing figure. It has been suggested that the bust was not finished because the plague disappeared before it was completed.

porticos. It is known as one of the earliest streets of this kind. It saw several reconstructions, the latest being by Justinian. Excavations have shown that owing to the debris which has been washed down from the slopes of the Silpius and deposited on it, it is now some 10 m below today's Kurtuluş Street, following the line of the ancient Seleucid wall. The mountain torrent was especially strong between the Silpius and the Staurin where it was named Parmenius, or Onopnictes ('donkey-drowner', today's Hacı Kürrüş).

Antioch was founded in a major earthquake zone and there was regular rebuilding under both its Hellenistic and Roman rulers. The fact that the city did not have a particular regard for Poseidon the earth-shaker, may have been the result of the frequency of tremors. Though almost nothing is left of this once great city, the stunning mosaics (all dating after Paul's time) brought to light from the excavations in Antakya (Antioch) and its suburbs, nearby Harbiye/Defne (Daphne) and Çevlik (Seleucia Pieria) give at least some idea of the prosperity and high living standard of ancient Antioch.[2]

By Paul's time the city was already spreading toward the level plain to the west of the Orontes River, which Strabo claims to have been navigable for about 40 km, until it reached the Mediterranean. This is confirmed from the fact that an Egyptian sea force sailing upstream had occupied Antioch in 146 BCE. Before entering the city from the opposite side the river split into two and created an island. This was not settled at Paul's time except for the hippodrome and palace which are said to have been built by Q Marcius Rex, the governor of Cilicia in 67 BCE. The channel of the river that stood on the mountain side was, in time, filled in and its trace was lost by the Middle Ages. Today the only visible remains on it are the poor ruins of the hippodrome and of a solid building enclosed in a wall, known by the locals as han ('inn').

Agricultural produce was bountiful in the warm climate and its location on trade routes helped to make Antioch an extremely wealthy city, attracting traders and artists from many countries. Antioch became the camp of one of the three or four legions stationed in Syria as early as the time of Augustus. The inhabitants according to Tacitus 'enjoyed having dealings with the soldiers they knew, and many of the provincials were linked with them by marriage and family ties'. The Roman soldiers who were based at the camps near Antioch were known to have been reluctant to leave the region. The wealth and luxury of the city were famed and the self-indulgent lifestyle of its inhabitants was immortalised by the first-century-CE Roman satirist Juvenal as he commented on the effect of oriental excesses on Roman life: 'The Syrian Orontes poured into Tiber long ago, carrying with it its language and customs, its flute-players and slanting strings; its native timbrels, and the girls ordered to sell themselves at the circus'. Although there is now almost nothing left to be seen from the city of Paul's time, when the apostle lived here many of the Hellenistic monuments and those built by the early Roman rulers must have stood.

The existence of nearby Daphne played an important role in Antioch's history; so much that the city was sometimes referred to as 'Antioch near Daphne'. When Hannibal sheltered with the Seleucids and came to Antioch in the summer of 195 BCE Antiochus III was absent but he found the king's son, future Antiochus IV, celebrating the games at Daphne, a fact which also implies the existence of a stadium and probably a theatre. Tradition has

[2] Displayed at Archaeological Museum in Antakya, the Louvre and over twenty museums or galleries in the US.

ANTIOCH ON ORONTES

Detail from the border of a mosaic pavement from Yakto near Daphne. Mid-fifth century CE. Archaeological Museum. Antakya. Although it dates some four hundred years after Paul's time the mosaic reflects the monuments and life of Roman Antioch. In front of 'the laboratory [workshop] of Martyrion' a servant pours wine for his master. Next is a group of a man, an elderly woman, and a young woman, who holds an object in her left hand, in familiar conversational gestures. A young boy holding a basket is in front of the 'Olympic Stadium'.

Next to the stadium is the 'Private bath of Ardabourious' which consists of two gabled buildings linked by a construction with a pyramidal roof and with some trees in its garden. The fact that the owner of the bath held the office of *magister militum per orientem* (commander-in-chief of the army in the East)in Antioch (450-57 CE) helps us to date the pavement. To the left are a rider and his servant as he turns his head backward clearing the way for his patron and on the other side of the door a man with a basket in his outstretched hand and a bundle under his left arm, perhaps about to enter the bath.

Mosaic showing Daphne being turned into a laurel tree, about to be caught by Apollo. From Daphne. Third century CE. The Art Museum. Princeton University. Princeton. New Jersey.

it that Apollo pursued the nymph Daphne here; the girl, being a priestess of the Mother Earth, and having been struck by one of Eros' lead-tipped arrows, could love neither a god nor a mortal, and was turned into a laurel tree (Greek *daphne*) by the goddess. At Paul's time the very tree into which the nymph was transformed was one of the attractions of the suburb. From ancient literature we learn that the oracle of Apollo at Daphne 'fell silent' in the fourth century when a martyrium was built at this spot and the bones of martyr bishop Babylas were transferred to it.

The site was famous for its cypress groves and sweet springs which are still the main source of fresh water for Antakya. In fact, the existence of such a rich nearby water source was one of the reasons for the choice of the site of Antioch. Seleucus I had consecrated the grove to Apollo, who was regarded as the second tutelary deity of his dynasty and Antioch (the first being Zeus), by building a sanctuary here. Ancient sources also mention the existence of a temple for Artemis. By the late Hellenistic and early Roman period Daphne had became a well-settled town. In Paul's days it was a very popular suburb with a Jewish population. In their effort to establish an ancient past for themselves the Antiochene Jews later created a tradition which placed the traditional meeting of Nebuchadnezzar II (605-562 BCE) of Babylon and the Sanhedrin at Daphne. In the reign of Antiochus IV the Jewish High Priest Onias III lived in or near Daphne when he was in trouble, sheltered in the 'sanctuary of Daphne' (2 Mc 4.33), probably that of Apollo. He was persuaded to leave the temple and was murdered.

From Acts 11.19 we learn that to such a cosmopolitan city — with its Greek and oriental cults and philosophies — came some of the Jewish Christians who were 'scattered by the persecutions that arose because of Stephen' in about 33 CE and preached 'the word to no one but Jews'. The Cypriots and Cyrenian Jews among them, however, could speak Greek and they preached the Gospel not only to the Antiochene Jews but to the Greeks as well. Thus from the very beginning the church at Antioch seems to have included both Jewish and non-Jewish Christians.

These years correspond to the reign of Gaius (Caligula; 37-41 CE) whose father Germanicus had been killed (poisoned?) in Antioch some two decades before. Caligula was then seven years old and staying with his father. When an earthquake took place in 37, shortly after Caligula succeeded to the throne, he immediately sent help to remedy the damage in Antioch and Daphne, very probably as a sign of his gratitude to the local people for the respect that they had shown to his father's funeral. Another important event of his reign was an outbreak of anti-Semitism. The tumult began at the circus, and spread to the other people of the city who attacked and killed many Jews and burned the synagogue. Just before his death Caligula decreed that a statue of Zeus, in his own likeness, be placed at the Temple of Jerusalem and caused wide unrest in Judea. The sentiment in Judea was probably felt first by the Antiochene Jews because the imperial letter would have been received by the governor of Syria who resided in Antioch.

After the violent feud in Alexandria (38-41 CE) for which he held the Jews responsible, Claudius tried to put an end to the enmity between the Greeks and Jews in Alexandria, reproaching the first and confirming the rights of the second. A copy of his decree was also sent 'to Syria' whose capital was Antioch, so that it would have a similar effect and thus improve the strained relations between the pagans and Jews.

One more important event of this period was the permission of the right to reestablish the Olympic Games in the city. It was granted in 43 CE after a request from the citizens of Antioch. The entertainment included theatrical and athletic competitions and other events and was held in the hippodrome. They are known as the longest-lived games, lasting until 520 CE.

Acts tells us that when the Jerusalem church heard that plenty of Gentiles had become Christians in Antioch, Barnabas was sent to the city. It is not known for how long Barnabas worked in Antioch alone. In Acts 13.1 the latter is mentioned as one of the prophets and teachers together with 'Symeon who was called Niger, Lucius of Cyrene and Manaean who was a close friend of Herod [Antipas] the tetrarch, and Saul'. When Barnabas saw that he needed assistance he went to Tarsus and fetched Paul and together they worked 'for a whole year'. From the words used in Acts 'when he had found him' one may conclude that having been rejected by his co-citizens Paul was not in Tarsus but probably proclaiming the Gospel in the country. Later Christian tradition records that at Antioch Paul and Barnabas preached in a kind of alley or street known then as Singon or Siagon ('jawbone'), probably called so because of its shape, by the pantheon. There is no information about the location where they preached or the pantheon. Although Acts says 'a great number' or 'a large number' were taught by the efforts of Paul and Barnabas it is difficult to make an assessment in numbers from such words. Still, it is generally accepted that the creation of a substantial nucleus of Gentile Christian minority in the church of Antioch was due to Paul's efforts. When their number increased following the popular practice of the time to refer to the partisans of a famous person as 'Herodians', or 'Pompeians' (supporters or partisans of Pompey), the term Christians,[3] a Greek word with a Latin ending, first came into use originating in the city to describe the followers of Christ, as distinct from the Jews (Acts 11.26) sometime before the 60s CE. It is not known if the word was first self-designation or used by others. The new term comprised all the known terms used until then to refer to the believers of the new faith: brethren, witnesses, those of the way, saints, etc. The coinage of the word also shows that at the beginning Christianity was regarded as a sort of social club. It is also very probable that Paul and Barnabas, together or separately, visited the Syrian countryside and proclaimed the Gospel. In most of the places they visited there were in addition to Aramaic-speaking Jewish Christians, Greek-speaking Jewish Christians who had to flee from Jerusalem after the martyrdom of Stephen. Paul and Barnabas may have created the nuclei of Christians here. North Syria was rich in ancient and wealthy cities each probably with a Jewish population perhaps with a synagogue. Although the Roman road building in Syria had not yet begun the urban centres had been connected by ancient routes since antiquity. Some places like Alexandria (İskenderun), Rhosus (Arsus), Seleucia Pieria (Çevlik), Nicopolis (Islahiye), Cyrrhus (Nebi Uri), Beroia (Aleppo), Zeugma (Belkıs), Dura-Europos (Salihiye), Chalcis on Belus (Is/Qinnesrin), Epiphania (Hama) and Hierapolis/Bambyce (Mambij) may have been places where the apostles proclaimed the Gospel.

Ancient road connecting Antioch to Rhosus (Arsus) over Kızıldağ avoiding the Assyrian Gates (Belen Pass).

The chronology of events at some stage of development according to Acts and what is learned from Paul's letter to the Galatians does not agree, but for the subject of this book it is circumstantial. Effort has been spent by scholars to conform the two sources and obtain a complete picture of events. Luke says that after the famine under Claudius, Paul and Barnabas took the famine aid to Jerusalem. Ancient sources mention a few famines which took place in the reign of Claudius (41-54) and some of them would have been effective 'all over the world' known to Luke. It may not be possible to guess which famine Agabus prophesied owing to the Spirit in Acts 11.27. Paul's

[3] Greek *christianoi,* 'Christians' or 'Christus-people'. The word was later modified to 'Chrestos' (Greek 'good, useful') by perhaps some Gentile Christians who may not have known the meaning 'anointed' that it carried for Jews and may have regarded this a more suitable name for a deity. 'Chrestians' appeared along with 'Christians'.

Kureş bridge on the river of the same name in Yayladağ on the Antioch — Laodicea route.

Burial towers of Amrit (Marathos). Sixth century BCE. They are locally known as *meghazil* ('spindles') and among the oldest surviving monuments on the Phoenician coastal route.

saying in Gal 2.2 that he went to Jerusalem 'in accord with a revelation' is regarded by some as being related to the revelation of Agabus. This famine may have struck Egypt and Palestine, Syria including Antioch and its environs around the years 44-46. The Antiochene Christians sent aid to Jerusalem to relieve the stress there. Since the revelation took place before the famine it is difficult to guess when exactly the help was sent.

Jerusalem was some 400 km from Antioch and the cities were connected by two ancient roads which both, at Paul's time, had a string of Roman colonies. One of these routes leaving Antioch by the Beroia (Aleppo) Gate followed the course of the Orontes by the skirts of the Anti-Lebanon Mountains as far as the Bekaa Valley. It ran by way of Apamea, Epiphania (Hama), Emesa (Homs) and Heliopolis (Baalbek). This road continued by way of Damascus where the caves were popular hideouts of the bandits at Paul's time and after and may have been the source of the expression 'a den of thieves' (Mt 21.13). The second and more popular road left Antioch by the Daphne Gate and crossing the skirts of Mount Casius by its eastern foothills and following the bed of the Nahr el-Kabir descended to Mediterranean at Laodicea by the Sea (Latakya), a city founded by Seleucus I and again named for his wife. This was a well-trodden route, well known in the journeys of Assyrian kings and Alexander the Great. In Paul's time some of the population still spoke Phoenician. It continued by way of Antaradus (Tartus), Tripolis, Byblos (Jebeil) and Berytus (Colonia Julia Augusta Felix/Beirut) from where an overland extension by way of Heliopolis (Baalbek) reached Damascus and on to Jerusalem. After Berytus the coastal route continued by way of Sidon (Saida), Tyre (Tyrus), Ptolemais/Acco and Caesarea. The earliest milestone on the route dates from 56 CE and was found near Beirut. It mentions the building of the road from Antioch to the new colony of Ptolemais. This was, normally, the road by which the Roman forces stationed in northern Syria would travel to Palestine when required. It was possible to reach Jerusalem by any of the last two stations by using long-established trails.

Although the amount of aid that Paul and Barnabas took to Jerusalem is not known, it was important to show the strong ties which existed between the Christian communities in the two cities and the concern of Antiochene Christians for the mother church at Jerusalem. Josephus' remark about the expensive gifts sent to the Jerusalem Temple by the Antiochene Jews may imply the wealth of later Antiochene Jews as well. The wealth of the Church of Antioch is important for the fact that whether Gentile or Jewish Christians,

Grotto-Church of St Peter. Antakya. This cave is on the slope of Mount Staurin, Mountain of the 'Cross'. Named thus after a cross which is said to have appeared in the sky above the mountain following an earthquake in 526 CE the eastern

extension of Mount Silpius is traditionally regarded as a meeting place of early Christians. The grotto was given a façade, probably in the eleventh century after the Crusader conquest, since which time it has been the Church of St Peter.

it was these people who financed Paul's missionary journeys at the beginning, although later Paul himself worked and received money from some of the churches he founded. Scholars, dwelling on the difficulties and expense involved in transporting bulky goods overland in antiquity, believe that the aid was in the form of cash by which grain would be bought perhaps at black market prices in Jerusalem and distributed. From Acts 12.25 that Barnabas and Paul 'completed their relief mission' we understand that they stayed in Jerusalem for a considerable length of time. Some scholars believe that this visit is the same that Paul mentions as being his second visit to Jerusalem (after his conversion) in Galatians. If this was so from the letter we learn that it was during this trip that Paul also met James, Peter and John in Jerusalem. The Jerusalem church would surely have heard that Paul claimed his apostleship independently of it and preached to Gentiles and Jews a somewhat liberated Gospel. Now Paul had even brought Titus, one of his uncircumcised Gentile converts to the city. There were plenty who were against the Gospel that Paul preached and their open opposition would have been against Paul's idea of a united church of Jews and Gentiles. Meeting the three pillars of the Jerusalem church privately Paul received their approval of his mission to the Gentiles such that it was agreed Paul and Barnabas should continue in the same manner to preach Gentiles (uncircumcised) and Peter to Jews (circumcised). Paul and Barnabas also were not to neglect collecting funds for the poor at the Jerusalem church.

The apostle Peter is associated with Antioch in several ways. Paul in his letter to the Galatians tells us how he met Peter in Antioch and clashed with him over the Jewish dietary requirements. Jerusalem was not distant and Peter may have visited Antioch more frequently than this to help the missionary work here. He may have also stopped at Antioch during his traditional journeys to or from Rome or Corinth. 1 Pt assigns the apostle Pontus, Galatia, Cappadocia, Asia and Bithynia as his field of evangelization. Some think that 'the another place' to which he disappeared in Acts 12.17 was probably Antioch. While some of the early Christian writings mention him as the founder of the church at Antioch, some say he was its first bishop, a tradition which have been based on the fact that he may have won the conflict with Paul and may have stayed at Antioch and dominated the church.

SELEUCIA PIERIA

Simplified plan of Seleucia Pieria.

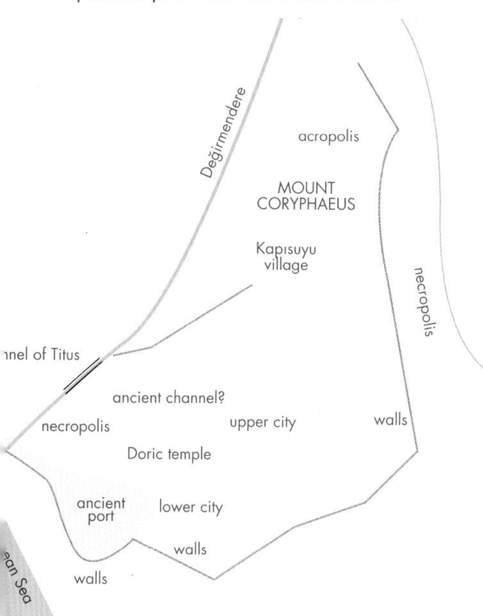

Seleucia (in) Pieria (Çevlik) was founded partly on a rocky promontory projecting from Mount Coryphaeus (Musa Dağı, 'Mountain of Moses'; 1,255 m), the southernmost extension of Mount Pieria (Kızıldağ, 2,240 m), and partly on its skirts below, some 10 km away from the point where the Orontes pours into the Mediterranean at the foot of Mount Casius (Keldağ, 'bald mountain', 1,739 m). In the archives of Ugarit and to the Hittites this mountain was known as Hazzi. It is one of the two deified mountains (the other being Namni) in relief on which the Hittite storm-god Teshup stands in the rock-sanctuary of Yazılıkaya near Hattusa. According to legend, while Seleucus I, Nicator (312-281 BCE) was sacrificing for Zeus on the Casius an eagle snatched part of the sacrificial offering and carried it to the place where the new town would be built. It was named after himself and known by the name of nearby Mount Pieria, originally the name of a mountainous region in Macedonia, but also as Seleucia in Syria. It was chosen as a capital before the foundation of Antioch and was one of the nine cities which the King named after his dynasty. The site had a sheltered inner harbour and an impregnable acropolis which was surrounded by one of the strongest fortifications of the Hellenistic period. The King's successor, Antiochus I (281-261 BCE), however, realizing that a coastal city was open to attacks from the sea, and lacking a strong navy, preferred to move the new capital to Antioch from where the inland trade routes also could be controlled. The city changed hands between the Seleucids and the Ptolemies. The invasion of the latter in 146 BCE is referred to in 1 Mc 11.8: 'Plotting evil against Alexander, King Ptolemy [Philometer] took possession of the cities along the seacoast as far as Seleucia-by-the-Sea'. During the final stage of Seleucid history the city was free and stood against Tigranes when he occupied Cilicia and Syria, owing probably to its topographical advantages which were sometime later complimented by Strabo as being 'a notable fortress and is too strong to be taken by force'.

The inner harbour of Seleucia was created by enlarging a natural basin at the mouth of a stream which is now known as Değirmendere. Shortly after Paul's time this became the most important Roman port for the Syrian fleet in the east from which the armies campaigning against first the Parthians and later the Sassanians, were supplied. Later, under Vespasian (69-79) and then Titus (79-81), and Domitian (81-96) and finally completed in the following century, an artificial water course was constructed to divert this stream from the harbour to prevent it from being silted up. This is a canal of some 1,400 m long, the final 130 m. of which was tunnelled through the rock to a height and width of 6 metres. Thus the torrent of Değirmendere poured into the open sea instead of the narrow port, which is now completely silted up. The cutting of the so-called 'tunnel of Titus' was the greatest project that Romans ever undertook in the provinces. Inscriptions which have survived on its walls, and which give the names of Vespasian and Titus, originally must have also included Domitian. Other inscriptions record that the work was done in sections and with the participation of some of the Roman legions stationed in eastern Anatolia. Some inscriptions also show that further work was done by soldiers of the legions under Antoninus Pius in about 149. Still, in the long run this would not have saved the harbour and it was by the sixth century blocked completely. A long and strong wall, made of various kinds of large limestone blocks, reinforced with towers, surrounded both the port and the lower city which was found between the port and the higher city with the acropolis. Today stretches of this wall survive on the eastern side where the acropolis slopes down toward a brook. In addition to the spur through which the tunnel went the gentle skirt on this side also served as the necropolis. On the west side, flanked by the Değirmendere, the city ends with a cliff and did not require strong

Commemorative inscription at the northern end of the tunnel of Titus in Seleucia Pieria. First century CE. In Latin it reads *divus Vespasianus et divus Titus f c*, that is 'Divine Vespasian and Divine Titus made it'. It is thought to have been carved after the death of both emperors. The word in the lower right corner in Greek reads '444', a date which in the Seleucid calendar corresponds to 131/2 CE, some fifty years after the reigns of the two emperors who built the tunnel.

Tunnel of Titus. Northern end.

fortifications. In its history after Paul's time the city seems to have shared the good and bad times of nearby Antioch. The mosaic pavements brought to light show the existence of residential quarters both in the upper and lower cities.

The city may have been one of those to which Greek-speaking Jewish Christians fled after the martyrdom of Stephen. This was the port from which Paul and Barnabas together with John Mark sailed to Cyprus and beyond on their first missionary journey.

Rock-cut Roman family tomb. Seleucia Pieria. 39/40 CE (dated in Greek on the door lintel). The niche to the right shows a standing woman. The window to the lower left, the crosses and the unfinished apse below the door were added later by the hermits who used the site.

Walls of the silted inner port. The tunnel of Titus goes through the height to the left. To the right is the beginning of the upper city.

Doric temple. Upper city. Looking toward the Mediterranean and Mount Casius.

Rock-cut stairway mentioned in the *Histories* of Polybius between the lower and upper cities.

Hellenistic fortifications.

Outer port. Looking toward Mount Casius.

Roman rock-cut tombs (Beşikli Mağara, 'cave with a cradle').

PONTUS/EUXINE SEA
(BLACK SEA)
Amastris
Heraclea
Bosphorus
Hebrus
Axios
Styrmon
THRACE
Byzantium
Chalcedon
Nicomedia
MACEDONIA
Pangaion 1,956
Nestus
PROPONTIS
(MARMARA)
BITHYNIA
Ancyra
Philippi
Neapolis
Nicaea
Sangarius
Doberus?
Ascania
Amphipolis
Hellespont
Cyzicus
Prusa
Dorylaeum
Tembris
Gordion
Edessa
Pella
Allante
Thassos
Palaipolis
Apollonia
Ludias
Thessalonica
Samothrace
Midaum
Germa
Pessinus
Beroia
Aloros
Imbros
Ergasteria
MYSIA
Rhyndacus
Tuzgölü
Tatta
Aigai
Methoni
Tenedos
Ilium
Cotieum
Pydna
Scepsis
Hadrianoutherai
Hadrianeia
Aezanoi
Amorium
GALATIA
Haliacmon
Lemnos
Alexandria
Troas
Neandria
Pionia
Cadı
Docimium
Dium
Assos
Adramyttium
Macestus
Olympus 2,911
Prymnessus
Tempe
ASIA
Synada
THESSALY
Lesbos
Mitylene
Pergamum
PHRYGIA
Anthius
Philomelium
Larissa
Antioch
Lagina
Laodicea
Iconium
Meander
Pharsalus
Hermus
Cogamus
Neapolis
Karadağ 2,228
Thaumacoi
Philadelphia
Limnai
Kilistra
Sardis
Apamea
Lystra
Nicopolis
Scyros
Apollonia
PISIDIA
Pappa
Lamia
Smyrna
LYCAONIA
Cayster
Hierapolis
Ascania
Malos
Karalis
Laranda
Chios
Nysa
Adada
Posala
Actium
ACHAIA
Delphi
Euboea
Ephesus
Tralles
Antioch
Sagalassus
Cremna
Pednelissos
Thebes
Laodicea
Colossae
Lebadia
Magnesia
Comama
Eurymedon
Calycadnus
Eleusis
Cestrus
Samos
Priene
Marsyas
Aspendos
PAMPHYLIA
Megara
Athens
Andros
Perge
Side
Piraeus
CARIA
Cibyra
Corinth
Tenos
Miletus
Attalia
Coracesium
Macronisi
Icaros
Acrocorinth 570
Cenchrea
Myconos
Sunium
Delos
Pharmacussa
Halicarnassus
LYCIA
Olympia
Cos
Anemurium
Naxos
Myra
Xanthos
Chelidonium
Cnidus
Sparta
Nisyros
Symi
Rhodes
Andriace
Patara
Tylos
Lindos
IONIAN SEA
Malea
Carpathos
Cythera
Nea Paphos
CRETE
Salmone
MEDITERRANEAN SEA
Cnossos
Phoenix
Gortyn
Fair Heavens
Cauda
FIRST JOURNEY
• Cities mentioned in Acts

FIRST JOURNEY

Antioch on Orontes — Seleucia Pieria — Salamis — Paphos — Perge — Pisidian Antioch — Iconium — Lystra — Derbe — Lystra — Iconium — Pisidian Antioch — Perge — Attalia — Antioch on Orontes

In the year 46/47 Paul set out on his first missionary journey from Antioch on Orontes. His travel companions were Barnabas and John Mark.

Barnabas' was both a Levite, namely a member of a Jewish priestly family, descended from Aaron, the brother of Moses and a Hellenistic Jew from the diaspora. He could speak Greek and was familiar with Gentiles. His name was Joseph. His given name, Barnabas (Hebrew *barnaba,* 'son of a prophet') may infer a role as a teacher or prophet, son of 'prophecy'. In Acts his name is interpreted as 'son of consolation'. He had previously 'sold a piece of property that he owned, then brought the money at the feet of the apostles' (Acts 4.37). Barnabas had introduced Paul to Peter and James, the Lord's brother and related to them Paul's conversion story when the apostle fled from Damascus to Jerusalem about a decade before (Acts 9.27). It was also Barnabas who had gone from Antioch to Tarsus, found Paul and explained him what was being asked from them. Barnabas was a native of Salamis and would have known the island well, hence perhaps the decision to go there. John Mark, who is usually identified both with 'Mark the cousin of Barnabas' of Col 4.10 and with Mark, the writer of one of the Gospels, probably owed his participancy in the journey as the third member of the group to the necessity of having a young assistant in such missions; to take care of the minor travel arrangements, carrying messages, baptizing converts and the like. It has been suggested that if John Mark was the unnamed young man of Gethsemane 'wearing nothing but a linen cloth' who left his garment 'behind and ran off naked' (Mk 14.51-52), he must have seen the previous events here and known Jesus personally and thus could help the preaching of his companions as an eyewitness; first-hand news of Jesus' life, miracles, death and resurrection would attract the attention of listeners.

Although the distance between Antioch and Seleucia was no more than 15 km as the crow flies, the region was rugged and overland communication through the mountains was not easy. There is no information about the popular route of Paul's time. The road of the later Roman period diverted from the road which led to Daphne and Phoenicia. After zigzagging over rough territory it descended to the Orontes and, crossing it at today's Sinanlı village and skirting the height which would later be named after Simon Stylite the Younger as the Mountain of Simeon (Saman Dağı) to the east continued in the direction of Seleucia Pieria following today's motor road. It was more than a day's walk. Paul and his friends may have also sailed downstream by the Orontes to reach Seleucia, which was easier and took only a day. There, according to the fifth-century apocryphal *Acts of Barnabas* they had to wait for three days to find a boat bound for Cyprus which was located some 100 km away.

The memory of the missionaries was later commemorated by pilgrims by the naming of the two breakwaters of the outer port of Seleucia Pieria after Paul and Barnabas, until they disappeared under water. Cyprus, the island to which their first journey took them, owing to its location at centre of the eastern Mediterranean, had been a kind of crossroad for ancient civilizations. It was less than a day's journey from Seleucia Pieria with fair winds. Geologically the island's southern part was a part of Africa while the northern ranges belonged to the Alpine chain. The two pieces of land had risen and created the island .

The island's earliest inhabitants are thought to have been immigrants from the Syrian and Cilician coasts. On clear days the silhouette of the Troodos chain (Tragodos; 1,170 m) is visible from these countries; and thus small rafts must have been sufficient to take the first settlers there.

The rich copper deposits of the island are thought to have been utilized since the beginning of the Bronze Age, sometime around 3000 BCE, and have given the island its name (Greek *kypros,* 'copper'). Oxhide-shaped copper ingots brought to light by underwater archaeology show that, in addition to agricultural produce such as wine, corn and olive oil, this metal was produced and exported from the island. Being on ancient trade routes the island was influenced by the Anatolian cultures and the civilizations of Mesopotamia, Egypt, Crete, Greece and Sicily. Kition (Citium; Larnaka), its capital and the most flourishing city of the Bronze Age, is thought to have been the Alasiya mentioned in Hittite and Egyptian cuneiform tablets. The OT term 'kittim' referred to the inhabitants of this city and was later used for Cypriots in general and eventually for Greeks and even Romans. Like Anatolia, Greece, the Aegean islands and the Levant, in the 1190s BCE Cyprus suffered the destruction of the Sea Peoples. Some of these immigrants may have also settled on the island. The strongest Greek element introduced to the ancient culture of Cyprus dates from this period. When the island recovered from

Palaestra of the gymnasium of Salamis. Augustan period (27 BCE-14 CE).

the Dark Age (1200-800 BCE) it was ruled successively by the Assyrians, Phoenicians, Egyptians, and the Persians.

The Greek city-states which were established on the island took a short respite after the conquest of Alexander's navy in 333 BCE. Meanwhile *Petra tou Romiou*,[1] where Aphrodite (Greek *aphros*, 'foam'; *Aphrodite*, 'foam-born') is said to have born or annually renewed her virginity, some 20 km to the southeast of Palai Paphos, had traditionally become the residence of the goddess. During the Hellenistic era the island was under the hegemony of the Ptolemies of Egypt. This was a peaceful and prosperous period in the island's

[1] The name means 'stone of the Romans', for the Greeks of the Byzantine era designated themselves as *Romaioi*, 'Romans'.

history. After it became part of the Roman Empire in 58 BCE it was first attached to the province of Cilicia and later given to Cleopatra. Finally to complete the control of the Levant directly it was made a proconsular[2] (senatorial) province by itself in the reign of Augustus in 22 BCE. A large Jewish population was known to have moved to the island after Augustus leased all of the copper mines to King Herod the Great in 12 BCE for the half of their revenue. Philo of Alexandria says that the island was 'full of Jewish colonies'. Thus, at the time that the ship carrying Paul, Barnabas and John Mark sailed into the harbour of Salamis the island was a part of the Roman Empire with a Roman governor.

Although the Romans had made Nea Paphos the capital of the province and the residency of the proconsul after Salamis was destroyed in an earthquake in 15 BCE, situated on the side of the ancient Phoenician trade ports Salamis was still the most important city on the island. At the time that Paul, Barnabas and Mark entered Salamis it boasted the fundamental public buildings of a large Hellenistic *polis*: a theatre and a gymnasium both built by Augustus were being enlarged during this period. The city also had one of the most famous temples of Zeus. Claudius had permitted the Salamians to call their city by his family title: Sebaste Claudia Flavia.

Acts informs us that the island was one of the places that some Christians had escaped to after the stoning of Stephen, and preached Christianity there. However, in the beginning as was the case in Antioch, it was to 'no one but Jews' that they had proclaimed the Gospel. In literature the existence of Jews on the island is first mentioned in the circular letter that was said to have been sent to the kings in Cyprus by the 'Roman consul' (1 Mc 15.23). Acts 11.20 tells us that there were some Cypriot Christians among those 'who came to Antioch and began to speak to the Greeks as well, proclaiming the Lord Jesus'. Much later in Acts 21.16 one of the Cypriot converts is mentioned as 'Mnason, a Cypriot, a disciple of long standing' at whose house Paul would stay on the way to or from Jerusalem as he returned from his third missionary journey.

There is not any information about the content of the message of Paul and Barnabas in Cyprus but that they proclaimed the Gospel in synagogues. They

[2] From Latin *pro consule*, 'proconsul'. Among the Roman provinces originally only Africa and Asia were governed by governors of senatorial status; by consuls after their year of office in Rome. With the increase in the number of provinces proconsular power was extended to governors holding military command who had never actually been consuls.

may have stayed here a few weeks. Ancient literature mentions the existence of fifteen major centres of habitation on the island in this period and there were probably Jewish communities in most of them, the largest one being perhaps in Salamis. The Cypriots probably knew more about Barnabas, whom they later regarded as their patron saint, than Paul. Excavations at Salamis have not yet brought to light any synagogue of Paul's era or later but just inscriptions with the word *archsynagogues*, a word which is usually interpreted as referring to someone of influence among the Jewish congregation even it does not carry an official status. All of the early synagogues must have been destroyed following the big Jewish revolt which began in Egypt and spread to the island (115-17 CE). When the rebellion was suppressed 'no Jew was allowed to appear on the island' by the order of Trajan.

Church built over the tomb of St Barnabas near Salamis. Byzantine period. Cyprus.

Acts 13.6 says that Paul's party travelled across the island or 'through the whole island' to Paphos. The expression, probably, is used to imply that in addition to those of Salamis and Paphos, some of the other Jewish communities were visited. Later traditions such as the apocryphal *Acts of Barnabas* state that they visited Lapithus (Lapta) along the northern coast of the island where an 'idol festival' was being celebrated then and they were not received well. They continued 'through the mountains and came to the city of Lampadistus' which is now identified with the resort of Kalopanayiotis village some 70 km to the southwest of the island's present capital. During their wanderings they had to take refuge in 'the village of the Ledrians' from the Jews who opposed them. Ledra (Ledroi) is the ancient name of Lefkosia (Nicosia).

The Tragodos range which occupied the western half of the island was almost impossible to traverse and the journey to Paphos could, normally, be made following the road which encircled the island. The southern coastal route was shorter. From Salamis it ran to Ammocostos (Famagusta/Gazimağusa), Citium (Larnaka), Amathus, Neapolis (Lemesos/Limassol), Curium (Kourion/Episkopi), Palai ('old') Paphos (Kouklia) and reached Nea ('new') Paphos.

Palai Paphos was founded in the 1300s BCE by immigrant Greeks. Nea Paphos, located about a day's walk farther, was founded by the city's last King Nicocles toward the end of the fourth century BCE, and under the Roman rule it had become the capital of the whole island.

In Nea Paphos, where a well-established Jewish community is thought to have existed, they may have begun preaching at the local synagogue and in

Icon of St Barnabas. Twentieth century. St Barnabas Museum near Salamis. North Cyprus.

time their new message may have reached the ear of the island's governor. Paul and Barnabas were summoned to speak in the presence of the Roman governor, proconsul Sergius Paulus (Latin *Paullus*), who had a Jewish sorcerer named Elymas Bar-Jesus.[3] During this period the employment of magicians or sorcerers by rich people was as common as worshipping one or more deities or cults. The governor was disposed toward philosophy and as he had shown interest in what Elymas represented, he wanted to hear about the cult of the new itinerant teachers. To the magician, Paul must have appeared as a rival and he tried to prevent his patron from hearing the apostle's preaching. Paul, calling upon the power of the Holy Spirit, temporarily struck blind the sorcerer. This miracle so impressed the governor that when he 'saw what had happened he came to believe, for he was astonished by the teaching about the Lord' (Acts 13.12).

It has been speculated that Paul employed the method which would have been used by the magician himself; fixing his eyes on his opponent, cursed him so that Bar-Jesus, at least temporarily, lost his eyesight. It has been also suggested that the phrase in Acts may refer to 'spiritual blindness' which later led to the story of 'actual blindness' of the magician. The conversion of Sergius Paulus, however, could not have had an immediate role in the spread of Christianity in the island, because proconsuls were usually appointed for one year periods and there was no reason why the Cypriots should follow the religion of the Roman administrator.

From this point on, in Acts, the apostle is not referred to as Saul, but Paul. Some scholars believe Luke decided that this was the most appropriate place to bring Paul's name forward in his narrative. It has been also suggested that here the change of the apostle's name refers to a change in his role; from being a Jew among Jews in the Semitic world of Judea, to a Roman citizen in the hall of a Roman proconsul, in the Gentile world of the nations. Thus Saul, his ancient royal name, had lost its importance. This is accompanied by the fact that it is Paul, but not Barnabas who was the leader of the trio, filled by the Holy Spirit who was the spokesman at the meeting. The fact that Acts gives just the *nomen* (family name) and *cognomen* (surname) but not the personal name (*praenomen*) of the proconsul has created

[3] Elymas is thought to be the Hellenized form of the Aramaic *alim*, 'wise', or 'magician', the Hebrew patronymic *ben* ('son') is Arabic *bin*, Aramaic *bar*.

Inscription which mentions the mother-in-law (*socrus*) of one Sergius Paullus from Pisidian Antioch. Yalvaç Museum. Since the *cognomen* (surname) of the person to

whom it belonged is missing it is impossible to find out the complete identity of its owner.

problems in identifying this person and efforts of various scholars to establish a connection with him and similar names encountered in Cypriot epigraphy have given no result. Such that in a dedicative inscription copied by scholars about a century before near Soli (Soloi/Morphou) one Apollonius says that his father served during the governorship of Paullus. Further reading of the inscription, however, has shown that this Paullus served in 126 CE under Hadrian. Another inscription from Kythrea (Hagios Dimitrios) which mentions a governor with the name of Quintius Sergius has been dated to the time of Caligula (37-41). Effort has been made to identify the 'Sergius Paulus' of Acts with L(ucius) Sergius Paullus, one of the five guardians of the Tiber that Claudius had appointed to prevent it from flooding, mentioned on a boundary stone. Sergius Paullus is an extremely rare name and the persons who bore it may have been members of the Sergia tribe who owned large estates in Galatia. It has been speculated that the Roman proconsul may have suggested that Paul should go to Pisidian Antioch where he had relatives and estates and may even have given Paul letters of recommendation.

At present the site of Nea Paphos is occupied by the village of Kato Paphos. A Cypriot legend maintains that the apostle was imprisoned and scourged here before his encounter with the governor. A broken column in the former Church of Chrysopolitissa (also known as of St Cyriacus) is said to have been used to tie up Paul and lash him 39 times. The tradition of 'columns of flagellations' seems to have been inspired by Paul's words in 2 Cor 11.24 that five times at the hand of the Jews he was scourged 'forty lashes minus one'. This kind of punishment is known to have belonged to ancient synagogue discipline. Acts 5.40 informs us that the apostles were punished thus already for speaking 'in the name of Jesus' in Jerusalem. Paul was, however, not one of them. According to Dt 25.2-3 forty stripes, but no more, may be given to a man whom the judge found guilty, in order not to disgrace his relatives 'because of the severity of the beating', and that one stroke was usually skipped to prevent miscount so that the regulation may not be broken. With the standards of the time this was regarded as a mild punishment. It has been suggested that the expression and probably also the number of strokes derived from the type of whip, which had 39 cords tied in three bands of thirteen cords. Acts does not give any information as to how Paul was punished like this five times. It has been suggested that while some of these persecutions may have taken place during the known missionary

'The founder Mopsus of Delphi, son of Apollo'. 120/21 CE. Inscription from the Roman city gate of Perge.

journeys some may have been in his unknown years when he preached the Gospel in Damascus, Cilicia and Syria. When Paul preached his so-called 'uncircumcised' Gospel at synagogues it was impossible to separate Gentile godfearers from Jews. The latter regarded Paul's message both offensive and against the agreement that would be reached between him and James, Peter and John, 'the three pillars' sometime later in Jerusalem such that preaching to Jews was the mission of Peter, and they may have punished him in the Jewish way. Although, if disclosed, his Roman citizenship may have shielded him against such beatings some believe that sheltering into it may have been regarded as a denial of his Jewishness and closed to him the doors of the synagogues.

After a few years Barnabas returned to his island together with John Mark. Tradition has it that he was martyred at Salamis aged probably about 61 and secretly buried. The apocryphal *Acts of Barnabas* mentions a synagogue which was 'near the place called biblia, where Barnabas, having unrolled the Gospel which he had received from Matthew his fellow-labourer, began to teach Jews'. His traditional tomb was discovered in 489 in the reign of Zeno together with the manuscript of the Gospel according to Mark, placed

Hellenistic gate. Looking toward the city and acropolis. Perge.

Graffiti on a column. Perge. Byzantine period. An angel in flight, holding a torch approaches a cross shown on top of a stepped column.

on his chest by its author, and a small church was built over it. A tradition holds that the apostle was killed by stoning in Salamis by the Jews who were incited by Bar-Jesus, the magician at Nea Paphos.

From Cyprus Paul, Barnabas and Mark sailed to Perge in Pamphylia. The latter was a narrow coastal plain between the Taurus chain and the Mediterranean shore extending, at the time of Paul, from the River Melas (Manavgat Çayı) to the Lycian heights beyond the plain of Attalia. It had been settled by people of Luvian origin and later by Greeks. The latter arrived here after the great upheavals of the1190s BCE and later regarded Trojan heroes like Mopsus, Calchas and others, who were spread around the Mediterranean after the fall of Troy, as their ancestors. Among its prosperous cities were, in addition to Perge, Attalia (Antalya), Side and Coracesium (Alanya), the last being the headquarters of the Cilician pirates until they were wiped out by Pompey in 67 BCE.

Perge may have been the destination of the ship's captain, a situation with which the apostle and his friends seem to have complied. It was about 12 km inland. Ancient literature informs us that in the first century CE the Cestrus (Aksu) that ran to the east of Perge, having no delta, was navigable from the sea and vessels sailed or were towed up against the slow moving current to a wharf some 4 km from the city. A more convenient arrival port which was connected to Perge by a road was Magydus (near Lara) about 10 km east of Attalia. At the time of Paul's arrival Pamphylia was a part of the Roman province of Lycia-Pamphylia and Perge was entering an era of great prosperity. The city's limits had already moved from the original settlement on the acropolis to the southern flat plain. Although most of today's remains and what has been uncovered date from the centuries following Paul's visit, some of the Hellenistic city such as the walls, which were first built by Antiochus III (223-187 BCE), the theatre and the circular Hellenistic towers of the main (southern) gate stood here in Paul's time. If one walked on the main street at the skirt of the acropolis to the left one would have reached the palaestra which C Julius Varus Cornutus had built and dedicated to Claudius, the reigning emperor of the time. The most famous and celebrated sanctuary of Paul's time was the Temple of Artemis of Perge which was described by Strabo as being 'near Perge on a lofty site, to the temple where a general festival is celebrated every year'. This site was possibly the large, low (60 m) and flat acropolis which was first settled in the Bronze Age. Today its scanty remains

Climax ('ladder'), the crossing point on the Via Sebaste at the Döşeme Pass (looking south) perhaps the border between Pamphylia and Pisidia. The worn-out inscription on the milestone to the left in Latin reads 'The Emperor Caesar Augustus, son of the god, pontifex maximus, consul for the 11th time, designated for the 12th time, hailed imperator for the 15th time, with tribunician power for the 18th time, made the Via Sebaste. His legatus pro praetore Cornutus Aquila supervised the construction. 139 (miles).' The distance is from Pisidian Antioch, at the time the terminal point of the highway. In the background to the right is a cistern.

include in addition to the traces of the original settlers, rock-cut cisterns, fortifications and several churches.

Apart from Paul's brief visits and his preaching here, little is known about early Christianity at Perge. Otherwise, even the OT information (1 Mc 15.23), where the Roman consul sends letters to the rulers of the Pamphylian cities, among which Side is mentioned, not to oppress the Jewish population, is hypothetical, one would expect the existence of a Jewish population of smaller or larger size in each of these ancient and prosperous settlements. In this stage of the narrative the name order also begins to change from 'Barnabas and Saul' to 'Paul and his companions'. The apocryphal *Acts of Barnabas* mentions a two-month stay here. In Perge John Mark left them to return to Jerusalem. In Acts there is no indication why Mark acted like this.

It has been speculated that if the original prospect of the mission did not extend beyond Cyprus, Mark was not satisfied with the change of plans, and specifically with Paul's growing enthusiasm for preaching to Gentiles who were not proselytes. Whatever happened in Perge, the event affected Paul's faith in John Mark. Paul and John Mark were eventually reconciled. Mark visited and ministered to him when he was in captivity in Rome. Many years later in Col 4.10 Paul said 'Mark the cousin of Barnabas (concerning whom you have received instructions; if he comes to you, receive him)' and in 2 Tm 4.11 he says 'Get Mark and bring him with you, for he is helpful to me in the ministry'.

Some scholars believe that the reason for Paul's moving to southern Galatia was chronic malaria or a disease he had contracted in his childhood or later although its effect is not mentioned until Paul's said 'you know that it was because of a physical illness that I originally preached the Gospel to you' in his letter to the Galatians (4.13). This would not have been surprising for the fact was that his hometown and the rest of Cilician plain were infected with mosquitoes to an extent that even the early arrivals in the region preferred to settle on the foothills of the Taurus rather than the fertile flats. Otherwise, for winning new converts the cosmopolitan coastal cities of Pamphylia, each with a Jewish community and a synagogue most probably with godfearers, were certainly more favourable than the scarcely populated Phrygian highlands. Whatever his sickness was, the apostle's words make it clear that fresh mountain air was better for it than the hot and humid coastal plain. It has been speculated that if the governor of Cyprus, Sergius Paulus, was related to Pisidian Antioch, after he heard about Paul's illness during his encounter with the apostle he may have even recommended the Phrygian spas with which he

Bülüç Uçuran bridge on the Perge-Adada route. The Çandar bridge on the same route to the north is now left in the Karacaören dam lake but surfaces when the level of the water drops.

Inscription from Yazılı Kanyon ('inscribed canyon'). Third century CE. In Greek Leontianos son of Leontianos invokes Apollo, friend of wayfarers.

was familiar. Paul's words to the Galatians (4.15) that they 'would have torn their eyes and given them' to him are interpreted as referring to the fact that the sickness affected his eyes which were probably in very bad condition when he first reached Galatia; unless the expression was used as a literary convention to show that they were ready to sacrifice their most valuable member for the apostle. Whatever his disease, to which he later referred as a 'thorn of flesh' or 'a messenger of Satan' (2 Cor 12.7), was its marks could not be hidden by his tunic or cloak and it showed on his face, hands or head. The fact that he could proclaim his Gospel for a long time despite the persecutions he suffered in southern Galatia show that it was not constant.

The narrow passes of the Taurus chain were closed through the winter months, and thus Paul and Barnabas are thought to have begun journeying north before snow began falling. Pisidian Antioch was situated along the southernmost fringe of Phrygia and the mountains which ran parallel to the Mediterranean did not give easy access to the interior. The Roman road of the time which connected the Pamphylian plain to the city was the Via Sebaste. It was built by the governor Cornutus Arruntius Aquila in 6 BCE and named in honor of Augustus (Greek *sebastos,* 'augustus' or 'exalted-one'). It began at Side and ran by way of Perge in the direction of Climax (Döşeme Pass). Crossing the first line of the Taurus here it continued to Comama (Şeref Höyük) encircling Lake Ascanius (Burdur Gölü) on its west side, by way of Apollonia (Uluborlu), to the northern shore of Lake Limnai (Eğirdir Gölü) and reached Pisidian Antioch. Around the time that Paul was born the Romans had begun pacifying the Pisidian heights and by the middle of the first century the main travel and transportation routes were safe. To go to Pisidian Antioch from Perge one would normally use this highway, an easy and safe route for the fact that on it there were staging posts and towns where travellers could replenish their provisions, take baths, change money, etc. Consequently some scholars believe that Paul may have used this thoroughfare during his trip to and from Pisidian Antioch.

Gate at Taşkapı ('stone gate') Fortress. Sütçüler.

Ceremonial steps with an altar. Roman era. Malos (Sarı İdris).

It has been speculated that although travelling on a well-kept Roman road would have been more convenient if Paul were sick, eager both to leave the humid plain as quickly as possible, and reach Pisidian Antioch where he expected to make new Gentile converts, he may have taken a shorter route. In addition to the surviving tradition of Paul's name on this trail, the desire to imagine an indefatigable missionary fighting his way through the deep ravines and over the rocky mountains of Pisidia may have played a role in the growing popularity of this idea. There seems to have been a trail which after leaving Perge went to north for some 15 km where it crossed the Cestrus near today's Çatallar, which may have been the last supply station before a traveller began ascending to north and followed the bed of Kırk Geçitler brook, a branch of the Cestrus flowing from northeast. This track was not designed for cart traffic and is called in Turkish Kırk Geçitler, ('forty crossings') because of the number of crossings between the two banks of the river. The route, whose eastern trail has been run over by a forestry track, still serves for some nomads in late May when they take their flocks to the northern highlands. Some of it has been left under the Karacaören dam lake. After Çandır village the route enters into a long ravine which has come to be known as Yazılı Kanyon ('inscribed canyon') because of the inscriptions left along the rock-cut track. These inscriptions at a rock-cut shrine show that the site was dedicated to Apollo. Somewhere below today's Sütçüler the track left the canyon to climb to a high stronghold known as Taşkapı and continued to Adada. This was the most important ancient city on this route and is still known by the local villagers as 'Kara Baulo' or 'Karabavlo' ('black Paul') where later a church was perhaps dedicated to him. To the north, somewhere near today's Sipahiler the route joined a similar mountain track coming by way of the Eurymedon River (Köprüçay) and continued in the direction of Pisidian Antioch possibly by way of Timbriada (Asar Kale near Aksu), Sofular village, Malos (Sarı İdris) and Gelendost, following after this point the course of the Anthius. Among the hypothetical routes drawn for Paul none of them fits better to his allusions in 2 Cor 11.26.

On such a hard trail travelling some 200 km across the Taurus may have taken several weeks or more. Paul and Barnabas probably joined a group of travellers going in the same direction, and waited until a crowd big enough to discourage the bandits from attacking them was gathered. Roman power was far from providing security on such mountain trails, especially those which run through notorious regions like the Pisidian heights. The tribes

A section of the ancient road ascending the Aktepe mountain from its south just before entering Adada.

which lived in the region had been known as wild people since ancient times. The natives of Herodotus who wore crimson puttees and carried oxhide shields, spears and helmets decorated with ears and horns of an ox, in bronze among the forces of Xerxes when he invaded Greece, are thought to have been Pisidians. During the chilly nights Paul's party probably made big fires and set sentries against both bandits and wild beasts.

After they lost the battle of Magnesia (190 BCE) against Rome, the Seleucids had retreated to south of the Taurus and the Seleucid hegemony in Pisidia including Antioch was taken over by Pergamum, Rome's most faithful ally of the time. In the centre of the peninsula beyond Antioch after their defeat by Gnaeus Manlius Vulso, assisted by Pergamum Galatians ruled as a vassal kingdom of Rome. This lasted until the establishment of the province of Galatia which took place when their last King Amyntas (37-25 BCE) fell during a fight with the Pisidian mountain tribes known as the Homonadeis who occupied the heights to the east of Lake Trogitis (Suğla Gölü). The pacification of the Pisidian heights was achieved by the consul Publius Sulpicius Quirinius[4] who is said to have left no man free in the countryside and forced the younger generation to adopt Roman customs. The only information about this war

Roman bridge on the Eurymedon near Timbriada. Early second century CE. The cave sanctuary known as Zindan mağarası ('dungeon cave') belonged to the Mother

Goddess. The statue of the river god Eurymedon found here is now displayed in Isparta Museum. The cave in its later history housed an early Christian church.

comes from Strabo. It is thought to have taken in place sometime in the last decade of the first century BCE.

Establishing colonies in the provinces enabled Augustus to obtain cheap or free land for his retired soldiers and thus saved him from the cash payment that they were to receive at the end of their long military service. These colonies were settled by Italian war veterans who may have been in time supplemented by immigrants from home and administered by Roman political and social institutions. Their function was to guard the Roman military routes against the Pisidian mountain tribes and provide the Roman army with sound bases. Pisidian Antioch was the first colony in the region, perhaps established shortly after 27 BCE and named Colonia Caesarea Antiochia.

Pisidian Antioch (Yalvaç) lies on the slope of a mountain overlooking a fertile valley northeast of Lake Limnai (Eğirdir Gölü), by the River Anthius (Yalvaç Çayı) which flows into the lake. The city is thought to have been founded by Antiochus I, Soter ('saviour'; 281-261 BCE). Its early natives were perhaps Phrygians and Greeks. Its later inhabitants, probably in their effort to establish a Greek origin, claimed descent from colonists from Magnesia on Meander. It was situated in the southernmost part of Phrygia known as Paroreius ('along the mountain'), and called 'Antiochia ad Pisidiam', Antioch 'near' 'toward' or 'next to' Pisidia in order to distinguish it from a number of Antiochs that the Seleucids had founded.

There is as yet no trace of any ancient road entering the city and the only monument which lies outside its walls seems to be the stadium. Normally, one would expect the existence of impressive sarcophagi of important personages flanking the road before it entered such a Roman colony. The necropolis has not yet been located. The main entrance of Antioch was from the western side. The triple-arched marble gate, whose impressive ruins have survived to the present, was dedicated to Hadrian and his wife Sabina in 129 CE when they were on a visit to Anatolia. Research and surviving fragments have shown that in front of its four piers on both sides the gate

[4] Quirinius is known to have held another post in Syria around 6 CE and held a census in Judea proper (not in Nazareth which was Joseph's native city in Herod Antipas' territory). Since Lk 2.1-7 mistakenly connects his name with the time when Jesus was born, some scholars have tried to accommodate a previous or first governorship of Syria for Quirinius earlier than 4 BCE, the death of Herod, so that the date of nativity in the time of Herod can be validated.

Simplified plan of Pisidian Antioch.

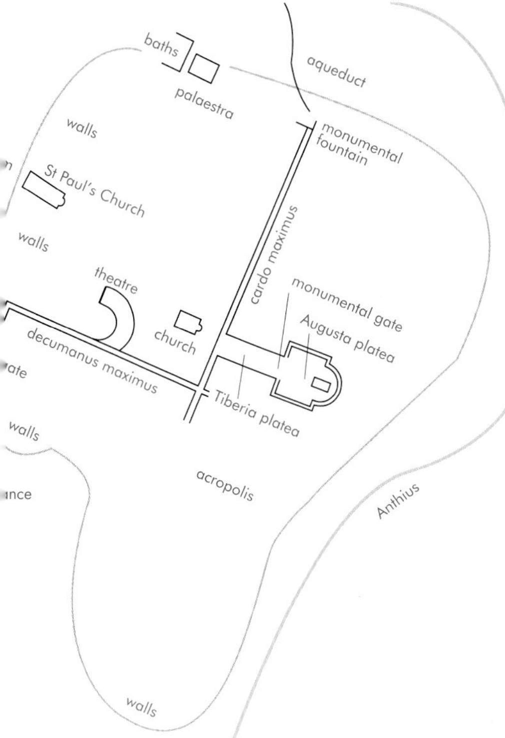

was decorated with statues. Above, it bore the inscription of dedication and winged Victories (Nikes) and genii, hippocamps, tritons and weapons in relief. The main street, which began here had a decorative water channel in its middle. The city of Paul's time was smaller. The fortifications which have survived to the present were built some two hundred years after Paul's journeys. They seem to have been built in haste because the construction work shows, in addition to well-dressed ashlar blocks originally belonging to the fortifications of the Hellenistic city, or the Augustan colony, reused material of various sorts including interesting epigrams. After making a turn toward the city centre the road became the *decumanus maximus*, the main east-west street of any Roman city. The theatre of Paul's time by which it ran was smaller. Close to the centre of the site this street met the *cardo maximus*, the main north-south street at a right angle. At Paul's time the centre of Antioch was the *Tiberia platea* ('broad street of Tiberius') and the *Augusta platea*, ('broad street of Augustus'). The first of these was a short colonnaded thoroughfare with shops and dining or drinking parlours on both sides. It was built in the reign of Tiberius (14-37 CE) and dedicated to him.

Access to the second square was gained by a monumental gate (propylon) with three openings, the earliest known example of a triumphal arch in the east. The entrances were reached by a stairway of twelve steps and in the front of each of the four Corinthian piers stood a fountain. Research and the fragments of the inscription which once bore letters in bronze above the central arch have shown that it was dedicated to Augustus sometime after 2 BCE but before his death in 14 CE. The rest of the surface carried reliefs of deities, weapons, war ships, winged Victories and genii and figures of Pisidian slaves and tritons (Yalvaç Museum). The fragments of the *Res Gestae* in Latin, a document of the 'deeds' of Augustus which were discovered hereabouts are thought to have come from the lower sections of the inner faces of the central two piers. This massive gateway gave access to the *Augusta platea*, which housed sanctuary of the imperial cult of Augustus, and Dea Roma, the goddess of Rome. The low hill beyond to the south of the sanctuary was the acropolis (1,235 m) of the city, now with scanty ruins from the Byzantine era.

At a later date, possibly in the fourth century, a large church was built behind the row of shops opposite the *Tiberia platea*. Narrow paths which left these two main streets on both sides produced a grid-plan (Hippodamian) with residential quarters placed in the rectangles created by their intersecting

Augusta platea. 2 BCE-14 CE. Pisidian Antioch. The sanctuary consisted of a courtyard surrounded on all sides by a colonnade whose semicircular section was double-storey and partly cut from the natural rock. The large holes which have survived in the rock surface belong to the wooden beams which supported the floor of the second storey. The temple building faced west. It began with a stairway of twelve steps carved of rock. The steps led to an entrance placed behind four Corinthian columns at the front and one on each side. The gabled pediment was decorated with acanthus scroll and garlanded sacrificial bull-heads, now scattered on the site. Behind this on a rectangular podium, again cut from the living rock, stood the cult room housing the statue of a deity. Below this a treasury room was built. After the establishment of the Christianity the site served for outdoor worshipping.

lines. Some of these districts bore the same names as those in Rome. What has survived gives the impression that the main streets were not colonnaded for their complete lengths. The public buildings seem to have been built of stone or marble and opened to the main streets. On the northern side the *cardo maximus* ended with a monumental fountain (nymphaeum) which was associated with an aqueduct that brought water to the city from the springs some 10 km to the north. Both the fountain and aqueduct were built during the first half of the first century CE. Normally, the street would have ended at a main entrance on this side whose trace has not yet been found. The dates of the Roman bath which seems to have been incorporated in the walls and the palaestra, both to the northwest, are not yet established.

The ruins of a second church, now named after St Paul, survive by the western edge of the site. What is visible today belongs to a fifth-sixth century building. It consisted of a narthex divided into two by a row of columns, and a nave separated from the aisles by a row of thirteen columns on each side. The main entrance was on the north side where the existence of an L-shaped portico can be distinguished. On the other side there was a cistern. Excavations have shown the existence of a previous church about half a metre below the floor of the visible ruins. The Bishop Optimus mentioned in the mosaic floor of this earlier church is known to have represented the city at the Ecumenical Council of Constantinople in 381. The evidence makes the church one of the two datable edifices of the early Christian era, the other one being the Church of St Babylas (387 CE) near Antioch on Orontes. Two other inscriptions which cited from Ps 43.4 'Then I will go into the altar of God', and 'the God of my gladness and joy' belonging to this early church also survive, buried. There has been no evidence found to show that the church was ever a synagogue. Beyond the church to the north the hollow of the stadium which stood outside the city walls can be distinguished.

Some scholars think that although physical preoccupations may explain Paul's preference of preaching the Gospel to the people in the cool heights rather those in the damp and hot Pamphylian lowlands, this is not enough to explain why he did not go from Perge to any of the closer cities such as Cremna or Sagalassus but headed toward Pisidian Antioch. The proconsul of Cyprus, Sergius Paulus who had been converted to Christianity by Paul a few months ago is thought to have been related to the Sergii family of Antioch, colonists from Italy. It is perhaps this contact, with all the possibilities it

St Paul's Church. Looking north. Fifth-sixth centuries. Pisidian Antioch. Its apse is oriented toward south.

Mosaic inscription from the floor of the church below that of St Paul's. Pisidian Antioch. Late fourth century CE. In Greek it informs us that Eutychianus and Idomeneus, a church reader, fulfilled their vows to God [of paving the floor mosaic] when Optimus was bishop.

(opposite) Base (height 2.5 m) of a statue of Claudius from Pisidian Antioch. 45/46 CE. Yalvaç Museum. Following the Emperor's titles in Latin the inscription informs us that the statue was dedicated by Caristanius Fronto Caisianus Jullus, formerly an administrator of the city to celebrate the victory and safe return of Claudius from his campaign to Brittany in 43 CE.

suggested, that was one of the reasons for the apostle's visit to Pisidian Antioch where he hoped to make similar converts of high status. Later developments in Acts show that changing or adapting his missionary route when such an opportunity rose was not unusual for the apostle.

Antioch was the most Romanized among the Pisidian colonies. Its official language was Latin. Although the town was the largest in the region, with a population of some 10,000 inhabitants, there is no information about the size of the Jewish community. From what is told in Acts we learn that on the sabbath Paul and Barnabas went to the synagogue,[5] sat down with the rest of the congregation and prayed. If there was a synagogue at the time of Paul or later, it may have been located outside the city, close to the Anthius, water being indispensable for Jewish rituals. The Jewish community here, as elsewhere, may have been using a house converted into a synagogue like the one discovered at Priene. After the prayers and the usual readings they were invited to address the assembly. According to Jewish custom, as Jesus had done many times before, a person was free to speak in the synagogue. Paul shared his knowledge of the scriptures with his audience and added his belief

[5] Greek *synagogue*, as it is used in Acts, may refer to a 'building' or 'congregation'.

in the death and resurrection of Jesus. According to Acts 13.16 he began his sermon by saying 'Fellow Israelites and you others who are God-fearing, listen'. Normally the word godfearing could be used as an introductory term just to gain the goodwill of the audience, and does not necessarily show the existence of Gentile sympathizers. Here, however, it is regarded to indicate that in addition to Jews and proselytes, Gentiles who were attracted to Judaism were allowed into the synagogue at Pisidian Antioch, a situation which was made clear by 'many Jews and worshippers' in Acts 13.43.

Whether it was a large urban centre like Antioch on Orontes, or Thessalonica, or a remote colony like Pisidian Antioch, the Jewish population of the settlement was usually subject to anti-Semitism by the majority of its inhabitants. On the other hand there were some Gentiles attracted by the monotheism and morals of the Jewish religion and characteristics such as the existence of a holy book and a weekly day of rest. In Acts such people are referred to by expressions like 'God-fearing' or 'God-worshipper', or just as 'worshipper'. It is sometimes difficult to understand if the word is used for Jews meaning 'pious' or 'devout' or to refer to the existing Gentiles. The latter were not proselytes, which would require circumcision, a requirement which possibly made the mentioned number of proselyte women higher than men, plus the ceremonial bath and practicing of the other Mosaic observations, including a pilgrimage to Jerusalem to sacrifice at the Temple. The godfearers even though they did not observe Jewish obligations were allowed in the synagogue. It is, however, difficult to figure out their level of involvement with the Jewish religion. Their status in the synagogue seems to have been lower than Jews. According to Acts Paul met them in almost all of the synagogues in which he preached. Their number would have been higher than the proselytes and it has been thought that, in addition to his own race, the existence of such Gentile groups has been the reason why Paul chose synagogues to preach for the first time wherever he went.

Paul told them what almost inevitably annoyed the orthodox Jews, that their Messiah (Hebrew *Mashiah,* 'anointed one'; Greek *Christos*) had already come, had been crucified by the Romans, at the instigation of their brothers in Jerusalem, and that he had risen from the dead. He was now the salvation of the whole world and Gentiles were as welcome as Jews into the kingdom of God. Surprisingly, despite his accusations of the Jews at Jerusalem, his address was received with enthusiasm and he was invited to preach on the next sabbath.

Dedications from the western wall of the sacred enclosure (temenos) of the sanctuary of the Anatolian moon god Men Ascaenus at Kara Kuyu ('black well') near Pisidian Antioch. Each niche probably imitates the architecture of the shrine, which housed the god's statue, and at its centre has a crescent moon, the symbol of Men. In the upper row the name 'Demetrius' in Latin is flanked by two names in Greek. The Latin letters LVS below are translated in plural as 'libentes vota solverunt' or 'fulfilled their vows gladly'. Scholars believe that the bilingual dedication belonged to three slaves of the same household. The temple was probably built in the mid-second century BCE when the area was ruled by the Attalids of Pergamum. At Paul's time it was entering into its most popular era. In the fourth century a church was built next to its ruins.

When subsequently, the Jewish members of the regular congregation opposed him, it was not because of the nature of his message but the numbers that had gathered to hear Paul. It has been speculated that the Jewish congregation were suddenly afraid of losing their privileged position in their synagogue and becoming a minority. Paul was no longer welcome in the synagogue. The incident made Paul and Barnabas say 'It was necessary that the word of God be spoken to you first, but since you reject it and condemn yourself as unworthy of eternal life, we now turn to the Gentiles' (Acts 13.46).

The Gentiles were obviously happy about Paul's message and carried his news to those they knew in the vicinity of the city; 'through the whole region', a remark which is regarded as a literary convention. The Jews, however, 'incited the women of prominence who were worshippers and the leading men of the city, stirred up a persecution against Paul and Barnabas, and expelled them from their territory'. It has been speculated that the Jews of the city realized that they could not make a judicial case against Paul because the Romans would not be interested in the domestic problems of Jews. They, however, may have exploited the women godfearers and some men of prominence among them saying that these two Jews were fomenting division,

Milestone serving as a tombstone in the cemetery by the Via Sebaste. Yunuslar village (Pappa/Tiberiopolis).

etc in their community and thus asked the help of their husbands and relatives some of whom may have had civic authority. Paul might have hoped that not only Jews but also Gentiles from important families would perhaps accept his Gospel. In the event, it was to the Jews of Antioch rather than to Paul, that these well-connected people, or at least some of them, gave support. Acts does not mention what kind of 'persecution' Paul and Barnabas faced here. When Paul later in 2 Cor 11.25 speaks about his sufferings and says 'Three times I was beaten with rods,' a magistrate's punishment, although the exact Roman jurisdiction of Pisidian Antioch is not yet known, the first case may have been here. Later they were expelled from the city. Nevertheless, some converts were made, and although their number may not have been high it was the first time a church of Gentiles, isolated from the Jewish community, was established. Thus shaking the dust from their feet, the dust of a country which had become impure by rejecting the envoys of God and kingdom of God, so as not to be defiled by a heathen community, Paul and Barnabas left. The expression has been used by Jesus in his teaching of the mission to the Twelve (Mt 10.14 and others) as testimony against the people who rejected the call to repentance.

At the time of Paul a short road crossing the Sultan range to the northeast connected Pisidian Antioch to the pre-Roman route which came from Ephesus following the Meander valley by way of Apamea (Dinar). This road led to Iconium crossing Philomelium (Akşehir; later addressee of the letter of Polycarp's martyrdom from the church at Smyrna), Lagina (Ilgın) and Laodicea Catacecaumene (Ladik). It was known as the Cilician Road, and about a hundred years before Paul's journeys Cicero had travelled on it writing letters in a carriage, in the direction of Tarsus, to take over his post as governor of the province of Cilicia. It was somewhere on this road near today's Ilgın that in 401 BCE the army of Cyrus the Younger had put a show charge for Epyaxa, Queen of Cilicia. It created such a panic that even the Queen fled in her carriage. However, to go to Iconium, in Paul's time one would normally use the Via Sebaste which had become a network connecting the Roman colonies with Pisidian Antioch as the terminal point, and served as the main artery between Pamphylia and Galatia. In addition to their function for transportation and communication such roads also symbolized the permanence of Roman power in remote regions and thus bore a symbolic value for the colonists from Italy. From Pisidian Antioch the Via Sebaste first ran to Neapolis (Kıyakdede village) in the direction of Lake Karalis (Beyşehir Gölü). Here it turned inland and began following the perennial springs along the undulating mountain skirts and by way of today's Selki and Pappa/ Tiberiopolis (Yunuslar village) went to Iconium. In the apocryphal *Acts of Paul* Onesiphorus comes as far as the point where the 'King's Highway', the Via Sebaste splits into two branches with one going to Lystra by way of Kızılören and Kilistra and the other to Iconium.

A section of the Via Sebaste between Yunuslar village (Pappa/Tiberiopolis) and Konya.

Takkeli Dağ, ('Mount of Thecla'), 'the mountain with *takke* (a kind of hat)' after the ridge which crowns it. The other one is named after Philip (apostle or evangelist) who according to one tradition travelled to Hierapolis and Ephesus by way of Iconium in his missionary work.

By Paul's time Iconium had already a very long history and is thought to have been Ikanuwa of the Hittite texts. When it was visited by Paul and Barnabas it was a *polis* known as Claudiconium after the Roman colony (Colonia Julia Augusta Iconium) which Claudius had founded next to the ancient city. If Paul and Barnabas used the Via Sebaste, a walk of some three to four days, for about 100 km, would take them to Iconium. Acts 14.1 informs us that here 'they entered the Jewish synagogue and spoke in such a way that a great number of both Jews and Greeks came to believe'. Paul probably stayed in the city for several months, 'for a considerable period'. However, not all the Jews believed and the Christian message gave rise to argument and division in the city, rather than to brotherly love, a development which recalls the situation at Pisidian Antioch. Hearing that their adversaries were planning to stone them, Paul and Barnabas fled. It was after all Jesus' advice that 'When they persecute you in one town, flee to another' (Mt 10.23.) Although Acts does not refer to Gentiles among the congregation at the synagogue at Iconium either as proselytes or godfearers, their existence could be expected. From the fact that Luke reserves the title 'apostles' for the Twelve and Acts 14.4 and 14 are the only cases the term was used for Paul and Barnabas, meaning envoys, has led some scholars to think that for the Iconium episode unless he employed the word in the dictionary meaning, 'envoys' sent by the Antioch church, Luke may have used a source for the events here. The only other material relating to Paul's stay in Iconium is the story about him and Thecla in the apocryphal *Acts of Paul*. Later tradition has named the easternmost of the two conical mountain peaks which command the landscape of the city after Thecla.

When they fled from Iconium, Paul and Barnabas seem to have found themselves on the Via Sebaste to Lystra which was located some 30 km south. While some of the ancient sources locate Iconium in Phrygia, some place it in Lycaonia. It has been suggested that the name of the region comes from the Luwian Lukawani, 'inhabitants of Lukku'. Lystra was, however, geographically a part of Lycaonia.

Mound of Lystra. Looking west.

Acts 14.8-12 tells us that 'At Lystra there was a crippled man, lame from birth, who had never walked'. He listened to Paul speaking, who looked intently at him, saw that he had the faith to be healed, and called out in a loud voice, "Stand up straight on your feet". He jumped up and began to walk about. When the crowds saw what Paul had done, they cried out in Lycaonian: "The gods have come down to us in human form". They called Barnabas 'Zeus' perhaps because of his having an elderly and more impressive figure and Paul 'Hermes', because he was the chief speaker and younger. The Lycaonians ethnically were different from the Phrygians and spoke a different language. It was not possible for Paul to understand what was said and perhaps he learned the meaning later from someone who could speak Greek. It is also possible that the locals switched to the little Greek that they could speak when they realized that the visitors could not understand them.

Obviously the people with whom Paul and Barnabas first came in contact were the uneducated locals and when Paul healed a cripple they were at first thought to be gods, and the people hailed them in their native tongue as Zeus and Hermes. Early Christian writings mention Barnabas as having a tall and imposing appearance and this must have caused him to be identified with Zeus. Paul, less significant than his companion, could be Hermes, the god with the gift of eloquence. Zeus (Roman Jupiter) and Hermes (Roman Mercury) were two of the anthropomorphic pagan gods worshipped in the region. The latter, herald and messenger of gods and protector of travellers was a well-known god whose shrines were encountered even by the roads. It is known that in some parts of Anatolia, Zeus was associated with other deities and epigraphic material from the region shows that he was frequently

Altar stone from Lystra with the name of the city. Second century CE. Konya Archaeological Museum. The inscription in Latin reads: 'Twice fortunate Lystra [Lustra],

a Julian colony dedicated [the altar] to the divine Augustus. Decreed by the city council'.

accompanied by Hermes. The grouping of divine names is known to have been special for the Lystra region. At Lystra Zeus was regarded as the protector of the grapevines and/or herds and represented as an elderly bearded figure sometimes accompanied by Hermes shown as a young male. The crowds' belief that the gods had arrived in their city in the likeness of men was not unrealistic. From ancient Greek literature we learn that from time to time immortals disguised in human form visited men to test their hospitality and the tradition of entertaining strangers lingered into the Greco-Roman period.

Although the very persons whom Paul and Barnabas encountered at this point may not have known it, their above-mentioned belief was a part of the ancient Greek mythology which associates the region with the visit of Zeus and Hermes during the time of the great flood as told by the Roman poet Ovid in *Metamorphoses* written a few decades before Paul was born:

'Jupiter visited this place, disguised as a mortal, and Mercury, the god who carries the magic wand, laid aside his wings and accompanied his father. The two gods went to a thousand homes, looking for somewhere to rest, and found a thousand homes bolted and barred against them. However, one house took them in: it was, indeed, a humble dwelling roofed with thatch and reeds from the marsh, but a good-hearted old woman, Baucis by name, and her husband Philemon, who was the same age as his wife, had been married in that cottage in their youth, and had grown grey in it together...So, when the heaven-dwellers reached this humble home and, stooping down, entered its low doorway, the old man set chairs for them, and invited them to rest their weary limbs; Baucis bustled up anxiously to throw a rough piece of cloth over the chair, and stirred up the warm ashes on the hearth, fanning the remains of yesterday's fire...Her husband had brought in some vegetables from his carefully-watered garden, and these she stripped of their outer leaves. Philemon took a two-pronged fork and lifted down a side of smoked bacon that was hanging from the blackened rafters; then he cut off a small piece of their long-cherished meat, and boiled it till it was tender in the bubbling water. Meanwhile the old couple chattered on, to pass the time, and kept their guests from noticing the delay. There was a beechwood bowl there, hanging from a nail by its curved handle, which was filled with warm water, and the visitors washed in this, to refresh themselves. On a couch with frame and legs of willow-wood lay a mattress, stuffed with soft sedge grass. Baucis and Philemon covered this with the cloths which they used to put out only on solemn holidays...Then the gods took their places for the meal.'

The meal that the poor couple prepared for the gods included various delicacies. After wiping the table with some stacks of fresh mint, Baucis placed wild cherries, radishes, cheese, eggs roasted in ashes, nuts, figs, dates, plums and wine. When the dinner was over Zeus and Hermes revealed themselves:

''We are gods'', they said, ''and this wicked neighbourhood is going to be punished as it richly deserves; but you will be allowed to escape this disaster. All you have to do is to leave your home, and climb up the steep mountainside with us''. The two old people both did as they were told and, leaning on their sticks, struggled up the long slope. When they were a bowshot distant from the top, they looked round and saw all the rest of their country drowned in marshy waters, only their own home left standing. As they gazed in astonishment, and wept for the fate of their people, their old cottage, which had been small, even for two, was changed into a temple: marble columns took the place of its wooden supports, the thatch grew yellow, till the roof seemed to be made of gold, the doors appeared magnificently adorned with carvings, and marble paved the earthen floor'.

The news of the wonder worked by the two strangers spread through Lystra and the priest of the Temple of Zeus hurried to find sacrificial bulls bearing garlands. Paul and Barnabas tore their garments in the customary Jewish reaction against blasphemy and the most common expression of grief in ancient Near East (Mk 14.63 and others). In answer to the pagan Lycaonians the apostle, 'Hermes', called upon their experience and knowledge of God, who at last had given a supreme revelation of himself, to turn 'from these idols to the living God', the advice which he would later repeat in Athens.

The events in Lystra give us an idea of how things were in a small Anatolian pagan town at the time of Paul's missionary journeys. Paul and Barnabas may have encountered many a similar settlement and experienced similar events during their travels. A similar incident would later happen in Malta where Paul's ship was wrecked during his journey to Rome. The event at Lystra also brings to mind the centurion Cornelius falling at the feet of Peter in Caesarea when he is greeting the latter in a manner appropriate to a deity (Acts 10.25). Both archaeological finds and ancient literature show that if there was one thing that Anatolia of the time was not short of, it was gods and goddesses. This was a period when politics, social and economic life, fortune and the future of people were all integrated into religion. Be it a metropolis like Ephesus or a countryside town like Lystra, sanctuaries and altars of smaller or larger size could be seen everywhere.

Thus Paul and Barnabas were expelled from Lystra too, at the behest of a delegation of Jews from Pisidian Antioch and Iconium. Paul was stoned and left for dead outside the town. Later in his letters the apostle would refer to these events saying 'once I was stoned' (2 Cor 11.25) and also 'persecutions, and sufferings, such as happened to me in Antioch, Iconium, and Lystra, persecutions that I endured' (2 Tm 3.11). Acts does not say if Paul was successful in Lystra. The people who were eager to regard them as gods changed their opinion of the two and stoned him. There is no mention of a synagogue. The disciples, who are mentioned gathered around him, thinking him dead, are not named. Later we learn that a family of a grandmother, Lois, mother, Eunice, and son, Timothy accepted the Christian faith (2 Tm 1.5). The grandmother and the mother were Jewesses. The latter had married a Greek. Their son Timothy would become a travelling companion of Paul during Paul's other journeys and in some cases serve as his secretary.

Polönü ('Paul's frontyard'). Kilistra.

The location of Lystra (Hatunsaray) has been identified by the discovery of a stone altar, standing in its original site, which gives the name of the site as Lustra. Its inscription indicates the existence of a temple dedicated to Augustus in the city which may have been the same as the Temple of Zeus referred to as being 'at the entrance to the city' (Acts 14.13). It has been speculated that the mound may have even been Tarhundassa, the capital of the kingdom of the same name of the Hittite period; otherwise the site did not gain any importance even after it was made a colony by Augustus with the name of Julia Felix Gemina Lustra.

Ancient road from Laranda (Karaman) to Ilistra (İlisıra/Yollarbaşı). In the background is Mt Posala (Pusula).

The memory of Paul's visits to the region seems to have survived in the settlement of Kilistra (Gökyurt village), some 15 km northwest of Lystra situated on the secondary road which diverted from the Via Sebaste. The open area in front of a group of cavities which include a small elaborately-carved rock-church is still known in Turkish as Polönü, or 'Paul's frontyard'. The church probably belonged to the monastic community who lived in the nearby rock-dwellings and was dedicated to the apostle. Inscribed grave stones have shown that the history of the site goes back to Paul's time, perhaps earlier. Christianity at the site seems to have flourished in the ninth-eleventh centuries together with the Cappadocian churches.

Mound of Derbe looking west. It is approximately 23 m high, 330 m long and 220 m wide, and had been occupied since the Iron Age.

Gravestone of Michael, Bishop of Derbe. Sixth century CE. Karaman Museum. Karaman.

Derbe was, however, the only place where Paul was not persecuted. The town was located some 150 km to the east of Lystra and it may have taken Paul and Barnabas four or five days to reach it. This section of the Via Sebaste was unpaved and avoiding the wasteland of the plain, first ran south as far as today's Akören. Here turning eastward it ran through today's Akarköy and Özyurt (Posala) which has given the name Pusula to the nearby mountain. After this point descending to the plain it took a straight course and crossing Kazımkarabekir (Prygoi?) and Ilistra (İlisıra/Yollarbaşı) and following todays motorway after the Ottoman bridge of Karasu it reached Laranda (Karaman). Laranda was, most likely, the last staging post of Paul and Barnabas before reaching Derbe. The administration of the region in this period is not clear. Somewhere near or at Laranda the territory of the province of Galatia may have terminated and the client Kingdom of Commagene which belonged to Antiochus IV began. The King had received eastern Lycaonia and a section of Rough Cilicia at first temporarily under Caligula. Later in 41 CE Claudius made Antiochus' rule over this region permanent.

Acts just mentions that they preached the gospel and made many disciples. Later, when Paul, in Gal 4.14 said 'you did not show disdain or contempt because of the trial caused you by my physical condition, but rather you received me as an angel of the God, and Christ Jesus' he may have had in mind particularly the people of Derbe. Also, later when he refers to the past 'persecutions, and sufferings, such as happened to me in Antioch, Iconium, and Lystra' in 2 Tm 3.11 Paul does not mention Derbe among these cities.

The site of Derbe (Kerti Höyük, near Ekinözü village) was located owing to an inscription discovered here, and no spade has yet touched the mound. There is almost nothing known about the history of the settlement except the

Limestone block with the name of Derbe from the city. Second century CE. Konya Archaeological Museum. The surviving part of the inscription begins with the seventh line and in Greek reads 'the gods of Derbe having manifested themselves, the council

and people, in the time of Cornelius Dexter, the governor [dedicated this altar].' Sextus Cornelius Dexter is known to have served as the governor in the region in 157 CE and the altar is dedicated to Antoninus Pius (161-80).

fact that in the first century BCE the town served as headquarters for the Isaurian bandit Antipater until he was killed by the Galatian King Amyntas (37-25 BCE). From the later Byzantine literature we learn that the name of the city meant 'juniper' in Lycaonian.

At this point of the journey Paul and Barnabas decided to return. Taking the Gospel further north into Galatia proper where people spoke their own tongues in Phrygian or Celtic dialects would have been difficult because of the language problem. In addition, research and archaeology to date have brought little evidence about the existence of Jewish diaspora in northern Galatia. The people of southern Galatia were more Romanized than the north and when others or themselves said 'Galatians' this carried a territorial sense rather than referring to the common pejorative ethnical characteristics of the original Galatians (Celts).

Paul and Barnabas had already diverted from their original mission itinerary. From Derbe they could have travelled overland to Antioch on Orontes by way of the Cilician Gates. This might have been more practical than going back through the cities of the furious Jewish communities they had visited or by the deep gorges of the Cestrus River. Later development of Roman roads in the region shows that there were a number of trails by which one could transverse the Taurus to the Mediterranean shore. The most popular route after diverging at Laranda and crossing the mountains at Coropissus (Dağ Pazarı) reached the bed of Calycadnus (Göksu) at Claudiapolis/Ninica (Mut). From here one could follow the river bed as far as Seleucia on Calycadnus (Silifke) on the Mediterranean or turn east to descend the coast by way of Diocaesarea (Uzuncaburç). In 401 BCE when Cyrus the Younger sent back the Queen of Cilicia to Tarsus escorted by his soldiers 'by the quickest route to her own country' the latter may have used one of these mountain routes. It is surprising that Paul and Barnabas did not take any of these tracks because Paul, owing to his long Cilician sojourn, may have been expected to have been familiar with most of Rough Cilicia.

Neither did they try the Cilician Gates. If winter was approaching they may not have wished to force the Cilician Gates. Writing in 50 BCE when he served as the governor of Cilicia, Cicero says 'Snow makes the Taurus impassable before June', a statement probably concerning only Roman troops with baggage trains but not the individual travellers. From Derbe Paul and Barnabas retraced their steps on the Via Sebaste to Lystra, Iconium,

Pisidian Antioch and Perge. On their return they possibly avoided speaking at the synagogues but stayed at the houses of their converts and at each of these places 'They strengthened the spirits of the disciples and exhorting them persevere in the faith'. The early history of all of these early churches is clouded in darkness.

The visits to these inland cities, with the exception of Pisidian Antioch, were probably accidental. Paul's missionary objective was directed to the well-populated urban centres, often situated on the coast and thus accessible by sea. Despite his failure in the region, however, Paul's determination would not permit him to forget the Galatians and he would visit them again and again on both his second and third journeys. Shortly after his return from the first journey the apostle heard about the apostasy of his first Galatian converts and wrote to them.

Acts 14.25 informs us that Paul, on his return from this journey from Pisidian Antioch went to Attalia after preaching at Perge. It does not give any information concerning new converts or whether they were persecuted at Perge. It is not known whether Paul's purpose in going Attalia was to proclaim

Dağ Pazarı Church. Dağ Pazarı (Coropissus) Late fifth century CE.

the Gospel there, something he had missed when he first arrived in Pamphylia from Cyprus, or just to find a vessel bound for Seleucia Pieria from where they could easily travel to Antioch on Orontes. Attalia is thought to have been founded by Attalus II (159-138 BCE) of Pergamum when he campaigned against Selge in Pisidia in 158 BCE. The site had the best harbour in the region and at the time of Paul's visit was a thriving Roman port. Among the ruins which are visible today there is nothing which dates back to the time of Paul except the ancient harbour which is still in use.

It was now almost two years or longer since Paul and Barnabas had begun their journey. They had been to places in some of which nobody had yet heard of the Gospel: Salamis, Paphos, Perge, Pisidian Antioch, Iconium, Lystra, Derbe and so many other places not mentioned in Acts. In most of these places Paul had established churches of which all or the majority were Gentiles, with Jewish minorities, unlike the model of the church of Antioch on Orontes, where in the beginning the majority were Greek-speaking Jewish Christians. As the ship carrying Paul and Barnabas was slowly towed out of the harbour of Attalia Paul and Barnabas had covered about 2,000 km, mostly on foot during this first journey. After this point and as far as Seleucia Pieria the sight of aged snow-capped ridges of the Taurus would accompany them. Thus Paul and Barnabas returned to their departure point, Antioch on Orontes (also called 'in Syria') and they 'spent no little time' there (Acts 14.28).

Ancient port. Antalya (Attalia).

MINISTRY IN ANTIOCH ON ORONTES

After his return to Antioch Paul received the news that some agitators were preaching a different Gospel than his among the churches in Galatia. Although their origin is not mentioned these are generally thought to have been some Jewish Christians from Jerusalem, 'some of our number' (Acts 15.24). These claimed that Paul was a flatterer and inconsistent in his teaching. The preachers whom he calls 'false brothers', probably referring to Abraham's words about the practice, insisted that the converts should be circumcised and also claimed that Paul was not an original apostle and his Gospel was wrong. In this manner they managed to divert some from Paul's Gospel. Thus he wrote to 'the churches of Galatia' a letter which was meant to be read at any church in the region.

Paul was so upset at the news that at the beginning of his letter he skips the usual blessing and salutations and saying 'I am amazed that you are so quickly forsaking the one who called you by [the] grace [of Christ] for a different Gospel' expresses his shock and disappointment. It was probably less than a year since they had received him 'as an angel of God, as Christ Jesus'. They would have plucked out their own eyes to give him. Although his expression 'stupid Galatians' or 'Are you so stupid' is not a usual manner of address, Paul is so shocked that he does not have time for pleasantness. The liberal manner with which he used adjectives like 'lazy, stubborn, untrusting' may indicate that Paul had failed in converting members from the higher levels of society and the people whom he addresses were lower class people. Paul blames them for foolishness in listening to those who preached that the observance of the Mosaic law was necessary for becoming Christian.

Despite its distance from Rome, archaeology and ancient literature have shown that Galatia was one of those regions where the Roman imperial cult was strongly established. At Paul's time the most evident representation of the imperial cult in Galatian cities were the sanctuaries dedicated to Augustus and the goddess Roma, personification of Rome, and becoming a Christian denied but did not protect a person from performing the obligatory worship to the imperial cult. This was the most important civic duty of a resident and for the Roman law its negligence was sacrilege and treason and punished by death. In addition, the Roman rule was suspicious of organizations, especially those established by members of lower classes. Even the clubs

Mosaic of Evil Eye from Antioch. Turn of the second century CE. Archaeological Museum. Antakya. The evil eye is represented together with the most powerful talismans against it. A naked goblin is carrying his talismans, a pair of skewers in each hand. He is not looking at the evil eye to avoid its dangers but his apotropaic element, an erect phallus, is turned against it. It has been suggested that when Paul said 'who has bewitched you' in Gal 3.1 he was referring to the ancient notion of the evil eye which was very common around the Mediterranean; something that his native hearers could easily understand. Those who envied their salvation had cast the evil eye on them. The inscription KAI ΣY ('And You') shows that the owner of the house to which this mosaic belonged wishes his guests the same thing, good or bad, that they would wish for him.

Evil Eye from a Roman quarry near Seleucia Sidera (Bayatlı) in Pisidia. Its inscription includes the common formula KAI ΣY. The destroyed section possibly had an ithyphallic goblin.

which were authorized, such as burial organizations, were not allowed to meet more than once a month. Christians' Sunday meetings made them very susceptible and from Pliny the Younger, who wrote some seventy years after Paul's time, we learn that their gatherings fell under the general prohibition. Apart from such problems scholars have commented that the simple salvation theory of Paul with only a baptizing ceremony was not a match for the elaborate pagan rituals and Judaism offered rituals as rich and more ancient than paganism. Now Paul was away and there was no one to exhort them. The Jewish Christians on the other hand, were protected by their ethnicity whose most distinguishing mark for the Romans was circumcision and their sabbath meetings which had been permitted since the time of Julius Caesar. According to Paul some Jewish Christians regarded circumcision as an instrument 'only that they may not be persecuted for the cross of Christ' without obligation to the other requirements of the Mosaic law, and asked non-Jewish Christians to do the same in which case they would be regarded by authorities as Jewish proselytes. Paul emphasized that if they only practiced the circumcision but skipped the other obligations of the Mosaic law they would be cursed.

Fragment from the *Res Gestae*, the 'deeds' of Augustus which was displayed at the monumental gate of his sanctuary at Pisidian Antioch. Yalvaç Museum.

Paul told them about the agreement reached between him and the three pillar apostles in Jerusalem during his previous visit. From Paul's letter we also learn that Peter came to Antioch, perhaps during one of his missionary journeys. Since he went 'to another place' in Acts 12.17, except for Paul's remark here and what is revealed by 1 Cor 1.12 that he may have stopped at Corinth, there is nothing known about Peter's movements. Paul says that Peter did not mind sharing meals with Gentile Christians and until some persons sent by James came to Antioch from Jerusalem, he was living like a Gentile. Even if the very complicated prescriptions detailed in the Book of Leviticus may not have been generally practiced in the first-century-CE Jewish world, what was applicable segregated Jews from Gentiles. The main reason why Jews were against sharing meals with Gentiles was the fact that much of the meat which would have been available to the latter at the market came from the sacrifices to pagan deities. Also prohibited was the meat of strangled animals because the pagan practice of strangling an animal, instead of cutting its throat, increased the risk of blood in the flesh. The prohibition against blood is already contained in the previous one. Some Jewish groups to prevent such dangers provided their own food. The details of the Jewish argument are not known. It is obvious that the Jews worried that the unknown meat which would have been served to them could be contaminated by idolatry. However, by stopping table fellowship with Gentile Christians the Jewish Christians indirectly forced the former to adopt the Jewish customs unless they wanted to survive as a separate church. In the long run the practice would have resulted in two groups of Christians who could not meet for the Lord's Supper. Paul blames Peter and those Jewish Christians who joined him with hypocrisy for the fact that they were doing, from Paul's point of view, something they did not believe in, under the pressure of the Jerusalem church. When they met in Antioch Paul criticized Peter for stopping sharing food with the Gentiles: 'I said to Kephas[1] in front of all, "If you, though a Jew, are living like a Gentile and not like a Jew, how can you compel the Gentiles to live like Jews?" '. Even his co-worker Barnabas

[1] Greek *Petros*, 'rock'.

complied with it. After all, he been sent to Antioch by the Jerusalem church and was unable to ignore it. Paul, nevertheless does not tell us Peter's reaction. Either Peter realized that he was wrong and repented, or as being in a superior position than Paul preferred to ignore the latter. If the problem had been solved as Paul wished it, at the time of writing the letter, he would, perhaps, not have neglected mentioning it to his apostate Galatian converts.

The rest of the picture is obtained from Acts 15 where we are informed that 'some' came to Antioch from Judea and preaching to Gentiles, claimed that circumcision was necessary if they wanted to become Christian. Although it is not explained, these preachers would have been Jewish Christians who were related to the ones that travelled to Galatia, mentioned in Paul's letter to the Galatians. A party among the Jewish Christians of Jerusalem were obviously angry and wondered how Gentiles being uncircumcised, with impure eating and immoral marriage habits and without any information about the scriptures, could be allowed to be their co-religionists. They claimed that people who did not observe the regulations of the law of Moses on such matters could not adhere to Christianity. This reaction may have been even regarded as normal by some of the proselyte Gentile Christians, but unwelcome to others who had accepted just some or none of the Mosaic requirements, the latter probably being mostly converts of Paul and Barnabas. The social standing of Gentile Christians probably differed in each congregation in accordance with the sort of observances of the Mosaic law that they practiced. Acts, without mentioning Jewish purity laws governing food, says that in Antioch 'no little' controversy arose, concerning circumcision. Luke's presentation of Barnabas debating with Judaizers together with Paul is regarded as an effort to diminish the conflict between the two.

The church at Antioch decided to send Paul and Barnabas and some others to the Jerusalem church to learn the thought of 'the apostles and presbyters about this question'. Provided 'by the church' of Antioch in about 49 the two took the route that they probably were familiar with and travelled by way of Phoenicia and Samaria. Arriving in Jerusalem they discussed such matters with the elders and apostles among whom Peter and James are mentioned.

Circumcision had been in practice in Syria or Africa since remote antiquity and although biblical tradition claims it to have been practiced since the patriarch Abraham, it may have been first introduced into the Semitic world by the Jews at the time of the Exodus. It was originally indicated by a tattoo showing that the

Inscription from the former church of St John at Selçuk near Ephesus. Byzantine period. In Greek it reads 'Jacobos [James] the Pope'. It is interpreted as 'James, the first Pope'. Scholars think that it reflects the belief in the Eastern church that James was the first Pope against the claim by the Western church in Rome for Peter.

circumcised person was a member of the tribe.[2] The law of Moses required that all male Jews be circumcised in infancy, on the eighth day of birth. The obligation had come to be regarded as more important during the later history of the Jewish nation when they lived under the rule of the Babylonians and Persians who did not practice it, and gained a religious meaning (Gn 17.14). The Jewish Christians claimed that all the converts to Christianity had also to be circumcised. The OT refers to the employment of primitive flint knives for the operation. At that time it was also a dangerous and painful operation especially for adults some of whom regarded it as a form of emasculation. At the Jerusalem Council Peter reminded the others that this problem had already found its answer in Caesarea by the vision of the centurion Cornelius which ended up with Gentiles receiving the Holy Spirit just as Jews.

James, accepting Peter's words about the unnecessariness of circumcision for non-Jewish Christians, said they should observe the basic requirements of the law of Moses governing purity, so that as long as they abstained from meat sacrificed to idols, meat of strangled animals, and also from blood in any flesh, and avoided marriage within forbidden degrees of affinity there was nothing to prevent them from becoming Christian. Although the complex obligations of the Jewish law seems to have been reduced to a few prohibitions, in reality, these were nothing but the repetition of some of the major regulations of the law of Moses, detailed in the Book of Leviticus.

In the conclusion summarized thus by James in Acts 15 there is no word about circumcision, still one may conclude that even if it was not abrogated its application may not have extended beyond Palestine. It is known that with the resolution of these matters pagans did not rush to be baptized, but their resolution would ultimately determine the character of the doctrine and practices of Christianity and help its spread.

The Jerusalem Council also decided that Paul and Barnabas should continue to preach to Gentiles and Peter to Jews. Following the meeting Judas, who was called Barsabbas, and Silas were chosen to accompany the apostles to Antioch with a letter to the Gentiles in Antioch, the capital and other places in the province of Syria and Cilicia, stating that Barnabas and Paul had been chosen, together with Judas and Silas, to take the message of resolution at the Jerusalem Council.

[2] The wedding ring, according to some scholars, originated from the practice of wearing the cut foreskin, later to be replaced by a ring.

PONTUS/EUXINE SEA
(BLACK SEA)
Amastris
Heraclea
Bosphorus
Hebrus
Axios
Styrmon
THRACE
Byzantium
Chalcedon
Nicomedia
MACEDONIA
Pangaion 1,956
Nestus
PROPONTIS
(MARMARA)
BITHYNIA
Ancyra
Philippi
Neapolis
Nicaea
Sangarius
Doberus?
Hellespont
Ascania
Tembris
Gordion
Thassos
Amphipolis
Cyzicus
Prusa
Dorylaeum
Edessa
Pella
Allante
Apollonia
Palaipolis
Germa
Ludias
Samothrace
Aisepus
Dascylium
Midaum
Beroia
Aloros
Thessalonica
Ergasteria
Pessinus
Tatta
Aigai
Methoni
Imbros
MYSIA
Rhyndacus
Pydna
Lemnos
Ilium
Hadrianoutherai
Cotieum
Nicolia
Haliacmon
Dium
Tenedos
Scepsis
Hadrianeia
Aezanoi
Amorium
GALATIA
Alexandria Troas
Satnioeis
Pionia
Olympus 2,911
Neandria
Assos
Adramyttium
Macestus
Cadı
Akroinos
Docimium
Lectum
Prymnessus
Tempe
THESSALY
Larissa
Lesbos
Mitylene
Pergamum
ASIA
Synada
Philomelium
PHRYGIA
Lagina
Laodicea
Antioch
Iconium
Meander
Pharsalus
Hermus
Cogamus
Neapolis
Karadağ 2,228
Limnai
Kilistra
Thaumacoi
Philadelphia
Pappa
Lystra
Sardis
Apamea
Nicopolis
Apollonia
PISIDIA
Scyros
LYCAONIA
Lamia
Smyrna
Cayster
Hierapolis
Ascania
Malos
Karalis
Actium
Nysa
Sagalassus
Adada
Laranda
ACHAIA
Chios
Tralles
Antioch
Posala
Euboea
Delphi
Ephesus
Cremna
Colossae
Laodicea
Pednelissos
Aulis
Lebadia
Thebes
Magnesia
Comama
Calycadnus
Eurymedon
Eleusis
Athens
Samos
Priene
Marsyas
Cestrus
PAMPHYLIA
Megara
Andros
Aspendos
Piraeus
CARIA
Perge
Side
Corinth
Tenos
Miletus
Cibyra
Attalia
Coracesium
Macronisi
Icaros
Acrocorinth 570
Cenchrea
Sunium
Myconos
Pharmacussa
LYCIA
Delos
Olympia
Halicarnassus
Anemurium
Cos
Myra
Naxos
Cnidus
Xanthos
Chelidonium
Symi
Andriace
Sparta
Nisyros
Rhodes
Patara
IONIAN SEA
Tylos
Lindos
Malea
Cythera
Carpathos
Nea Paphos
CRETE
Salmone
Cnossos
MEDITERRANEAN SEA
Phoenix
Gortyn
Fair Heavens
Cauda
SECOND JOURNEY
• Cities mentioned in Acts

SECOND JOURNEY

Antioch on Orontes — Derbe — Lystra — Galatic Phrygia — Mysia — Alexandria Troas — Samothrace — Neapolis — Philippi — Amphipolis— Apollonia — Thessalonica — Beroia — Athens — Corinth — Cenchrea — Ephesus — Caesarea —Jerusalem — Antioch on Orontes

According to Acts 15.36, 'After some time' the Gentile mission, although with limitations, now accepted, Paul decided for a second missionary journey to 'all the cities' that they had visited during the first journey. Paul wanted to see with his own eyes how his first converts in the churches of southern Galatia were doing since he wrote them a while earlier. Later developments show that he did not have a plan after this point. Barnabas, despite the problem reflected in Gal 2.13 agreed with him; but they went their separate ways, ostensibly because they disagreed over the suitability of John Mark. At this date Paul had not yet forgiven Mark's desertion in Perge. 'So sharp was their disagreement that they separated' (Acts 15.39). While Barnabas and John Mark went again to Cyprus, Paul left Antioch perhaps in 49 or 50, accompanied by Silas. The latter's name is a shortened form of Sylvanus, a Roman deity of wild places and the forest. The Silvanus of Paul's letters is regarded to have been the same person. In Acts 15.22 he is mentioned as one of the leaders of the church at Jerusalem and in 15.32 a prophet. His Roman citizenship is implied in Acts 16.38 after the jail episode in Philippi.

From Antioch there was only one major overland route to central Anatolia. This had been in use centuries before Paul's time and is still being used. Paul must have frequently marched on it during his long sojourn in 'Syria and Cilicia'. After they left the city the apostle and Silas, probably following the route of the present-day motor road, skirted the Amuq (Amık) plain, where the Seleucids once kept their elephants, until they reached the Amanus Mountains, the southernmost extension of the Taurus. They must have climbed the endless winding roads, and crossing the mountain by the Syrian/Assyrian Gates (Belen Pass, 800 m) descended to the Mediterranean coast, to Alexandria near Issus (İskenderun), another city founded by or for Alexander the Great. From this point on the ancient route followed the narrow strip of land left between the sea and the Amanus. The site where the mountains almost touched the shore, a narrow point which would later be named as Jonah's Pillars, was also known as the Portae/Portella ('narrows'), where a section of one of the piers of a Roman

Motor road entering from Antioch into the Assyrian/Syrian Gates (Belen). The narrow path along the cliff across was in use until some thirty years before and possibly followed the ancient route.

gateway survives. Later tradition regarded the site as the spot where Jonah was belched out by the great fish 'upon the shore' (Jon 2.11). The rest of the ruins which have survived belong to a medieval fortress whose origins perhaps go back to the Seleucid era or earlier. Paul and Silas must have continued their march through the battle ground of Issus where Alexander the Great defeated Darius (333 BCE) at the mouth of the Pinarus (Deli Çay/Payas Çayı). If they began in the early spring this walk may have been one of the most difficult in Paul's travels for the fact that even after a brief shower on the mountains the torrent made the smallest brook swollen and impassable. The road after running through Baiae (Payas) and Issus (Kinet Höyük) entered into the flats of Smooth Cilicia by way of the Amanid Gates (Kara Kapı).

The Cilician plain is fed by the rivers Pyramus (Ceyhan) and Sarus (Seyhan) and by changing their courses and silting since prehistoric times they had already turned the flat land into an expanse of lagoons, lakes and marshes infected with malaria. Here began the Alea plain of Homer where Bellerophon, hated by gods and men, once, 'eating his heart out' wandered all alone. Later literature informs us that 'In length it is sixteen days' journey, its breadth to the mountains two'. In Paul's time one would normally have reached Tarsus by crossing the Pyramus at Mopsuestia (fancifully translated 'hearth of Mopsus', Misis/Yakapınar) and continued by way of Adaniya on Sarus. The two major cities of Cilicia, Adana and Tarsus, have preserved their original names to the present.

From Antioch it would have taken more than a week to reach Tarsus. It is very probable that Paul visited some of his kinsmen or friends here and supplies were refreshed for the long trip awaiting them. One could travel from Tarsus to interior Anatolia either by way of the Cilician Gates or using one of the mountain trails which ran through Rough Cilicia. The latter was probably a region where the apostle spent much of his time when he had to flee from Jerusalem many years before. Most, or all, of the churches here perhaps owed their existence to Paul's missionary work and he would have visited and exhorted them travelling to southern Galatia by way of these familiar Christian communities; consequently this was perhaps a more attractive idea than the long solitary march through the Cilician Gates.

The popular ancient route followed the path of the Roman road, which would later be known as the Via Tauri. Leaving Tarsus it ran toward the Cilician Gates by way of Mopsucrene ('fountain of Mopsus' over the rugged foothills of the Taurus. In Paul's time the Cilician Gates (Gülek Boğazı, 1,050

A stretch of the Via Tauri between Tarsus and the Cilician Gates. Across the pavement on the rock ('Yazılıtaş') is a worn-out road inscription in Greek.

Amanid Gates (Kara Kapı, 'black gate' because of its surviving black basalt stones). The remains of the ancient paved road can still be traced is for as the Ottoman caravanserai of Kurtkulağı. In ancient history the two long natural passes which connected the Amuq plain to northern Cilicia by way of Nurdağı/ Bahçe and Fevzipaşa/ Hasanbeyli were also known by the same name.

m) which provided the shortest connection between the southern plain and inland Anatolia was a narrow pass of several kilometres, 3 m wide. It was the main passage connecting central Anatolia to Cilicia and Syria and continued for about 50 km through the mountains following the bed of Çakıt Suyu/Pozantı Çayı. The earliest people whom we know fortified the pass were the Hittites, who called the heights Mount Muti. Crossing it in 401 BCE, Xenophon in *Anabasis* describes it as having 'consisted of a carriage track which was tremendously steep; impassable for any army if there was any opposition'.

Alexander found the pass almost undefended and as he entered it in 333. From the literature about Alexander we learn that one 'could have been crushed just by rock, if there had been anyone to hurl them down on his approaching troops. The road could hardly accommodate four armed men abreast, and a mountain ridge overhung a pathway which was not only narrow but at many points ruptured by numerous streams that flowed over it, emanating from the mountains'. For the most of the pass the pathway was cut into the living rock and followed the bed of a brook which then flowed into the Cydnus. Podandos (near Pozantı) is the only station that we know about until one crossed the mountains.

After coming out of the gorges the road forked into two branches and while the first one continued toward Tyana (Kemerhisar) from where it went to either Ancyra (Ankara) or Caesarea (Kayseri), the second one turned to west and ran in the direction of Derbe by way of Cybistra (Ereğli) and Sidamaria (Anbar village). To the north lay central Anatolia, a dry, vast, high plateau known at the time of Paul as Axylon ('steppe'), a part of Galatia. Livy says that it was called 'Axylon ('Woodless')' because 'it produces no wood at all, not even thorns or any other fuel; the people use cow dung as a substitute for wood'. In Paul's time the Romans had not yet begun building the roads which cut across the flats of central Anatolia. Since Persian times, the armies after entering the heart of the peninsula — from west or east — avoided crossing it. Research has shown that it was once, some ten or fifteen millennia before, until the end of the last ice age (Halocene), occupied by an inland sea. In time when temperature rose and evaporation increased, the springs which fed the sea disappeared and the present-day Tuz Gölü ('salt lake') known in Paul's days as Lake Tatta was left. Strabo says that 'on account of the congealing of the salt, the birds who touch the water with their wings fall on the spot and are thus caught'. The earliest farmers of the plateau also

Ancient bridge on the Pyramus (Ceyhan) at Mopsuestia. Ottoman construction possibly built at the spot of its Roman antecedent. View from the acropolis.

Road inscription at the Cilician Gates. 217 CE. In Latin it reads 'Imp Caesar Marcus Aurelius [Antoninus Pi]us Felix Invictus Augustus, montibus caesi[s] viam latiorem fecit. ΟΡΟΙ ΚΙΛΙΚΩΝ'. After giving the titles of a Severan emperor, known to have been Caracalla, it informs us that he 'made the road wider by cutting back the mountains' at 'the Boundaries of the Cilicians', the last

part added in Greek. The construction work is thought to have been carried out for the movement of the Roman army and supplies for the Emperor's eastern campaign against the Parthians which ended with his death at Carrhae (Harran) in the spring of 217. Originally, the road was about the same level with the inscription.

Milestone from ancient Podandos, some 25 km north of the Cilician Gates. Now placed at Pelit restaurant near Pozantı. 217 CE. The inscription in Latin reads 'The Emperor Caesar Marcus Aurelius Severus Antoninus Pius, fortunate, August, conqueror of Parthians, Britons and Germans, chief priest, in the 20th year of his tribunician power, hailed imperator thrice, four times consul, proconsul, father of his country repaired the Via Tauri which was dilapidated with age, by levelling mountains, smashing rocks, widening carriageways and building bridges. From the Gates 15 miles'. The last sentence is repeated in Greek. The emperor mentioned in the inscription is known to have been Caracalla.

appeared hereabouts some seven millennia before our era at places like Çatal Höyük near Konya or Aşıklı Höyük near Aksaray (Archelais). In Paul's days where water supplies permitted it could give adequate grain harvests, but much of it was a dusty dun-coloured expanse which became a barren waste at the centre. Since their invitation from Thrace by Nicomedes I of Bithynia to serve as mercenaries against his rebellious brother during the first quarter of the third century BCE, the region had become the home of the warlike Celtic tribes or Gauls, and was named Galatia. Originally forming a military aristocracy, the Gauls remained a minority of a population that was largely native Phrygian and Cappadocian. Livy writing a few decades before Paul's journeys tells us that before going into the battle against the Gauls of Galatia Manlius Vulso described them: 'Their tall physique, their flowing red locks, their vast shields and enormous swords, together with their songs as they go into battle, their howlings and leapings and the fearful din of arms as they batter their shields following some kind of ancestral custom — all these are carefully designed to strike terror'. At the time of Paul's travels the province's capital was Ancyra, and Tavium (Büyük Nefes village, Yozgat) and Gordion were its most important other two cities. Galatia entered into Roman rule in 189 BCE. The population of the region was mostly Phrygians and Cappadocians known to have resisted Greco-Roman culture and maintained their language and identity. The ruling Celtic aristocracy was perhaps the most Hellenized section of society.

For the regions of Paul's evangelistic activities in Galatia Luke uses ethnic regional terms such as Lycaonia or Pisidia. At the time of Paul's journeys Lycaonia was the southern part of the province of Galatia which was established in 25 BCE following the death of the last Galatian King Amyntas. It was a largely pastoral area, with large flocks of sheep and goats and other animals, even wild asses (now extinct) and wild sheep. Water lies in some 15 to 50 m depth. The journey of Cyrus the Younger and his army through this area in 401 BCE may be regarded as the earliest contact of the native population with Greek culture. Although the region would be subdued by Alexander the Great's general Perdiccas, the actual penetration of Greek language and culture had to wait for the establishment of the Seleucid cities which were later supplemented by Roman colonies. When Paul came this way, many people spoke their own tongues, although as elsewhere, Greek was the common language. Even though a network of Roman roads traversed it, the region remained remote, and its few cities were situated along the major Roman road. In addition to the Sergii, to whom Paul's first known Gentile convert Sergius Paulus of Cyprus belonged, Italian families such as the Caristanii, Calpurnii or Cornuti are known to have held large estates in the flats. The aristocracy at Rome mocked their members who owned land in this remote region. Most of the Bible teachers believe that when Paul said 'Galatia' the apostle could not have meant Galatia proper where he had not been, and as he referred to the Christians in Thessalonica or Philippi as 'Macedonians', here he referred to the churches he had established in southern part of the province of 'Galatia', which was geographically located in southern Phrygia and Lycaonia.

The security that the Augustan peace which the Romans claimed kept 'the corners of the whole world free from the fear of robbers' was not absolute and ancient literature shows that the cities of Lycaonia were open to the attacks of the highlanders of the Taurus. During the Byzantine period the inhabitants of Rough Cilicia were called Isaurians. These people were politically and culturally isolated from those who occupied the lowlands on both sides of the mountains and reciprocal animosity underlined their relations. Some of them were known to have raided the rich coastal settlements in Paul's time. Basil the Great of Caesarea (330-79) informs us how, at his time, the highland barbarians raided Lycaonia and made their captives swear oaths to pagan gods and taste food sacrificed for pagan deities. The order of the cities in Acts 16.1, 'Derbe and Lystra', has been interpreted by some scholars to imply a geographical itinerary which began from the east, probably travelling by way of the Cilician Gates. Thus, it is very probable that Paul and Silas, making use of the relative safety that the Roman roads provided, traced the first mission's route, the Via Sebaste from Derbe to Lystra, Iconium and Pisidian Antioch, the last two not being mentioned by Luke. Sometime in this period when the province was ruled by

Fortress-treasury of Deiotarus (about 80-50 BCE). Peium (Tabanlıoğlu Kalesi) on the Hieros (Girmir) River near Beypazarı, Ankara. He was the most powerful Galatian tetrarch at the time of Pompey/Caesar.

the governor Annius Afrinus (49-54 CE) he permitted two of the cities to use the Emperor's name and they were called Claudiconium and Claudioderbe. The Temple of Augustus in Pisidian Antioch was completed in 50 CE and its triple gate dedicated to Claudius. Except for at Lystra the apostle's activities during his second missionary journey through this region are not known.

Some wonder if Paul's insistence on visiting a region like Galatia, devoid of large cities and urban elites and perhaps many synagogues, again and again, can be interpreted, in addition to an unyielding strain of character, in light of his failure or limited success with the Galatians. They also wonder if the uneducated locals could understand Paul's complicated scriptural polemics. From his remark in 1 Cor 16.1 we learn that he also ordered the 'churches of Galatia' to collect funds for the Jerusalem church. Although he had been stoned at Lystra this had taken place about one or two years earlier. Here Paul was joined by a young disciple, Timothy who had perhaps known Paul from his previous visit to Lystra. Timothy's father was a Gentile, but mother was a Jewish convert to Christianity and of whom the brothers in Lystra and Iconium had spoken highly (Acts 16.2). In spite of Paul's belief that circumcision was not necessary for salvation, a fact which was officially established by the Jerusalem Council, and at the time a person who had a Jewish mother and a Gentile father was regarded a Gentile, out of respect for Jewish sensibilities he had Timothy circumcised (Acts 16.3). After all, the latter would be working for Paul's Gospel not just for Gentiles but Jews as well. The latter's mother was a Jewess and the Jews that Paul would have

Roman road near Sandıklı, Afyon.

come across would have been offended meeting an uncircumcised half-Jew. Timothy, although not circumcised, probably had been raised in the manner of a Jewish youth. It has been speculated that although his behaviour seems to contradict his words 'if you have yourselves circumcised, Christ will be of no benefit to you' (Gal 5.2), Paul might have wanted to avoid unforeseen problems when preaching to Jewish communities. The words in 2 Tm 3.10-11 that Timothy also endured Paul's persecutions at Lystra may refer to the fact that Timothy was a witness of the events which took place here during Paul's first journey. Timothy would become Paul's secretary and envoy for some of the apostle's special missions, writing his letters and conveying them to the believer groups that he established in each city.

The valleys which flanked the beds of the Hermus, Cayster or Meander, rich in cities with Jewish communities, where Paul could preach, provided easy access from Phrygia to Ephesus, at that time the capital of the province of Asia. Paul was prevented from going in this direction 'by the Spirit' (Acts 16.6). This may have taken place somewhere near Apamea (Dinar) close to the territory of province of Asia, where the road from Pisidian Antioch met the other ancient arteries of communication. The hills around Pisidian Antioch were the southern extremity of the Phrygian plateau. Paul, Silas and Timothy must have travelled through the bleak Phrygian uplands which were never short of sweet water springs and towns established in the pockets of the mountains. Acts 16.6 informs us that 'They travelled through the Phrygian and Galatian territory' using both the ethnic and administrative name of the same region, translated usually as 'Galatic Phrygia', which may imply an ancient route which went north by way of Synada (Şuhut), Prymnessus (Süğlün), Docimium (İscehisar), Amorium (Hisarköy), Pessinus (Ballıhisar), Germa (Karacapaşaören near Babadat) and Midaum (Midas City) toward Dorylaeum (Şar Höyük near Eskişehir) on the Tembris (Porsuk) River. The last city was the main exit from the central plateau into Mysia and Bithynia. However, from Prymnessus a shorter route by way of Akroinos (Afyon), Meiros (Malatça/Demirözü) and Nicolia (Seyitgazi) also led to Dorylaeum. The remains of the Roman roads and bridges on both of these routes and the rest of the region are from after Paul's time and the possible routes that Paul may have taken are no more than conjecture. The region they travelled falls partly into Phrygia which the Romans called Epictetus, ('new acquired'), and was popular with its spas which would later be frequented by visitors from different parts of the Roman world. Some scholars suggest that Paul may have not missed the opportunity of visiting some of these to improve his health and may even have chosen this route for that purpose.

Somewhere probably near Dorylaeum (Şar Höyük, Eskişehir) they were about to turn north to enter Bithynia but the Holy Spirit prevented Paul from advancing in this direction. Bithynia had become Roman soil, a Roman province in 74 BCE when Nicomedes III bequeathed his Kingdom to Rome. In 63 BCE Pompey had joined it to the province of Pontus. If Paul had continued he would have reached the populated cities of Prusa (Bursa), Nicaea (İznik) and the capital of province Nicomedia (İzmit) and finally Byzantium. Prevented from going northward they travelled west through the Mysian heights to Troas.

Simplified plan of Alexandria Troas.

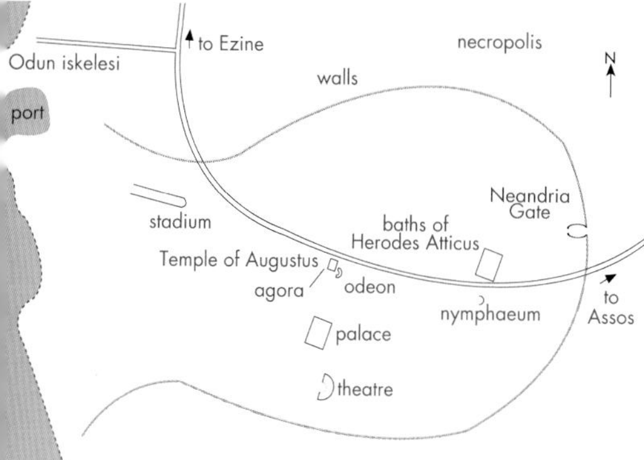

Acts 16.8 saying that 'they crossed through Mysia and came down to Troas' adds nothing about the route they took. Central Mysia was a huge mass of mountain ranges covered with thick pine forests, separated from each other by the beds of, from west to east, Aisepos (Gönen Çayı), Enbeilos (Karadere) and Macestus (Simav Çayı) all flowing into the Propontis following the northeast-southwesterly alignment of the mountains. It was not a populated land and few were the settlements that could be reached only by following the river beds. Some like Ergasteria (Balya/Maden) or Argyria (Gümüş Maden) owed their existence to the nearby silver mines. If one wanted to travel from one river bed to the other one would have to walk over mountains devoid of settlements and roads and through small patches of arable land.

There is almost no information about the road condition in the region when Paul crossed it. In travelling through such an uninhabited territory safety would have been more important than logistics for a small party and Paul may have tried a relatively known trail. Later development of Roman roads shows that if he wanted to avoid crossing Bithynian soil he may have advanced first to Cotieum (Kütahya), following the course of Rhyndacus (Kemalpaşa Çayı) to the west in the direction of Hadrianeia (Dursunbey/Balat) and on to Hadrianoutherai (Balıkesir) from where one could either continue a northwestern or a western route. The first, following the watersheds of the Macestus went to Cyzicus (Erdek) by way of Dascylium (Ergili) and encircling the mountain masses by following the shore of the Propontis reached the Aegean, Ilium/Troy and Alexandria Troas. The second route went toward Adramyttium (Edremit) by way of Pionia (Gömeniç). Following the coast by way of Antandros (Devren/Avcılar) and Gargara (near Arıklı) it

Eastern gate of Alexandria Troas in the direction of Neandria. It is thought that after coming out of the gate the road forked into branches going in the direction of the Scamander valley, Neandria and Assos.

A stretch of the Roman road which is today known as Ulu Yol ('great road') between Neandria and Alexandria Troas.

reached Assos and avoiding Cape Lectum (Baba Burnu) by going through Smintheium (Gülpınar) turned north in the direction of Alexandria Troas. This would however be going up to Troas instead of coming 'down' to it as Acts says. After Gargara a second road turned toward Ilium/Troy following the bed of Scamander. If one took this road and went to Alexandria Troas by way of Neandria (Kayacık village) this scenario would have brought one 'down' to the latter. Neandria was founded at the top of Mount Çığrı (500 m), the highest spot in the region. Although it lost its importance after the foundation of Alexandria Troas it must have still been an important town in Paul's time. A soft descent of some 30 km, a walk of less than a day, led to Alexandria Troas. The route crossed the undulating land where later Turkish villages were founded at the spots with water sources. The Roman road, whose remains are still visible, was in use until a few decades ago and called by the local people Ulu Yol, ('great road'). Just before climbing to the Neandria Gate at the place where both sweet water springs and hot spas exist today it was joined by the Roman road coming from Assos by way of Smintheium.

Troas, also known as the Troad, was the name of the northwestern projection of Anatolia into the Aegean. It extended north from Adramyttium (Edremit), to the Hellespont (Dardanelles). Among its mountains the highest was Mount Ida (Kaz Dağı, 1,767 m) by which the Scamander (Karamenderes) flowed, and where Paris once acted as the arbitrator for the beauty contest which is said, ultimately, to have led to the Trojan War. The major cities of the region were Assos, Alexandria Troas and Ilium/Troy. Alexandria Troas was founded in about 310 BCE by Antigonus Monophthalmus ('one-eyed'), a general of Alexander who had inherited central Anatolia after the latter's death, and who named the settlement Antigonia. We are informed that the settlement was populated by people who were moved here from the nearby towns such as Scepsis (Kurşun Tepe) or Neandria. After defeating Antigonus at Ipsus (near Afyon) in 301 BCE, together with the Seleucid King Antiochus I, Teos ('god'), the victor, Lysimachus, the general of Alexander who had taken Thrace, renamed the city in honour of Alexander and added the word 'Troas' to distinguish it from the other Alexandrias. The city soon became the most important port for travelling across the Aegean. It was made a colony: Colonia Augusta 'Troadensium' or commonly 'Troas' by Augustus and by Paul's time

Temple of Augustus. First century BCE. Alexandria Troas.

with its small but well-protected artificial harbour it had become the major trading and communication post between Asia and Europe.

Alexandria Troas is now one of the largest Pauline cities with most of its remains still under the soil. Since excavations are just beginning our information about this large and overgrown site is very limited. Ancient literature mentions a fortification wall of some 8 km and this is regarded to imply a population no less than thirty thousand people. The city did not have a height which could be referred to as acropolis but was spread on the undulating land. Recent excavations have brought to light the ruins of the foundations of a temple which is thought to have been built in the reign of Augustus, perhaps dedicated to the divine Julius and the goddess Roma, and the agora. The odeon is situated next to the temple. The remains of a monumental fountain and the baths which were built by the Greek tycoon Herodes Atticus, who served as a special administrator in Asia and who was the richest and most influential political figure of Athens in the middle of the second century, have also survived to the present. Roads in the direction of Ilium/Troy, Neandria and Smintheium and Assos departed from the gate whose ruins survive to the present. Early visitors inform us about the existence of the main gate of the city away from the harbour on the east side. The high hills between Assos and Alexandria Troas supplied the type of stone known as Troad granite that became popular especially after the mid-second century CE. It was exported in the form of monolithic columns and the pieces which still rest around the jetty of the harbour belong to columns abandoned in the course of transportation.

Roman quarry of Yedi Taş ('seven stones') or Yedi Uyuyanlar ('seven sleepers') near Alexandria Troas.

In Alexandria Troas the apostle saw a vision telling him to go to Macedonia. It has been suggested that this was an allusion to Luke. Some hold that, since Luke was with Paul, the vision may have been that of Alexander the Great who wished but failed to unite the western and eastern cultures of his time under a single flag. The first encounter of Luke, the narrator of the so-called 'we-sections' in Acts, and Paul is thought to have taken place here. This meeting was very probably accidental because until he reached the border of Bithynia, the apostle had not yet decided which way to travel. Luke was a Greek physician, very probably the 'beloved physician' of Col 4.14, and according to one tradition 'by birth' from Antioch on Orontes, a hypothesis thought to have originated from confusing him with Lucius of Cyrene mentioned among the first church officials at Antioch. Eusebius' words 'Luke, by birth an Antiochene and by profession a physician' also refer to an eastern tradition. Generally, he is regarded as a native of Macedonia who practiced his profession on both sides of the Aegean and whom Paul first met at Alexandria Troas. He may have already been Christian because of the fact that according to Acts the apostle was then forbidden to preach in Asia by the Holy Spirit. It has been suggested that Luke's parents may have obtained Roman citizenship when Julius Caesar granted it in 46 BCE 'to all medical practitioners' resident in Rome. In the Roman world of the time doctors were often slaves or freedmen and it has suggested that Luke's unknown ancestor may have received the name of his master (Lucius, of which Lukas is a diminutive) when he was manumitted. It is probable that the party, now of four, decided to cross to Macedonia on the initiative of Luke who was familiar with the region. It is not known if Paul's sickness played a part in Luke's becoming a permanent companion of Paul during the last section of his journeys.

Some scholars believe that although Luke begins narrating the events as a member of the group it is difficult to know exactly if he simply used 'we', first person plural, as a literary device common for the time to colour the incidents. The realistic way that the events are recounted after this point give the impression that even if he was not there during the 'we' events, he may have used another eyewitness' story. Acts does not mention any ministry in the city

Ancient harbour. Dalyan (Alexandria Troas). Across the Aegean is Tenedos (Bozca Ada). Some fifty years after Paul's time Ignatius' vessel would also wait here for the change of the wind to depart for Neapolis 'at any moment'.

during this first visit to Alexandria Troas. The apostle would revisit the city during his next journey and preach the Gospel.

The destination of Paul's party was Philippi across the Aegean. Sailing directly to the opposite coast from Anatolian harbours was not easy. In summer the heat rises to its maximum intensity, around 40° C. When the masses of the warm air lift, all of a sudden cool air of the north or northeast, from the Black Sea, rushes into its place violently. Herodotus calls it 'Hellespontian' and says that it raises 'a confused sea like a pot on the boil'. The wind is commonly known as *meltemi*. The captain may have waited for the southerly wind which blew less than the northerlies and even for it to drop a little until he ventured out of the sheltered port of Alexandria Troas. It is probable that with the large degree of leeway by the islands on her way Paul's ship had to make about 300 km, a voyage of two days, to reach the opposite side of the Aegean. The vessel must have been one of those small ships which hopped from one island to the other carrying merchandise of any kind, dropping and picking up passengers who wanted to visit the local shrines or their relatives. Acts, however, says Paul's vessel sailed 'straight to Samothrace' without making stops at the other islands on her way.

Sailing north with the proper winds Paul's ship must have first rounded Tenedos (Bozca Ada). Many centuries earlier the Greek fleet hid itself under the lee of the island after leaving the wooden horse on the Trojan plain before the final attack. The expression 'chopped it through with a Tenedos axe', used for anyone stubbornly refusing to be spoken to, was contributed to ancient speech by the island. In *Politics*, Aristotle, in his list of examples of cities with unusual opportunity for nonagricultural employment mentions Tenedos with a large class of ferrymen.

On the Asian side, although it was sacked by the Romans in 85 BCE, the restored Temple of Athena rose above the city walls of Ilium/Troy. The inhabitants of the city were granted permanent exemption from tribute by Caesar, a decision which would be confirmed by Claudius in 53 CE, as being the supposed founders of the Roman race. The two already worn-out mounds which would later be claimed to be housing graves of Achilles and Patroclus should have easily been distinguished. Leaving Tenedos behind, the ship would come into the main current which swept into the Aegean from the mouth of the Hellespont. As the pilot continued north the current would become weaker and his ship would finally begin to use the shelter provided by Imbros (Gökçe Ada) against the north wind. Recent excavations have shown that it was settled as early as Troy. To the right stood the tip of the Thracian Chersenose which would later be known as the Gallipoli peninsula.

Samothrace, where the first leg of the voyage ended, was a large island whose summit dominated the sea. In the *Iliad* Poseidon watched the battle ground from the summit of today's Mount Phengari ('peak of the moon', 1,664 m) that commands a view of the Trojan plain, and encouraged the Achaians. The island was settled by immigrants from Lesbos or northwestern Anatolia who probably brought the cult of the Great Mother with them, and named the island thus to distinguish it from the Ionian Samos. Its major settlement was Palaipolis. Pliny the Elder, when he says that the island was devoid of harbours, was right because even the anchorage of Palaipolis was no more than a small natural inlet at the mouth of a brook and did not offer shelter for long stays. In fact unlike almost all the other Aegean cities, Palaipolis owed its existence not to a well-protected harbour but to the sanctuary of the Great Gods which occupied the foothills of the Phengari to the west of its walls. There may have been some pilgrims on Paul's vessel who wanted to disembark here. The origins of this sanctuary went back to the foundation of the city. Its small pantheon was headed by the Great Mother called Axieros. It was one of the most popular sanctuaries of the Hellenistic world and excavations have brought to light ruins of many shrines dedicated by different Hellenistic rulers. By the first century CE however, almost all of the ancient deities of the pantheon had lost their original identities and were syncretized with Greek gods, such as Axieros with Demeter and the demons Cabiri with the Dioscuri. The Cabiri watched over the ship-wrecked sailors and some of

Samothrace. Looking from north. The Byzantine tower, which can be distinguished close to the sea shore on the right, marks the place where the city of Palaipolis was situated. On the other side of the island, the eroded granite mass in the picture opens like a crescent and allows some cultivable land at its skirt.

the crew of the vessels docked at the harbour may have not missed the chance of visiting the sanctuary. The mysteries were not limited only to the elite but open to all kinds of people who were ready to keep their secrets. The happy afterlife that the mysteries offered made them very popular. There is no information about the initiation rituals except that a feast with plenty of wine, a hearing of confession of sins, sacrifices and libations were included. Philip II of Macedon is said to have met Olympias, future mother of Alexander the Great, here, during on initiation ritual and to have fallen in love with her. The sculpture of the Nike monument, or winged Victory (190 BCE) — now displayed at the Louvre — is the most familiar object from the island's history for the general reader. Placed on a marble ship's prow it had its own precinct above the theatre and was perhaps visible from the vessels sailing to the north of the island. The sanctuary offered asylum, and Perseus, the last King of Macedonia after he lost the battle of Pydna (168 BCE) to the Romans, sheltered here. Here he surrendered and was taken to Rome to be paraded as a peasant in chains.

Ancient (silted) port of Palaipolis.

In the morning, shortly after the captain gave start for Neapolis, Paul and his friends must have viewed the peaks of Mount Athos (2,220 m) to the southwest which would later become one of the most important centres of the Gospel that they were now carrying to Europe. On the mainland side the River Hebrus (Maritza/Meriç), which would later become the border between Turkey and Greece, flowed into the Aegean. Rounding Thassos to its north, an island famous for its marble in antiquity and where, according to Herodotus, the Phoenicians utilized gold mines as early as the sixth century BCE, they sailed into the port of Neapolis possibly before the darkness set.

The country in which Paul and his friends landed was called Macedonia, after its people the Macedons, later anglicized as Macedonians. The apostle would visit it again and again, and his extensive missionary activities here would be second only to those in Anatolia.

Macedonia was a land of high mountains through which perennial rivers ran. Its wide plains were cultivable and its pastures were perfect for animal husbandry. Its inhabitants were famous as horsemen. The large forests supplied excellent timber for shipbuilding. Its wooded mountains which produced gold and silver and other metals were also infested with all kinds of wild animals such as leopards, panthers, bears and lions. Herodotus tells us how lions descended on the camps of Xerxes' army as it marched through the Axius (Vardar) valley in 480 BCE and 'molested neither men nor other animals but just camels'. The valleys were mostly inhabited by large clans related to each other by common descent, language, and marriage. Although the structure of their city-states was similar to that of Greeks, they differed in the fact that they were subject to a king. The Macedonians spoke the Aiolic dialect of the Greek language. Other ethnic groups such as Thracians or Thessalians who lived in the region, in addition to their local tongues, also knew Greek. Persian sources of the late sixth century BCE mention the inhabitants among the nations who paid tribute to their Great King and call them *yauna takabara* ('Greeks wearing the hat') after their distinctive broad-brimmed sun-hat known as *kausia*. When Greek sources call the Macedonians barbarians they refer not to their language but their way of life, because they resented the Macedonian habit of polygamy and brother-sister marriage. It was nevertheless, these many inter-marriages which kept so many clans together and provided the unity of the Macedonians. By the Greek standards Macedonia was a backward country.

The Macedonian state was established in the sixth century BCE but reached its zenith when it was ruled by Philip II (359-336) and later his son Alexander the Great (336-323). During this period Macedonian hegemony extended to Athens and the rest of the Greek peninsula. Despite the failures which were caused by the wars of succession that took place after Alexander's death, the Macedonian monarchy survived and ruled a large part of the peninsula. In the last quarter of the third century BCE Rome, the alleged protector of the Greek states, began making a slow entrance into the eastern stage. The final aggressions, however, had to wait until Rome washed its hands of the Carthaginian feud, and came to an end with the defeat of the last Macedonian King Perseus at the battle of Pydna in 168 BCE. Macedonia became a Roman possession and split into four independent republics. At the time that Paul and his friends arrived however, these were united as the Roman province of Macedonia, and after many changes, in 44 CE together with Achaia was again made a senatorial province with a Roman proconsul whose seat was at Thessalonica.

Neapolis (Kavala), the port of Philippi, lay at the end of a wide bay protected by a small peninsula at Paul's time crowned by a statue of Aphrodite. It was the favourite port for travellers from central and northern Europe and those coming from Anatolia. Paul's party probably spent the night at a local inn and next morning joined the cosmopolitan traffic which travelled to the north on the Via Egnatia. Today an altar outside the Church of St Nicholas, which once stood along the water, traditionally, commemorates the place where they landed. The church is said to have, originally, carried the apostle's name and was turned into a mosque during the Turkish occupation. When the time that the building could again be turned into a church came, the fishermen who met the expense of the restoration cared more for their patron saint Nicholas than the apostle, and named it thus.

Acts does not mention any preaching in Neapolis but moves Paul's party to their next destination. Philippi, which was located about 20 km away, less than a day's walk to the north, was a small settlement originally founded as Daton by immigrants from the nearby island of Thassos. At the beginning it consisted of no more than a fortified acropolis on a rocky extension of Mount Orbelus. It was, however, captured and renamed after himself by Philip II in 356 BCE. The agricultural wealth of the settlement was supplemented by the gold mines of the nearby Mount Pangaion. Its native population was of mixed Macedonian and Thracian stock. About a hundred years before Paul's visit, in 42 BCE it was on the marshy plains extending outside the city's western walls that the two battles between Octavian (later Augustus) and Mark Antony against Brutus and Cassius had been fought and ended with the defeat and suicide of the last two. The town was made a Roman colony by Mark Antony and settled by some of his veteran soldiers and their families. After the latter's defeat at Actium (31 BCE) these were supplemented by Octavians' veterans and Antony's veterans evicted from Italy. The city was now named Colonia Augusta Julia Philippensium. The objective of the colony

Port of Neapolis (Kavala).

A stretch of the Via Egnatia near Neapolis descending from Mount Symbolium in the direction of Philippi.

was the protection of the Via Egnatia which was the only artery by which Roman forces moved to Anatolia and the east. Owing to the Roman soldiers and the concentration of Roman administrators the town developed a strong Latin character. Great fortified barracks were built at the top of the acropolis. Although agriculture continued to be the major sustenance of the town it also prospered by its share of the trade which passed along the Via Egnatia. There were also the Roman soldiers ready to spend their salary on the produce of the villagers and local artisans.

From the information in Acts some scholars conclude that Philippi's small Jewish community had no synagogue but a 'place of prayer' (*proseuche*) just 'outside the city gate along the river' water being an indispensable instrument of Jewish worship. It is not known if the anti-Semitism of the Philippians also played a role in the choice of this distant location. The settlement was not a commercial centre but a military colony and the number of Jews was not obviously high. Acts does not mention the presence of men when Paul visited them on the sabbath. Some scholars have remarked that the distance between the eastern city gate and the Gangites is more than the 'two thousand cubits in every direction' prescribed by Mishna for a sabbath day's mission, and the prayer place at Philippi may have been somewhere by the little stream Krinides that gave the settlement its local name Krinides ('springs') in the Hellenistic era. The 'place of prayer' mentioned in Acts may have been a private house used for this purpose or an open area perhaps with a kind of enclosure to provide some privacy. Paul, Silas, Timothy and Luke, after their arrival in Philippi, found their way to the Jewish community here. Acts 16.14-15 informs us that it was here that Paul came across 'a woman named Lydia, a dealer in purple cloth, from the city of Thyatira, a worshipper of God'. His meeting with this woman, who was named after her native country, is interesting in showing the Roman peace and lively commercial world of this period in the Aegean. She was selling purple-coloured cloth, a business which required capital. Lydia was famous with its textiles of many colours, especially those in the blue/red range dyed with madder root; so much so that the Lydians were credited with the discovery of wool dying. Thyatira (Akhisar) may have been the centre of the surviving Lydian weaving industry at that time. An inscription found in Philippi (now lost) read in Greek 'The city honoured from among the purple-dyers, an outstanding citizen, Antiochus the son of Lycus, a native of Thyatira, as a benefactor' and thus shows Thyatira as a weaving centre and famed for

View of the agora (forum) from the acropolis. Philippi. In the foreground is the basilica A (fifth-sixth centuries CE). The uncovered stretch of the Via Egnatia extends parallel and some 3 m below the asphalt road at bottom of the picture. The foothills of Mount Pangaion (1,956 m) begin to rise across the plain.

purple-dyed cloth. The information is reinforced by similar epigraphic material from Thyatira. Lydia was not a Jew but a proselyte 'worshipper of God', and now she found Paul's message far more appealing than Judaism. After a while Lydia was converted and baptized in the river together with her family. Paul accepted the invitation to stay at her house. It was probably Lydia who would arrange to send the apostle money when he had to move to Thessalonica, and 'more than once' perhaps when he was at other places such as Corinth or later in prison (Phil 4). A Julia Lydia is encountered in epigraphic material from Sardis (first century CE) and a Julia Lydia Laterane in Ephesus (first-second centuries CE) and in both cases the names belong to women with social standing.

One day, as Paul and the others were on their way to the place of prayer by the river they were followed by a slave girl. She was no ordinary slave but inhabited 'with an oracular spirit, who used to bring a large profit to her owners through her fortune-telling' (Acts 16.16) and it seems that she may have listened to Paul's sermons by the river. At the time fortune reading was a profitable profession. The Greek word for the spirit is *python* and this had a connection with the giant serpent that Apollo was reputed to have killed in

Traditional spot by the River Gangites where Paul converted Lydia and her family. Philippi.

River Gangites (the Angites of Herodotus). Philippi.

Delphi. She began following Paul and his friends, and calling out popular pagan formulas like 'These people are slaves of the Most High God [the epithet referring to Zeus], who proclaim to you a way of salvation'. She must have become annoying because Paul finally lost his temper and exorcised her. Although the girl may have been happy and grateful to the apostle, her owners, having been deprived of a valuable investment, were furious. They incited the crowd against Paul. It seems that Luke and Timothy were not present for 'they seized Paul and Silas and dragged them to the public square before the Roman authorities', the *duoviri* (Latin 'two men'; Greek *strategoi* or *archons;* magistrates or presiding-officers).

Although inscriptions inform us that much of what has survived to the present from the forum of Philippi dates from the reign of Marcus Aurelius (161-80 CE), its general appearance was not much different when Paul and Silas were brought here to face magistrates. Here from an elevated podium (Greek *bema,* Latin *rostra*) which stood to the northwest of the square the magistrates judged. Paul could be charged as a sorcerer because of what he had done to the girl and the Jews were famous as magicians and sorcerers; but at the time the attitude of Roman law to illegal magic was not clear. As Roman law did not have anything to say about exorcism, the owners of the girl saying 'These people are Jews and are disturbing our city and are advocating customs that are not lawful for us Romans to adopt or practice' (Acts 16.20) accused Paul and Silas with disturbing the peace and subverting the laws of Rome. While as an ethnic group the existence of Jews was tolerated by the Romans propaganda of Judaism was against the Roman law. The local Jews if they were involved would have been happy about the way that the matter was presented to the magistrates because the latter could not yet distinguish Jews from Christians and were not interested in a Jewish religious feud.

At this point Paul and Silas did not bring forward their Roman citizenship and demand a formal trial. There have been many speculations about why this was not done. They may not have owned such documents. Or at the moment they may not have carried them. Or, even if they did, their protest was probably lost in the angry voice of the mob in the market place. It has been suggested that Paul hid his Roman citizenship because he had not wanted to be seen as above the people to whom he preached, or to shelter something provided by the power whose immediate collapse he proclaimed. What would his non-Roman-citizen converts who were not protected by such

A stretch of the Via Egnatia which ran by the forum partly hidden by today's motor road. Philippi.

a privilege do under similar persecution? It is probable that even if the magistrates heard the protests of the accused they did not understand their nature and it was easier for them to keep the peace in the forum by sentencing and punishing the culprits on the spot. Surviving evidence shows that they were more powerful than the impression given about them in Acts. After all it was their custom and responsibility to respond to situations to maintain order. They may have ignored the identities Paul and Silas produced. From Josephus we learn that the procurator in Judea had some Jews who were of the Roman equestrian order 'whipped and nailed to the cross before his tribunal'. Or Paul may have foreseen that if their citizenship was disclosed at this stage this would be the beginning of long trial to establish the authenticity of their documents, something which would interfere with his missionary plans. In a Roman town, for those who frequented the forum the sight of criminals who were being beaten by the lictors was not unusual. This sort of punishment, *fustes*, was applied to free men and the information in Acts confirms what is supplied by ancient texts, that it could be heavy. The criminal, his back bared, normally, would be tied by both wrists to the whipping posts which stood in one corner of the forum. The lictors held before them a bundle of rods flanked by axes or fasces symbolizing Roman power and carried out the judgement of the court.

Later when the apostle said 'Three times I was beaten with rods' (2 Cor 11.25) the incident at Philippi must have been one of them. Thus Paul and Silas were stripped and beaten one by one and were dragged and thrown into the innermost cell of the jail. From the account of Luke we understand that the jail was in two sections, with the innermost part reserved for dangerous criminals. Here a prisoner's feet were clapped in stocks with the shackles attached to a chain which was fastened to the wall.

An earthquake should not have been regarded a rare incident by the Philippians because their city lay on an earthquake zone and was prone to frequent tremors of smaller or larger size. At that time, however, they were still surrounded by mystery, and by all the elements of superstition. Pagans attributed them to Poseidon, the earth-shaker. The bolts and hinges of the doors and the chains of the prisoners which secured them to the wall were pulled out. They were free. The jailer woke up and, terrified, rushed to the prison. At the time to lose a prisoner entrusted to one's care meant death. This is evident in Acts 12.19. When Peter disappears from the prison Herod Agrippa orders 'the guards' trial and execution. The jailer thought that all of

Roman cistern with two rooms, 'with an innermost cell' (Acts 16.24), which tradition regards as St Paul's prison. Philippi. Remains of a wall painting which showed

enthroned Jesus flanked by a pair of saints or angels survive. Later a chapel was built above the cistern.

his prisoners had escaped. Drawing his sword he tried to kill himself. Paul intervened and told him that nobody had escaped.

The jailer called his slaves for lights, and then rushed in and fell at the feet of Paul and Silas. He may have thought that these two men were under a god's protection in some way. Otherwise why they had not fled when the door of their cell flew open?

The jailer led Paul and Silas out into the main body of the prison where his slaves would by now have lit oil lamps. The other prisoners were once more secured. He , still unrecovered from the shock said 'Sirs, what may I do to be saved?' And they said, 'Believe in the Lord Jesus and you and your household will be saved'. In the small hours of the morning, he and his family and household slaves gathered around Paul and Silas who told them the basics of the Gospel. The jailer took the two, probably to the well in the outer court, and washed their wounds. He and all the members of his family were baptized. Paul and Silas were taken to his house and given some food. However, the two were still prisoners, and the guard probably took them back to the jail. The details of the incident of Paul's imprisonment and the following events at Philippi would become the leitmotif for martyrdom stories in later Christian tradition.

Next morning at sunrise the magistrates sent the lictors with the order that the two Jews should be set free and sent on their way. The jailer reported their message but Paul and Silas had no intention of leaving. Paul said that he would not leave the jail until he had a full apology from the magistrates. It is probable that the two produced the documents that proved their Roman citizenship when Paul said 'They have beaten us publicly, even though we are Roman citizens and have not been tried, and have thrown us into prison. And now, are they going to release us secretly? By no means. Let them come themselves and lead us out' (Acts 16.37). The apostle knew that the magistrates had violated Roman law and condemned two Roman citizens to be flogged. The lictors took Paul's message to the magistrates. The fact that the latter when they heard Paul's message were afraid, although not stated in Acts, may give the impression that Paul had made his Roman citizenship known but it had been ignored, because they had been put in prison and into the worst part of it which was usually used for common criminals. Otherwise when criminals did not disclose their Roman citizenship magistrates were not responsible for their acts. Wishing to get rid of these two Jews as soon as possible and silence the matter they rushed to the prison and

Dikili Taş ('upright stone'). Philippi. It was erected by the Roman officer C Vibius Quartus and in Latin marked a halting place referred to as the Co *Fons* ('spring of water') on the Via Egnatia.

apologized and begged them to leave the town for their safety could not be guaranteed if the mob got stirred up again. Thus, Paul and Silas came out of prison and went to Lydia's house and after farewell words with Lydia, her household and some other brothers, left for Thessalonica. The account of Acts about the length of Paul's stay in Philippi is not clear. While 16.12 reads 'spent some time in that city', in 16.18 the girl with an oracular spirit follows the apostle 'for many days'. In any case, the events which took place in Philippi would require a stay of several weeks.

Luke was left behind. Being a native of the country he was possibly able to practice his profession without hindrance from the local Jews and authorities and to continue Paul's mission. He does not seem to have met Paul again until some years later when Paul travelled through Macedonia during his third missionary journey. Thus, in Philippi Paul established his first Christian church in Europe.

Following the enthusiasm with which some Philippians embraced Paul's message one would expect Christianity to have flourished in the region in a short time. The scarcity of Christian tomb reliefs and their late date (post-Constantinian), in contrast to the popular continuity of pagan ones, the reliefs of various deities, especially the reliefs of Artemis/Diana and the elaborate shrines dedicated to the Roman god of nature Sylvanus, on the rocks of the acropolis in the period following Paul's visit do not confirm this. Some scholars speculate that the absence of any reference to a bishop in Polycarp's letter written in the 150s to Philippi may also point in the same direction, the relatively late development of Christianity in the region. The fact that in the apocryphal *Acts of Paul* and *Acts of Andrew* the Philippians are converted through a series of miracles may also point to a strong pagan trend, requiring miracles. The events in Acts, and the city's location on the Via Egnatia would make Philippi a very important pilgrimage site only after the time of Constantine the Great.

It was now almost a year since Paul had left Antioch on Orontes, when he, Silas and Timothy began walking in the direction of Thessalonica. The mention of two staging posts, Amphipolis and Apollonia, shows that the party travelled on the Via Egnatia perhaps spending a night at each of these places. The distance to their destination was some 150 km and the road, after leaving Philippi, continued northwest and encircling Mount Pangaion turned south. In Greek mythology the region into which they entered now was known as the land of the Edonians, whose King Lycurgus was driven mad by Rhea, and killed his own son. The first station, Amphipolis, some 50 km away, was founded in a large meander that the River Strymon (Struma) created before discharging itself into the Aegean a few kilometres farther on. The town's acropolis commanded the bend of the river and the valley beyond as far as the seashore where there was a port called Eion. On the landward side to the west a long wall connected the two points on the river's banks. In antiquity it was known as the *Ennea Hodoi* ('nine roads'), because of the number of the roads radiating from the town. It owed its prosperity to the Strymon, which provided access to the agricultural riches of the hinterland. Its inhabitants are also said to have collected tolls for crossing the river. Herodotus says that the magi in the army of Xerxes propitiated the great river by the sacrifice of white horses; probably cutting their throats into a pit so that the running water was not polluted. Herodotus, in his general description of the Eastern nations, says also 'when they learnt that Nine Ways was the name of the place, they took nine native boys and nine girls and buried them alive there'. In 497 BCE, Aristagoras of Miletus, the instigator of the Ionian revolt, had tried to settle here but was driven off by the Edonians. The settlement was later colonized from Athens in 437 BCE and named

Northern city walls, city gate and the bridge (under the roof) over the ancient bed of the Strymon River. Amphipolis. Under a modern roof is the substructure of fossilized pillars which have supported the bridge since pre-Hellenistic period.

Lion of Amphipolis. Research has shown that, originally, the lion decorated the roof of a mausoleum, which was in the form of a stepped-pyramid. The funeral monument is

thought to have been built in the last quarter of the fourth century BCE for Laomedon, one of Alexander's generals.

Amphipolis 'because it was surrounded on two sides by the River Strymon' and it became one of the most important urban centres in the district. In 387 BCE Philip II captured the city and used it as a bridgehead for his forces campaigning to the east of the river. At the time Paul and his friends walked into the city, probably by the Thracian Gate which stood landward to the north, it was the centre of the first district of Macedonia and it is surprising that Acts does not mention any missionary activity here. Paul, Silas and Timothy seem to have spent the night in the city. Next morning leaving by the south gate they perhaps skirted the Strymon and continued on the Via Egnatia. Once it crossed the foothills of the Cardylium range the road descended to the plain and ran a smooth route toward Thessalonica encircling the small lakes Volvi (Bolbe) and Koroneia on their south. Apollonia, (not the city which was located to the southwest) which was no more than an interim station, was some 40 km west.

Thessalonica (Salonica), situated about a day's walk from the last staging post was the most important city located almost at the middle of the Via Egnatia. It was also the terminal point of the main road which arrived from the northern interior following the bed of the Axios River. In the *Iliad* Homer calls the latter 'the clearest stream that flows across the earth'. The settlement was founded about 316 BCE by the Macedonian general Cassander on or very near an ancient settlement known as Therma and named after his wife Thessalonice, half-sister of Alexander the Great. Strabo says that Cassander, destroying the nearby towns, forced their inhabitants to settle in his new city. After the battle of Pydna in 168 BC the city became the capital of the second of the four districts of Macedonia and in 146 BCE, when the Roman senatorial province of Macedonia was established, its capital. In the first century CE it was an important port and industrial and cultural centre of Macedonia, also the residence of the governor of the province which encompassed Epirus and some of Illyricum.

The Via Egnatia after making a sharp turn to the north in the direction of the city — following today's motor road — entered by the Letaia (Lete) Gate and most probably continued toward the forum. The city was the northern trading centre of Roman Greece, with a cosmopolitan population and unlike Philippi it had protected its Greek character. It was built on a grid plan and today's 'Demetriou' and 'Egnatia' streets probably correspond to the *decumanus* and *cardo* of Roman times. Among the flourishing crafts was purple-dyeing, supplied by the molluscs of the fisheries in the region. The

Late-Byzantine city walls through which the Via Egnatia coming from Philippi entered the city by today's Lete Gate. Thessalonica.

Roman forum. Second century CE. Thessalonica.

population of the city at this time may have been close to 100,000 people. Almost all of ancient Thessalonica is buried under the modern city. From its walls, which date from the late Byzantine period, a section in the northeastern part goes back to the Hellenistic period. When Paul was here the sea was some 400 m further inland. Efforts to prove the existence of a forum dating back to Paul's time under the surviving remains of the Roman forum from the end of the second century CE have not given any result. Excavations carried out before the First World War showed that the city had had a Temple of Serapis since the third century BCE. Sparse as it is, the evidence about the existence of Jews in the city does not go back earlier than the late Roman period, perhaps the fourth century CE. Still, such a city would have had a well-established Jewish population and Paul guessed that he would find a synagogue. Late traditions either locate the synagogue in the crypt of the Church of Demetrius or near a spring in the district called Hagios Pavlos.

As usual Paul's immediate concern was to address the people of his own race wherever he went and the elders invited him to do so on the first sabbath that he was in the city. Here, Paul demonstrated by quotations from the prophets of the OT that Jesus had in many ways fulfilled every condition required of the Messiah. As is evident in his letters to the church here Paul was particularly absorbed in the doctrine of the second coming. Christ's return was imminent and everyone should live as if each day was the last before the judgement. Paul's discourses about the risen Christ probably did not surprise either the Jews or the Gentile 'worshippers of God'. But the Jews could not accept his words that the promised kingdom was even going to be for those who did not follow the law of Moses. Salvation by the deities was a familiar promise for Gentiles. The cults of both Dionysus or Orpheus, and Isis and Serapis were prominent in the region and all promised some kind of salvation beyond life in this world. Paul, however, was saying that this new God of his had really lived on the earth, in the physique of an individual, until he was crucified. His Gospel was accepted by a few Jews and more Gentile worshippers.

According to Acts Paul preached on three different sabbaths in the synagogue but was subsequently expelled from the city. 'Three sabbaths' is indicated as the period he spent preaching only in the synagogue. Some of his listeners, among whom there were Jews, Greeks and 'not a few' prominent women believed him. The apostle seems to have separately preached to Gentiles among whom he made many converts and thus stayed longer in

Milestone from the Via Egnatia found along the road to Langadas some 10 km from Thessalonica near the Gallikos River. Archaeological Museum. Thessalonica.

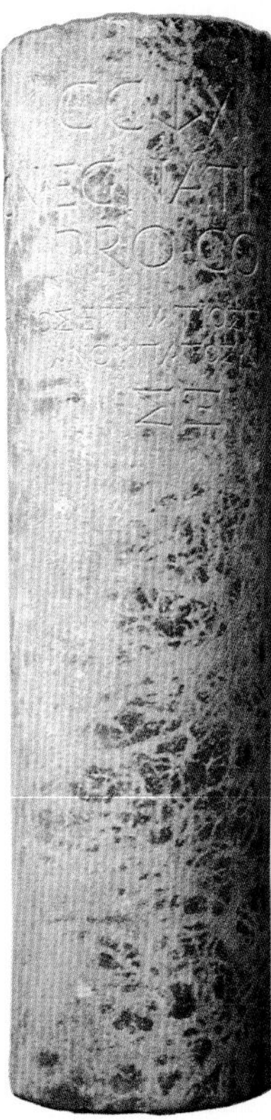

The bilingual inscription in Latin and Greek reads '260 miles [from Dyrrachium] Cnaeus Egnatius, son of Gaius, proconsul' who was the first governor of the region and built this section of the road in 146-120 BCE.

the city, perhaps several months. Despite his initial success Paul encountered here the familiar reaction and trouble. The Jews were jealous of Paul for his success with the worshippers and tried to prevent him 'from speaking to the Gentiles that they may be saved' (1 Thes 2.16). Not long after Paul and his companions arrived in the city, they 'recruited some worthless men loitering in the public square, formed a mob' (Acts 17.5). The agoras of ancient metropolises are assumed to have been the places where unemployed people hung around and were ready to do such things perhaps for a small fee. They tried to get hold of Paul and Silas and bring them before the people's assembly. Failing to find them in the house of Jason with whom Paul and his two friends had been staying, they dragged the Christians that they found before the magistrates, for whom Acts uses their pre-Roman title 'politarchs' because of the fact that the city retained its 'free' status. The charge was that these people had acted 'in opposition to the decrees of Caesar and claim instead there is another king, Jesus'. The charge of the Thessalonian Jews was a well-chosen political one; because this was exactly the message that Paul was proclaiming, the message of second coming which suggested to simple minds a great king would shortly arrive from the East and overthrow the Roman Empire in accordance with the traditional Jewish expectancy. Such apocalyptic expectations were prohibited both by Augustus and Tiberius. They probably knew about the Jewish agitations in Alexandria or Antioch which had taken place about a decade before. Also, the Jews in Rome had recently been expelled because of some kind of imaginary king about whom they could not come to an agreement among themselves and were probably afraid that Claudius' recent decree could be extended to their city, and tried to show their loyalty to the Roman rule. The provokers may have heard of the events at Philippi and known that Paul and his friend possessed Roman citizenship. Also, in addition to Jason, who was a well-known citizen, there were some 'prominent women' among those who shared this belief of the strangers. Thus, without taking the matter to the Roman proconsul residing in their city, it was decided to put down a bond to make sure that the apostle and his companion would not break the peace. Thus, Paul and his companion were thrown out of Thessalonica. In addition to the bail that was paid the conditions of release probably stated that Paul would not return the city. To make up for his absence Paul would resort to writing letters and sending his assistants. Later traditions claimed more than a single place as the spot where Paul preached at Thessalonica and that some of the present-day churches rose on the site of the synagogues. There is, however, no evidence to confirm any of these speculations. From Paul's words in 1 Thes 2.9 and 2 Thes 3.8 we understand that in Thessalonica, in addition to preaching, the apostle worked 'night and day' to support himself and his companions and 'not to burden' any of his converts.

Paul had to leave the city all of a sudden and at night. Timothy seems to have stayed in the background since he was not accused. Thus he could soon return to the city to finish Paul's work. It has been speculated that when Paul had to leave Thessalonica in hurry, he expected to return to this fertile field of evangelization soon.

Monument built over the steps from which Paul was said to have preached. Veria.

Beroia (Veria) was founded on the eastern slope of Mount Bermius and commanded the large plain watered by the Haliacmon and Ludias rivers. The majority of its population were Macedonians. Romans and perhaps Jews settled here after Rome divided Macedonia into four republics following their victory at Pydna and made Beroia the capital of one of them. In Paul's time, like Thessalonica its government was run by politarchs. The distance from Thessalonica to Beroia was some 80 km. The Haliacmon, Ludias and Axios were not fordable near the coast and until the late Roman period there was no road which cut across the plain. The Via Egnatia left the city near today's Axios Gate and continued in the direction of Pella and Edessa by way of ancient Allante (Nea Chalcedon). Paul's party may have spent the night here. A branch left the Via Egnatia at this point and ran almost straight to Beroia by the south of Lake Ludias and by way of today's Alexandria, avoiding the coastal marshes. From Edessa the road would continue to Lake Lychnidus (Ohrid) in Illyria where it forked into two, one branch going to Apollonia (Pojan) and the other to Dyrrachium (Epidamnus, former Durazzo, now Durres in Albania) with a distance of some 80 km between them. It has been suggested that it was during this journey that Paul wanted to continue to Rome. He went as far as the Illyrian coast of the Adriatic and changed his plans there.

Acts says the Jews of the synagogue at Beroia 'were more fair-minded than those in Thessalonica' and listened to Paul's message with pleasure and attention. They were more open and compared what they heard from Paul with the scriptures to see if he was telling the truth. 'Many of them became believers, as did not a few of the influential Greek women and men' and thus Paul founded a new church here. Tradition has accepted a podium of four steps, the topmost bearing the word 'Pavlos', in Veria as the

Roman road. Veria.

place from which Paul proclaimed his message. The apostle's peaceful stay here may have lasted a few months. But things changed soon. When the news of Paul's whereabouts reached Thessalonica the Jewish community there acted immediately. They, probably paying some people and sending them to Beroia, stirred up trouble and provoked others for a protest against Paul and he was compelled to leave. Although the details are missing Paul's letters and Acts agree that after this point his route ran to Athens and Corinth. The opposition at Beroia was directed against Paul himself, and did not extend to his two companions.

The apostle was escorted to the nearest sea coast by his newly converted brethren. The trips of Paul's assistants in this section of the journeys may be interpreted in several different ways depending on whether the text of Acts is accepted or Paul's letters. As he preached in Beroia, Paul's mind was still haunted by the problems of his Thessalonian converts. He had had to leave them without the proper farewells and he wondered what his converts thought of him after his sudden departure without any explanation.

At the time of Paul the road to the sea coast ran by the foothills of Mount Pieria of today, following the gorges, first to northwest by way of Aigai (Vergina) as far as Aloros (Angathia) where turning south it continued by Aiginion and reached the Aegean near Methoni (Nea Agathoupolis). The Thermaic Gulf (Thermaikos) was connected with all the major ports of the Aegean and Paul's embarking on a vessel bound for Athens was probably accidental. It has been suggested that if Paul travelled by sea the point of his departure may have been by way of Methoni, or Pydna (2,5 km south of Makrygialos) further south, or Dion/Dium at the northern foot of the Olympus (2,911 m). Scholars have noted that Acts usually mentions the harbour of departure when it is used for the first time and skips it on other occasions. In this case, however, surprisingly it just says 'to the sea coast' and does not mention any port and it is speculated that there may have been a reason for this. At the time, as now, the main road to Achaia after crossing the plain at a distance where the rivers were fordable, first ran by the sea coast following it as far as Tempe Pass where it entered the mainland. After the pass the road continued south by way of Larissa, Lamia and Thebes all with narrow passes where banditry was rife. The fact that Paul's Beroian escorts did not leave him alone but accompanied him as far as Athens may also point to an overland trip. The tradition which claimed an overland journey to Athens survived well into the nineteenth century when it was forgotten.

It is, however, generally accepted that Paul travelled to Athens by sea. The ship Paul took, after sailing along the mountainous coast of the Greek mainland would have turned west to come under the lee of of Euboea (Evvia) to escape from the northerly winds and entered into the well-protected Gulf of Eupirus (Evvoikos). In Paul's time, near Chalkis, where the island almost touched the mainland there was of a wooden bridge supported by a mole raised on the small island in the middle of the strait. Even the smallest contact with the Greco-Roman culture of the time would orient one with Homer and it is probable that Paul was familiar with the *Iliad*. It was hereabouts, at the Bay of Aulis, that the Greek fleet bound for Troy had to wait for a favourable wind, until Agamemnon decided to sacrifice his daugher Iphigenia. Paul's ship probably continued through the strait between the mainland and the island of Helena (Makronisi, 'long island'). Legend has it that the latter was the first port of call when they escaped and where Helen gave herself to Paris. Opposite the island on the mainland stood the silver mines of Laurion which were exploited at about the beginning of the fifth century BCE and became the major source of wealth for Athens. As the ship rounded Cape Sunium to enter the Saronic Gulf (Saranikos) the white columns of the Temple of Poseidon which was built some five hundred years before came into view. The approach to Athens from the sea was a breath-taking sight. None of the cities in which, until then, Paul had preached could compete with Athens either in antiquity or in the number and size of the sanctuaries that the city boasted. The 'sheer and strong-walled' acropolis was famous when Athens was no more than a collection of shanty houses at its foot. This last comment was true for the city of Paul's time. Athens would never become a city of colonnades or gardens like Antioch on Orontes or Ephesus, and owed its fame and splendour to the acropolis. In fact when Athenians said 'the city' they meant the acropolis and by Paul's time the latter had already a complicated archaeology going back to Mycenean times.

A late tradition claims that the apostle landed at Glyphada (ancient Aixone), which was the first anchorage on the coast for ships entering from the east, situated some distance from Athens. Another possible place of landing was the Bay of Phaleron where the city's warships docked in the past. However, Piraeus (Pireas) was the main port of Athens and most of the sea traffic ended or began here. In 86 BCE the Roman general Sulla laid siege to Athens and its port because of the fact that the city had a few years before taken sides with King Mithradates VI of Pontus. After Athens fell, the Greek army evacuated Piraeus and Sulla burned its magnificent arsenal and shipyards. In other words, at the time Paul walked from the port to the city not much was left from its so-called 'Long Walls', a double wall of some 12 km long which linked the port to Athens.

Although Pliny the Elder mentions Athens as one of the cities which possessed about three thousand statues the city's eclipse was in decline. The road from Piraeus which was at Paul's time flanked by sanctuaries and statues of various deities ended at the district of Kerameikos which was a monumental cemetery named after its community of potters. Crossing Kerameikos the road entered Athens by the Dipylon ('double gate'). This entrance, whose ruins have reached the present in the northwestern corner of the excavated area, consisted of two gates, each flanked by a pair of towers. Ancient literature informs us that the site was a hangout of the money-lenders and wine-sellers and prostitutes waiting for customers coming from Piraeus. The sacred road, which began at Eleusis, entered Athens by the sacred gate which stood next to the Dipylon. The road after this point ran through the agora and ascended toward the acropolis. Most

Dipylon. Kerameikos. Athens.

of what one could see on the acropolis of the apostle's time was built in about the middle of the fifth century BCE by Pericles using funds that were collected from the cities on the Anatolian coast and the islands on the pretext of protecting them against the Persian Empire. The height was crowned with the Temple of Athena, known as the Parthenon. Although its treasures and most beautiful sculpture had been removed to Rome and the number of bearded priests and priestesses in white costumes who attended Athena may have diminished, the Parthenon was still the pride of classical architecture. Its sculptures were carved by Phidias. The area encircling the Parthenon and skirts of the hill were covered with sanctuaries, temples and altars some with smoke rising from recent sacrifices. Following the Roman conquest an altar for the divine Julius and later a temple for Augustus together with the goddess Roma and later images of other Roman rulers had been added. The monumental gate to the acropolis was known as the Propylea. At the time of Paul's journeys Claudius had ordered the rebuilding of the stairs (Boulée Gate) leading to it. The temple called Erechthium, which bore the name of a legendary king of Athens, Erechthus,

Remains of the city wall of Athens built by Themistocles in 478 BCE. Kerameikos. Athens. The wall in the foreground is the first line of defence.

was also there. It housed the sacred robe of Athena, her ancient image in wood and the first olive tree which she had planted beside Poseidon's well, and which had grown again 'eighteen inches long' on the day after it was burned during the Persian conquest (480 BCE). The tree was the main attraction for visitors in Paul's time.

There was, as would be expected, a Jewish community with a synagogue for Acts 17.17 informs us that in Athens 'Paul debated in the synagogue with the Jews and with the worshippers, and daily in the public square with whoever happened to be there.'

Culturally Athens still boasted the most important schools of philosophy, which survived until Justinian the Great closed the last of them in 529, regarding the institution the last seat of idolatry in his Empire. The market place, or agora Paul entered after walking through Kerameikos was the social, intellectual and commercial centre of city. It was always crowded with people of every kind, slaves, prostitutes, merchants, students and also frequented by local and foreign philosophers and rhetoricians from different corners of the Mediterranean world. At the time of Paul's visit the ancient schools of philosophy, once represented by Plato or Aristotle, had been replaced by Stoicists or Epicureans or Cynics, perhaps somewhat nostalgic and poor Hellenistic substitutes of the originals. Although not much is known about them, some tried to guide human life and give it an inner security. Acts says that philosophers were eager to hear 'something new', and in the agora Paul got into discussions with them. Among those who listened to Paul there may have been also Platonists, Pythagoreans and others. Two of the most important stoas where such discussions took place in Athen's agora were built by Eumenes II (197-159 BCE) and Attalus II (159-138 BCE) of

Areopagus (In the middle above the trees and below the wall of acropolis). Athens.

Pergamum, who were regarded as the champions of freedom of east Greek cities.

The people who frequented the market place were used to new cults and mystery religions pouring from the East and some of them thought that Paul was 'a promoter of foreign deities'. A few of Paul's listeners were probably familiar with the monotheism, the type claimed by some philosophers of the time in which God manifested Himself under many names and forms, and some even believed this. Paul's words that 'the Lord of heaven and earth does not dwell in sanctuaries made by human hands' were not offending at all because they knew that temples as well as the statues or paintings were just symbols. They called Paul a 'scavanger' or 'babbler'. The word's Greek equivalent *spermologos* ('seed-picker') was used in vulgar slang for a man who picked the seeds of other men's ideas and then, without really comprehending them, used them as his own. Paul's words were meaningless for the people who were not familiar with the Jewish religion and some of those who listened to Paul probably thought that Jesus was a god and resurrection (Greek *anastasis*) a goddess. According to Acts some Athenians led Paul to the Areopagus, a rocky height which is situated between the acropolis and the agora, overlooking the latter. Athenians believed that this was the seat of the first trial of the murder of a son of Poseidon by the god of war Ares and thus was named after this deity. The burial gifts discovered in the rock-cut tombs on its slopes whose traces are still visible, have shown that the hill had an ancient history and like the acropolis, was a part of the Mycenean cemetery.

Boundary stone. The inscription in Greek reads 'I am a boundary marker of the Agora'. Agora. Athens.

Here in the past the Aeropagites, members of the council of Athens, met to watch over the laws. It was the place where the truth was established. On three sides of a rough courtyard its members sat on semi-circular rock-cut benches reached by a flight of rock-carved stairs which have survived to the present. Two prominent white rock-cut stones marked the place where accused and prosecutor took their stands. 'The natural stones,' says Pausanias 'where men on trial and the prosecutors stand' are named as 'the rock of Shamelessness and the rock of Arrogance', respectively. The stones of Pausanias have not survived. The last remains of the benches are buried under soil. Paul may not have fully understood the implication of this invitation. By the first century CE the council had been deprived of its original power of jurisdiction but the hill of Ares still meant in Athenians' eyes the seat of judgement. Nevertheless, Paul's situation at the Areopagus was evidently not a trial.

It has been remarked that by Paul's time the council had moved its meetings from the hill to the royal stoa whose few ruins have survived in the northwestern corner of the agora beyond the railway. Originally, this was an impressive building with walls on three sides and eight Doric columns at its front on the east side. Although when Acts says 'Then Paul stood up at the Areopagus and said' it is not clear if the word refers to the hill, it is generally assumed that Paul spoke here. It has been suggested that Luke may have wanted to present Paul's case, recalling the trial of Socrates who was accused of 'not recognizing the gods that the State recognizes and introducing other new divinities'; Paul in the role of a latter-day Socrates explaining the identity of the unknown god to his listeners.

Paul after complimenting his audience for being very religious people told them that as he walked through the Athenian shrines he had even seen an altar dedicated to 'an Unknown God'. Athenians were unable to see what was so strange about having an altar for an unknown god. Although research has not yet brought to light an altar such an inscription from Athens the existence of such altars, with or without inscriptions, was known by his audience and for them there was nothing unusual in Paul's reference. Among the ancient writers

Remains of Simon the shoemaker's shop by the agora. Athens. While the hobnails, bone eyelets and the like discovered here showed that the building was a shoe shop, the discovery of a fragment from a late fifth-century-BCE wine cup, incised with the name of its owner, Simon, led to speculations that the latter may have been Simon the shoemaker whom Socrates used to visit near the agora. Simon recorded what he remembered from Socrates' visits and his dialogues were published as 'Cobbler's Dialogues'.

Drawing of the royal stoa (stoa basileios) in its first period (Camp).

Remains of the royal stoa. Agora. Athens. The marble base at the bottom belonged to the foundation of its rear wall. At the front the building opened to the Panathenic way.

who mention altars dedicated to unknown gods Pausanias in *Guide to Greece* says that he saw altars of the 'Unknown Gods' near the harbour Phaleron and another similar altar at Olympia. It has been claimed that today's Chapel of Sts Theodoroi was built on the spot where Paul saw this altar. Apollonius of Tyana, visiting Athens at about Paul's time says he saw altars 'set up even in honour of unknown gods'. In addition to such an altar found at the Temple of Demeter in Pergamum where 'Capito, the torch bearer' dedicates an altar to the unknown gods, excavations on the Palatine hill of Rome have revealed an inscribed altar dedicated to an unknown god (Palatine Museum) dating from the beginning of the first century BCE. For the people of the Greco-Roman world the expression did not carry a monotheistic sense at all. Those who did not want to offend any deity whose rituals might possibly have been skipped unknowingly erected nameless altars for them, to placate them, recalling the Feast of All Saints on 1 November, which commemorates the saints whose names are not mentioned in the liturgical calendar. Paul knew that there was no connection between the unknown pagan god and the one true God that he preached. When Paul added that there will be a day that the God 'will judge the world' through a man he has appointed 'by raising him from the dead' his Greek audience who believed in the survival of soul but not the body began mocking. They thought that their time was wasted; but although it was doubtful if any of them would appear, they politely said 'We should like to hear you on this some other time' and left. Some, however, joined Paul as he was leaving. Among the few who believed Paul were Dionysius, a member of the council of Areopagus, and a woman named Damaris. It has been suggested that her name derives from *Damalis* ('heifer') and she was probably a low class woman since women, normally, except for slaves or old people did not frequent the agora. Dionysius was later known as St Denis the Areopagite, patron saint of Athens and as St Denys of France. Acts does not inform us why the apostle left Athens so fast. The expression 'While Paul was waiting for them in Athens' (Acts 17.16) may even lead one to think that this was the only reason why the apostle had stopped at Athens and he did not want to miss his chance of preaching the Gospel at the agora. There is no word about any persecution after the events at the agora of Athens and probably Paul, being unsatisfied with the number of converts, left for Corinth without waiting for long.

From Athens Corinth could be reached overland or by sea. The land route ran by way of Eleusis and Megara. His walk would have first taken him to Eleusis, famous for the Great Mysteries of Demeter. Although very rough this was a well-trodden trail by armies since the early history of Greece. After Megara the Gerania range blocked the way giving no room for any road but single precipitous passage called in antiquity 'Scironian Way' (Kake Skala, 'bad descent') on the side of the Saronic Gulf. The cliffs were named after Sciron the Corinthian who was said to have sat on a rock and forced the 'travellers to wash his feet: when they stopped the task he would kick them over the cliff into the sea, where a giant turtle' devoured them. The sea voyage for Cenchrea, the eastern port of Corinth was certainly shorter and easier.

Corinth owed its rich history to its geography. It consisted of a citadel on top of the height Acrocorinth (570 m) and the settlement associated with it on its northern slopes. Its impregnable citadel and strategic location between two gulfs made the city a crossroad of trade lines between Europe and Asia; also between central Greece and the Peloponnese. Its products such as pottery, bronze vases and textiles were sought-after as early as the sixth century BCE outside mainland Greece. It was once the only city in Greece whose naval power could challenge that of Athens. Strabo mentions its two harbours as 'one of which is near Asia, and the other near Italy'. The latter, man-made and called Lechaion, to which the city was connected by long walls on both sides of a main road, was on the Corinthian Gulf and the other, Cenchrea on the Saronic Gulf — hence the name in Latin 'bimaris Corinthus'. Having

View of the Saronic (right) and Corinthian gulfs from the Acrocorinth. The ruins in the foreground belong to the Temple of Aphrodite.

Western end of the *diolkos* where it reaches the Saronic Gulf. After their cargo was loaded on animals ships would be strapped to wheeled vehicles on this pathway, whose width was 3 to 5,5 m and were carried over the isthmus. Corinth. During the Persian attack in 480 BCE the Peloponnesians carrying 'stones, bricks, timbers, sand-baskets' day and night raised an earthwork along this pathway between the two ports Lechaion and Cenchrea to prevent Xerxes from invading the peninsula.

two harbours had created a city rich in warehouses, banks, taverns and brothels and a cosmopolitan and wealthy population of sailors, money-changers, merchants, soldiers of fortune and the like. Corinthians' immorality became proverbial, so that Corinthianise (*korinthiazomai*) became one of the common Greek verbs meaning to practice fornication. A typical Corinthian of Paul's time is described as 'a hater of the pious, bold in shameless deeds, never ceasing doing evil to his colleagues, prone to drunkenness, impatient'.

Since antiquity cautious traders preferred the safe transportation of the isthmus to the dangerous 300 km sea voyage round the Peloponnese, and ships were dragged from one gulf to the other on wheeled vehicles running on a marble tramway called *diolkos* (Greek *dielko*, 'haul-over'). The first of these tracks was built by the tyrant Periander (627-585 BCE). Cargoes of larger vessels could be carried on pack animals and reloaded on other vessels. Passengers often took a different boat at the other end. Heavier ships would sail round the Peloponnese. War ships were hauled over the causeway as early as the fifth century BCE. The Corinthians, who lived by hauling ships, believed in a prophecy that those who attempted to dig a canal were cursed. Among the ancient rulers who disregarded the curse

Upper Peirene where according to mythology Bellerophon bridled Pegasus. Acrocorinth. The oldest reference to the spring is by Herodotus. Strabo says that it

was 'always full of transparent, potable water' and figured out that the springs of Corinth were fed by Acrocorinth.

and thought of doing this were Alexander the Great, Demetrius Poliorcetes, Julius Caesar, Caligula and Nero who was the most energetic of all. He is said to have dug up the first earth with a golden spade and carried it away in a basket over his shoulder when he visited the city in 66 CE. Among the workers employed there were 'six thousand of the strongest Jews' sent by Vespasian following his subduing the district of Galilee. The work, however, halted after Nero committed suicide. According to Philostratus it was also rumourred that 'Egyptian men of science axplained to him [Nero] the nature of seas, and declared that the sea above Lechaeum would flood and obliterate the island of Aegina'. Today's 6 km canal was built in 1882-93.

Corinth, like Athens, had gone through its glorious history in the classical era some five hundred years before Paul's time. In 146 BCE it had been captured and razed to the ground by the Romans. Its people were sold into slavery; its riches including the statues which decorated its buildings and streets were carried to Rome. The city was a heap of ruins and lay desolate until Julius Caesar refounded and made it Roman colony in 44 BCE, the year that he was assassinated. It was, like the rest of the Roman colonies, resettled by veterans from the Roman army and Roman freedmen. At the time of Paul's visit it was the capital of the Roman province of Achaia and seat of the proconsul and in the midst of extensive construction.

Coming from Cenchrea one would walk the 10 km road and enter the city by the gate named after the port and go through the suburb of Craneum. This was a cypress grove where the gymnasium, and several sanctuaries were located. Alexander's famous encounter with the Cynic philosopher Diogenes of Sinope (400-325 BCE) is said to have taken place hereabouts. When Alexander asked if Diogenes, who had been lying in the sun, naked except for a loin-cloth, needed anything, the latter answered 'Yes, stand aside, you are between me and the sun!' A remark which later made Alexander say 'If I were not Alexander, I would be Diogenes.'

Much of what one sees today at the ancient site stood here when Paul lived in Corinth. The road entered the agora of the city by the mid-point of its eastern side. Sometime before Paul's visit the agora was divided into levels: the upper for civic and religious purposes and the lower one for commercial activities. By today's museum stood the sanctuary (today known as temple E) that was built by Augustus, the most important symbol of the presence of Rome. Among the edifices which stood at Paul's time the most conspicuous

Peirene. Corinth. This was the most important of the caves where the water coming from the Acrocorinth outflowed naturally, and it determined the site on which Corinth was founded, somewhat away from its harbour, and from the two gulfs. The Roman-period fountain house includes some small Ionic columns and worn parapets of the earlier period inside. Behind these there are long basins which were fed by the natural channels leading into the Acrocorinth.

belonged to Apollo. It had escaped the Roman devastation and reached Paul's time in good condition. During his stay at Corinth most of the apostle's time would probably have been spent at the agora which was being enlarged by Claudius. Paul met two of the most important of his future companions, Priscilla (a diminutive of the Roman name Prisca) and Aquila at Corinth. The latter was perhaps a freed Jew carrying a Latin name, originally from the Roman province of Pontus, and with his wife Prisca, had settled in Rome. Research has shown that Aquila was a popular name in Pontus. They were probably two members of the Jewish population that Claudius had banished from Rome in 49 CE, and although not mentioned in Acts, already Christians when Paul met them. The mentioning of Priscilla's name before her husband's (several times in Acts and twice in Paul's letters) was common for the period for women with higher status than their husbands. Paul, arriving at Corinth, perhaps asked for the location of tentmakers and having found Aquila introduced himself and received the invitation to stay with them. Although later Corinthians would complain that Paul refused their help, Paul made use of the hospitality of many wealthy Corinthians staying with them and probably using their houses for preaching.

Temple of Aphrodite at the topmost peak of the Acrocorinth. Unless it had other premises elsewhere the temple, as its ruins stand today, is too small to accommodate Strabo's 'more than a thousand temple-slaves, courtesans, whom both men and women had dedicated to the goddess'. It has been speculated that its female servants and their immorality are alluded to by Paul (1 Cor 6.9-20; 2 Cor 12.21).

The Roman historian Suetonius writing in the second century says 'Because the Jews at Rome caused continuous disturbances at the instigation of Chrestus, he expelled them from the city'. This is the first reference known in Latin mentioning the word Chrestus. Although Suetonius does not elaborate, the disturbances may have again been the reaction of orthodox Jews to Christian Jews on matters such as the observance of the Mosaic law and the acceptance of Gentiles into Christianity. The historian's reference is short and not clear. Jews were an acceptable ethnic group in the capital and scholars agree that Claudius, although not fond of Jews, was not the kind of man who would have banished them without a good reason. The Emperor seems to have followed the characteristic Roman attitude at the time of disturbances and punished all of the insurgent Jews, Christian or non-Christian, by expulsion. Whether non-Jewish Christians were included in the banishment is not known.

Thus Christians or not, most of the Jews Paul met at Corinth may have moved here when expelled by Claudius. Paul, as anywhere else, first went to his own race and 'when Silas and Timothy came down from Macedonia' he was still busy with trying to convert Corinthian Jews and godfearers he found at the synagogues. Again, the Jews, denying his arguments about Christ being the Messiah, rebuffed him. Paul responded with the traditional gesture, shaking off the dust from his clothes, and saying, ' Your blood be on your heads! I am clear of responsibility. From now on I will go to the Gentiles'. Some of the Christians here seem to have been wealthy and lived in large houses which could accept resident guests and serve as house churches and Paul taking up residence with one of them, a Titus Justus, a Gentile 'worshipper of God' whose house stood next to the synagogue, stayed in the city. The name of his host shows that he was probably a Roman or Latin, possibly a descendant of the settlers in the city when it was made a colony. Paul's words in his letter to the Corinthians that the Christian congregation here could afford to 'set aside and save whatever one can afford' for the poor at Jerusalem also implies that the Corinthian church was not poor.

During a part of his long Corinthian sojourn Paul seems to have lived like any other Corinthian wage-earner, mixing with the inhabitants of the city practicing his tentmaking. It has been claimed that his remarks to the Corinthians 'Who wants a vineyard without eating its produce. Or who shepherds a flock without using some of the milk from the flock?..these plowman should plow in the hope, and the thresher in hope of receiving a share' may have been inspired from his experiences with the Corinthian peasantry. Returning from their missions in Macedonia Silas and Timothy joined him at Corinth and helped him in his preaching. The sum of money that these two brought 'from Macedonia' enabled Paul 'to occupy himself totally with preaching the word'. It is likely that he abandoned his tentmaking at the same time as he moved into the house of Titus Justus. Paul had months

North basilica on the Lechaion road. First century BCE. Corinth. Some, speculating that a Roman governor would not hold courts in a public place such as the bema in the agora, the traditional spot of Paul's case, have suggested that he may have preferred to use in the proper Roman custom the tribunal (judgement seat) of one of the basilicas of the city, such as the south basilica (40 CE) which stood near where the road from Cenchrea entered Corinth. In the background on top of the hill is the Temple of Apollo whose origins go back to the fifth century BCE.

Bema upon which Roman officials were said to have appeared before the public at the agora. Corinth. Augustan era. Although Acts does not give any indication, traditionally, Paul is believed to have probably faced the Roman proconsul Lucius Junius Gallio here. At the apostle's time the structure had an entrance at its rear through three openings separated by massive piers and had a roof resting on columns. In the later period it served as a base for successive church buildings, and Christian graves were cut in its core.

of undistracted preaching and instruction and it seems almost certain that the majority of his converts were made among the Greeks and Romans.

A drastic change took place in the summer of 51. In July that year a new proconsul of Achaia, Lucius Junius Gallio, a brother of the philosopher Seneca and a friend of Claudius, was appointed. The appointment of Gallio at Corinth is confirmed by an inscription which came from Delphi and in which Claudius says 'my friend [Lucius] Junius Gallio, proconsul of Achaia'. This inscription is regarded as the single evidence discovered so far which would help establishing the exact chronology of Paul's journeys. In his writings the philosopher Seneca refers to his brother as a person of a pleasant character and disposition and says that he caught fever in Achaia. The subject inscription mentions Claudius as *imperator* for the 26th time. Since the latter was declared emperor for the 27th time on August 1 scholars claim that the inscription must have been set during the first seven months of 52, and that Gallio should have taken his post in Achaia in 51 CE. The illness Seneca mentions forced him to leave his post before the winter that year, before the sailing season was over and Acts seems to imply that he had only recently acquired this position when Paul was before him, after the apostle settled at Corinth 'for a year and half' (18.11) something which may imply that Gallio became governor of the province in

51 to serve for two years. The Jewish community seems to have imagined that with the change of government, they might find a Roman new to the office who would be willing to accede their request: removal of Paul from their city. They 'rose up together against Paul and brought him to the tribunal'. The charge laid against Paul was that he was trying to persuade people to worship God in a manner that was against the law.

For Gallio the problem looked like a different interpretation of some aspect of Jewish religion and did not involve any material offence. He was probably in Rome when the Jews were banished by Claudius two years before because of a similar feud among themselves. The case brought to him was individual and isolated and the Jewish community at Corinth, after all, probably like any other big city, had its own power to judge such cases. He concluded that 'If it were a matter of some crime or malicious fraud, I should with reason hear the complaint of you Jews; but since it is a question of arguments over doctrine and titles and your own law, see to it yourselves. I do not wish to be a judge of such matters'. Thus, the Jews were removed from the court. The Jewish community decided that the whole affair had been treated inefficiently by the leader of their synagogue, Sosthenes, who may have concentrated just on offences against the Jewish law instead of emphasizing in his accusation that Paul was proclaiming a doctrine that was a threat to the Roman emperor. The angry group, possibly of Jews, seized Sosthenes and beat him in front of the court; 'But none of this was concern of Gallio'.

Although Acts does not say anything about why Paul chose Corinth rather than any place else after leaving Athens, it has been speculated that the

Erastus inscription. Theatre square. Mid-first century CE. Corinth. Reused pavement block of two pieces incised to hold metal letters belonging to the inscription ERASTUS PRO AED S P STRAVIT which is reconstructed as ERASTUS PRO AEDILITATE SUA PECUNIA STRAVIT which in Latin reads 'Erastus, in return for his aedileship, at his own expense, laid the pavement'. It is speculated that he may have been the same person Paul speaks of as being the 'city treasurer' (Rom 16.23).

Synagogue inscription with seven letters reconstructed as 'Synagogue of the Hebrews'. Archaeological Museum. Corinth. The inscription comes from the foot of the stairs where the Lechaion road enters the agora. It is thought to have belonged to the upper lintel of a doorway of a synagogue, and dates from the second century CE, having been reused in the following century.

main reason for this was the opportunities a large cosmopolitan city with an important festival, the Isthmian Games, offered for evangelization, apart from the existence of a large Jewish congregation. It has been suggested that Paul may have visited Isthmia because in addition to missionary activity the games would give him and his tentmaker friends an opportunity to make money. During the festival, there was a big crowd from far-away lands and to accommodate them tents had to be pitched along the roads or in squares. Strabo says that 'further profits' came by way of the crowd for the renowned Isthmian Games which were held in the neighbourhood. Paul would also hear news of the churches he had founded in Anatolia and Macedonia from the visitors.

Corinth's past was rich in legends and names such as Oedipus, who killed his father and married his mother Iocaste unknowingly, or the legendary King Sisyphus, who was punished by rolling up the hill a huge block of stone which kept falling to the bottom just before he reached the summit. The Isthmian Games were established by Sisyphus in the remote Greek past. Driven mad by Hera, Athamas, the King of Orchomenos, tried to kill his son Melicertes (Melkarth) and the child's mother Ino. The latter jumped into the sea and was drowned together with her son. Zeus, however, deifying both the mother, and Melicertes as the god Palaimon sent the boy on a dolphin's back to the isthmus of Corinth. The games were held every two years for Poseidon and the boy-god Palaimon, who is frequently depicted riding a dolphin, and attracted visitors from all over the Greek world. By Paul's time the games, which had come to a halt after Corinth's destruction by the Romans, were reestablished. Scholars believe that if Paul went to the games this must be in 51 CE, and in April, or early May when they were held. Paul

Apse of the Byzantine church built into the walls. Isthmia.

Sanctuary of the Cyclops mentioned by Pausanias as being near the Temple of Poseidon. Isthmia.

Base of the shrine of Palaimon. Isthmia.

may have seen the procession to Isthmia for the celebration of the games (1 Cor 9.24-7), where he watched the runners. It is, however, difficult to say if his expressions related to gymnasium life such as 'runners in the stadium' or 'a perishable crown' are inspired by these or other similar games held in Ephesus or his hometown Tarsus, or Antioch on Orontes and Daphne, all famous for such festivals. The image of a racing athlete was frequently employed by Paul. Still, Paul knew that the listeners to his words at Corinth would immediately understand them. Some doubt that a large pagan crowd gathered for festivities would make a potential field for evangelization for Paul. They remind us that Paul mostly preached his Gospel in synagogues or house churches and preaching to crowds would have made him one of the itinerant teachers of the time from whom he tried to distinguish himself. His audience were the small parties or assemblies who listened to him in quiet isolated places such as in the houses of other Christians or where he worked.

Isthmia consisted of a high acropolis and sanctuaries and a stadium at its skirts, some 20 km to the east of Corinth. Except for the wall of its starting point whose ruins have reached the present, the rest of the stadium where these games were held is buried in soil, partly under citrus trees.

There is no information if Paul ever preached in the country outside Corinth. Writing at about the time of Paul Jewish Philo of Alexandria says that there were Jews 'in most of the Peloponnese'. Paul may have visited and preached the nearby towns or easily crossed to the islands. 1 Mc 15.23 and Josephus mention the existence of Jews in Delos. The ruins of a synagogue building, which is tentatively dated to the first century CE, has been uncovered in the northeast of Delos. Although not from Paul's time, excavations on Aigina have brought to light the ruins of a fourth-century-CE synagogue which may have been built on the remains of an earlier one.

Paul was, thus, able to continue his activities uninterrupted for 'quite some time' in Corinth after his trial. In the spring of 53 embarking on a ship at Cenchrea Paul left Corinth in the company of his fellow tentmakers Priscilla and Aquila. The two may have accompanied Paul to Ephesus, apart from their religious enthusiasm, in order to find more profitable business opportunities, for the city was famous for the manufacture of tents and marquees. This was a period when people travelled with relative safety and easily from one place to the other for different purposes. It is also suggested that at this time Paul's health was not good and the couple accompanied

Site of the Hellenistic and Roman stadium. Isthmia.

him as far as Ephesus. He was later to thank the people of Corinth for their treatment of him, and to confess that he had come to them 'in weakness and fear' (1 Cor 2.3). The words are interesting, for they can hardly refer to his treatment in Athens where he had been heard with scepticism but not with violence. It is possibly right to assume that the sum of events until then and his treatment in Macedonia had prepared him for further persecutions.

Seismic tremors have caused the land in the area of the harbour town Cenchrea to sink in some places as much as 2 m and the structures of the port which were mostly warehouses are now under water. On the pier which once joined the southwestern mole of the harbour to the land was the sanctuary of Isis, the Egyptian goddess of motherhood and fertility. From the submerged ruins of the sanctuary underwater archaeology brought to light 120 glass panels showing the harbour (Isthmia Museum). In Apuleius' *The Golden Ass* it is at Cenchrea that ass-shaped Lucius was initiated into the mysteries of Isis and transformed back into a human. In Paul's time the salt-water spring which was located near the bay was known as Helen's bath. The information in Rom 16.1, where Paul introduces Phoebe, 'a minister of the church at Cenchrea' shows that there was a Christian community here. Phoebe is thought to have been one of the leaders of the congregation in town, possibly an independent woman of wealth.

Thus according to Acts 18.18 Paul 'sailed for Syria'. Although not from Cenchrea but Piraeus, ancient literature mentions plenty of sea journeys to Ephesus. On his way to Cilicia for his assignment as the governor of the province in 51 BCE Cicero embarked on a Rhodian open vessel in the month of July. Cicero after admitting that travel 'by sea is no light matter, even in July' says that his ship made stops at six islands including Delos and Samos on the way to Ephesus, and the trip took 17 days. His return trip in October next year, during which he had to wait 'for calm spells to suit the Rhodian craft and the other long ships', took 14 days.

It was probably shortly after the sailing season began in early March that Paul sailed from Cenchrea. Acts 18.18 says that before sailing he 'had his hair cut because he had taken a vow'. In the Jewish religion vows concerning only hair were also regarded as a Nazirite vow. The reason for undertaking this vow is not known. It has been suggested that the apostle wanted to be at Jerusalem for Passover and had embarked at Corinth on a vessel which may have been full of orthodox Jewish pilgrims who had a similar plan, and

Cenchrea. On the other side are the remains of the harbour mole and warehouses. Above the last stood a Temple of Aphrodite. On this side stood the Temple of Isis. Today's ruins partly submerged in the water belong to a Byzantine church.

were hostile to the apostle. Paul may have felt it necessary to display his Jewish origins to his travel companions during such a long voyage. According to the Jewish custom one cut his hair when one was ill, or in distress and followed the prohibitions elaborated in the Book of Numbers (6). To unbind the vow he would shave his head and keep his hair to be presented as a burnt offering at the altar of the Jerusalem Temple and a sacrifice would be offered. Or he may have been sick. Since the Corinthian mission had been successful and there was no reason to be distressed, the vow Paul had taken is thought to have concerned his sickness at Corinth, another place infected with malaria. Later in Rom 16.1-2 when he introduces Phoebe of Cenchrea, who may have been the bearer of the letter itself, saying 'she has been a benefactor to many and to me as well' he may have been referring to his sickness there and Phoebe's nursing of him. The reason may have been the conclusion of a successful mission.

At the time that the ship carrying Paul, Priscilla and Aquila arrived, Ephesus was on the sea with its port close to the mouth of the Cayster River (Küçük Menderes). Strabo, writing some thirty years before Paul's arrival, says that the harbour was already silted up but not yet to a degree to prevent transportation. Paul's vessel sailed by the Hellenistic barracks which would one day be named St Paul's prison after him that stood on top of the hill to the south. Scholars have found the words of Luke in Acts 18.19 difficult to understand. Paul 'left them' and 'entered the synagogue and held discussions with the Jews'. It is not clear that if Priscilla and Aquila went to an already established church of Jewish and Gentile Christians or if they founded one. The existence of Gentiles at the synagogue of Ephesus is not mentioned and the place where it stood is not known. The evidence about the Jewish existence in the city is not much and dates from the later period. Paul was asked to stay longer. Promising that he would return one day Paul left Ephesus.

Priscilla and Aquila remained in Ephesus where they became prominent figures of the Christian community. It is also probable that Priscilla and Aquila went to Ephesus and stayed there to make preparations for Paul's third journey; because, eventually, one of the congregations at Ephesus met in their house (Rom 16.5). This unusual couple were deeply committed to their religion and Paul's mission. The apostle admits that at least once they 'risked their necks' for his life (Rom 16.3-4). During the absence of the apostle, Apollos (diminutive of Apollonius, a name particularly popular in Egypt during the Roman era), an Alexandrian Jew, who knew the scriptures well and was a good speaker came to Ephesus. He 'spoke and taught accurately about Jesus' but had not received baptism. The 'baptism of John' he practiced stands for 'baptism with water' as a symbol of repentance but not baptism in the name of Jesus.

Ruins of the church built on the remains of the Temple of Isis. Cenchrea. Its apse is in the sea to the right. Fourth century CE. The apse is partly submerged in the water.

The information given by Acts leads one to think that Apollos was preaching 'a Baptist sect' which perhaps existed separately, even in competition with the Christian church. Priscilla and Aquila, who had listened to him speak in the synagogue of Ephesus were impressed but also concerned about his lack of understanding of the power of the Holy Spirit, so they 'took him aside and explained to him the way [of God] more accurately. And when he wanted to cross Achaia, the brothers encouraged him and wrote to the disciples to welcome him' (Acts 18.26-27). The story of Apollos shows that in addition to Paul, there were other Christian preachers who frequented the metropolises of the Greco-Roman world.

Thus, from Ephesus Paul sailed for Caesarea. At Paul's time the latter was the most important harbour of Phoenicia and the capital of the Roman province of Judea and frequently mentioned in Acts.

Acts 6:3 informs us that Philip the evangelist was one of the 'seven reputable men' and was sent out from Jerusalem to Gaza' (Acts 8.26) probably at the time of Pontius Pilate (26-36 CE) to end up at Caesarea. The city is also the scene of the conversion of Cornelius, and the preaching of the Gospel to the Gentiles for the first time. In Acts 9:30 Paul leaves for Tarsus from the same port. This city is also mentioned briefly, as a stopover, toward the end of Paul's third journey where he stays at the house of Philip (Acts 21.8). It, however, became crucial in the last part of Paul's life, being his prison for two years. Caesarea continued to play an important role in the following centuries, after Paul. Several of the best-known church fathers were active in the city. Among them are Origen (185-254), who headed its famous library for 23 years and Eusebius (263-354) who wrote *The History of the Church* and compiled the *Onomasticon*, a book of place names in the Holy Land in the fourth century.

Acts 11.19 mentions Phoenicia as one of the regions where the believers fled and took the word with them, although 'to no one but Jews'. Paul must have been familiar with the region during his travels between Antioch and Jerusalem and even had preached here. In Acts 15.3 we are told that as they journeyed to Jerusalem for the Council Paul and Barnabas 'passed through Phoenicia and Samaria telling the conversion of the Gentiles, and brought great joy to all the brothers.'

At Caesarea Paul stayed just long enough to greet the brothers and 'went up' which means travelled to Jerusalem although geographicaly the latter was 'down' from Caesarea. When his work here finished he 'went down' to Antioch on Orontes, in similar logic, from Jerusalem to Caesarea through Samaria and to Ptolemais/Acco, Tyre, Sidon, Berytus, Byblos, Tripolis and Antaradus to Laodicea. From the last, an inland road ascending toward Mount Casius reached Antioch.

Ruins of the Hellenistic tower known as St Paul's prison probably since the seventeenth century. Ephesus. This is the westernmost point of the fortification circuit built by Lysimachus on Mount Coressus (Bülbül Dağı). It was square and divided into four rooms that served as barracks. An inscription on a reused marble block in the tower mentions the rental of a piece of land near the height which is referred to as *Astyagou Pagos*, 'the hill of Astyages'.

PONTUS/EUXINE SEA
(BLACK SEA)
Amastris
Heraclea
Bosphorus
Hebrus
Axios
Styrmon
THRACE
Byzantium
Chalcedon
Nicomedia
MACEDONIA
Pangaion 1,956
Nestus
PROPONTIS
(MARMARA)
BITHYNIA
Ancyra
Philippi
Neapolis
Nicaea
Sangarius
Doberus?
Hellespont
Ascania
Amphipolis
Thassos
Tembris
Gordion
Edessa
Pella
Allante
Apollonia
Palaipolis
Cyzicus
Prusa
Dorylaeum
Ludias
Thessalonica
Samothrace
Aisepus
Midaum
Germa
Beroia
Aloros
Pessinus
Methoni
Imbros
Tatta
Aigai
Pydna
Lemnos
Tenedos
Ilium
Ergasteria
MYSIA
Rhyndacus
Cotieum
Haliacmon
Dium
Alexandria Troas
Scepsis
Hadrianoutherai
Hadrianeia
Aezanoi
Amorium
GALATIA
Neandria
Satnioeis
Pionia
Macestus
Cadı
Docimium
Olympus 2,911
Lectum
Assos
Adramyttium
Prymnessus
Tempe
Larissa
Pergamum
ASIA
PHRYGIA
Synada
THESSALY
Lesbos
Mitylene
Philomelium
Cyme
Antioch
Lagina
Laodicea
Meander
Iconium
Pharsalus
Hermus
Cogamus
Neapolis
Elea
Limnai
Kilistra
Karadağ 2,228
Thaumacoi
Philadelphia
Pappa
Lystra
Scyros
Sardis
Apamea
Apollonia
Nicopolis
Smyrna
PISIDIA
LYCAONIA
Derbe
Lamia
Cayster
Hierapolis
Ascania
Malos
Karalis
Actium
Euboea
Chios
Nysa
Sagalassus
Adada
Posala
Laranda
ACHAIA
Tralles
Cremna
Chaironia
Ephesus
Antioch
Laodicea
Colossae
Pednelissos
Delphi
Thebes
Magnesia
Comama
Eurymedon
Calycadnus
Lebadia
Cestrus
PAMPHYLIA
Eleusis
Samos
Priene
Aspendos
Megara
Athens
Andros
Marsyas
Perge
Side
Piraeus
Trogyllium
Miletus
CARIA
Cibyra
Attalia
Coracesium
Corinth
Tenos
Icaros
Acrocorinth 570
Cenchrea
Macronisi
Sunium
Myconos
Pharmacussa
Delos
LYCIA
Olympia
Halicarnassus
Anemurium
Cos
Naxos
Cnidus
Myra
Xanthos
Chelidonium
Sparta
Symi
Andriace
Nisyros
Rhodes
Patara
IONIAN SEA
Tylos
Lindos
Soloi
Malea
Cythera
Carpathos
Nea Paphos
CRETE
Salmone
MEDITERRANEAN SEA
Cnossos
Phoenix
Gortyn
Fair Heavens
Cauda
THIRD JOURNEY
• Cities mentioned in Acts

THIRD JOURNEY

Antioch on Orontes — Galatia — Ephesus — Macedonia — Greece — Macedonia — Philippi — Alexandria Troas — Assos — Mitylene — Chios — Samos — Trogyllium — Miletus — Cos — Rhodes — Patara — Tyre — Ptolemais — Caesarea — Jerusalem

After some time in Antioch, perhaps in the spring of 53 or 54 Paul set out on his third missionary journey which would be the last and the longest. When he bid farewell to his brothers here the apostle did not know that he would not return to Antioch; this was the last time he saw them. Normally, after delivering the funds which were being collected from the churches of the diaspora to the Jerusalem church he would have been expected to terminate his journey again at Antioch. Now the main objective of his mission was again Ephesus the largest city and capital of the Roman province of Asia, to which the Holy Spirit had not allowed him to go and preach, and where he had stopped briefly toward the end of his previous journey. The fact that he did not travel by sea but land shows the importance that Paul gave to the churches that he had founded on this route. As in the case of his previous journey he travelled probably by the same route, by way of the Syrian Gates, Smooth Cilicia and Tarsus, and the Cilician Gates into Lycaonia. It is very probable that he visited Derbe, Lystra, Iconium and Pisidian Antioch and many unnamed places to see how the nucleus of the Christian community that he had established at each of these cities was doing. Although from 1 Cor 16.1 we learn that Paul had 'ordered the churches of Galatia' to save for the poor Christians at Jerusalem there is no information how and when the Galatian collection travelled to the city.

When, later, the apostle referred to Asia in his letters, his readers would have understood that this was the large province which comprised western Anatolia. At this time, it included the whole of the Aegean coast from Caria, through ancient Ionia and Aiolis to the southern shore of the Propontis (Sea of Marmara), a little east of Cyzicus (Erdek). It embraced Mysia and Lydia, and extended inland through the valleys and headwaters of the Hermus (Gediz), Cayster (Küçük Menderes) and Meander (Büyük Menderes) toward the Phrygian plateau and the eastern boundary with Galatia. It was the oldest and wealthiest of the Roman provinces of Anatolia and it contained several ancient and famous cities, including Miletus and Smyrna on the coast, and inland, the old Lydian capital, Sardis; further north was Pergamum, the former prosperous capital of the Attalids. The good climate and soil gave rich harvests and much of western Anatolia was well settled, particularly in the Hermus, Cayster and Meander valleys. The roads which ran along the river beds in the east-west alignment enabled the rural population to find a market for their agricultural produce and other merchandise in large coastal cities and the Aegean world beyond. The rivers have changed their courses since antiquity and it is not known if or when or to what extent they were navigable. At Paul's time the silting of the ancient harbours established at their mouths was already threatening the sea traffic. The popular route from Pisidian Antioch to Ephesus followed the path of the Meander and had a string of ancient and prosperous cities founded on commanding positions on one or the other side of the road. The apostle may have travelled by way of Apollonia (Uluborlu) to Apamea (Dinar), where the ancient routes from the four cardinal points of the compass met each other. The city also probably had the largest Jewish community in the region. The natives of Apamea believed that Philemon and Baucis of the Phrygian flood saved themselves by climbing to the nearby hill of Celaenae. The Jewish population, perhaps already by Paul's time, had begun to assume that the title 'kibotos' (Greek 'chest') that the city bore implying its richness, referred to Noah's Ark and regarded the hill as the place that it landed. To reach Ephesus one would normally continue to Colossae (Honaz), and Laodicea on Lycus (Goncalı), Antioch on Meander (Başaran Köy), Nysa (Sultanhisar) and Tralles (Aydın) and Magnesia on Meander (Menderes Manisası). The road from Laodicea to Ephesus was the middle section of the first Roman road in Anatolia that was built by Manius Aquillius and connected Pergamum to Side.

Early Christian church on the acropolis of Apamea (Dinar).

Even if there were some Jewish people in western Anatolia earlier, their number may not have reached substantial figures until the Seleucid King Antiochus III moved two thousand families from Babylon and Mesopotamia sometime toward the end of the third century BCE to Lydia and Phrygia. Josephus also informs us that these new settlers were given vineyards and grain fields, and allowed to establish separate groups from the locals who had recently supported Antiochus' rebel uncle Achaeus. They were the descendants of the Ten Tribes which were originally moved to Mesopotamia from Jerusalem in 597 and 586 BCE by the King of Babylon, Nebuchadnezzar II, and would be claimed to be separated from their brothers by 'the baths and the wines', that is by the luxuries of the Roman way of life according to

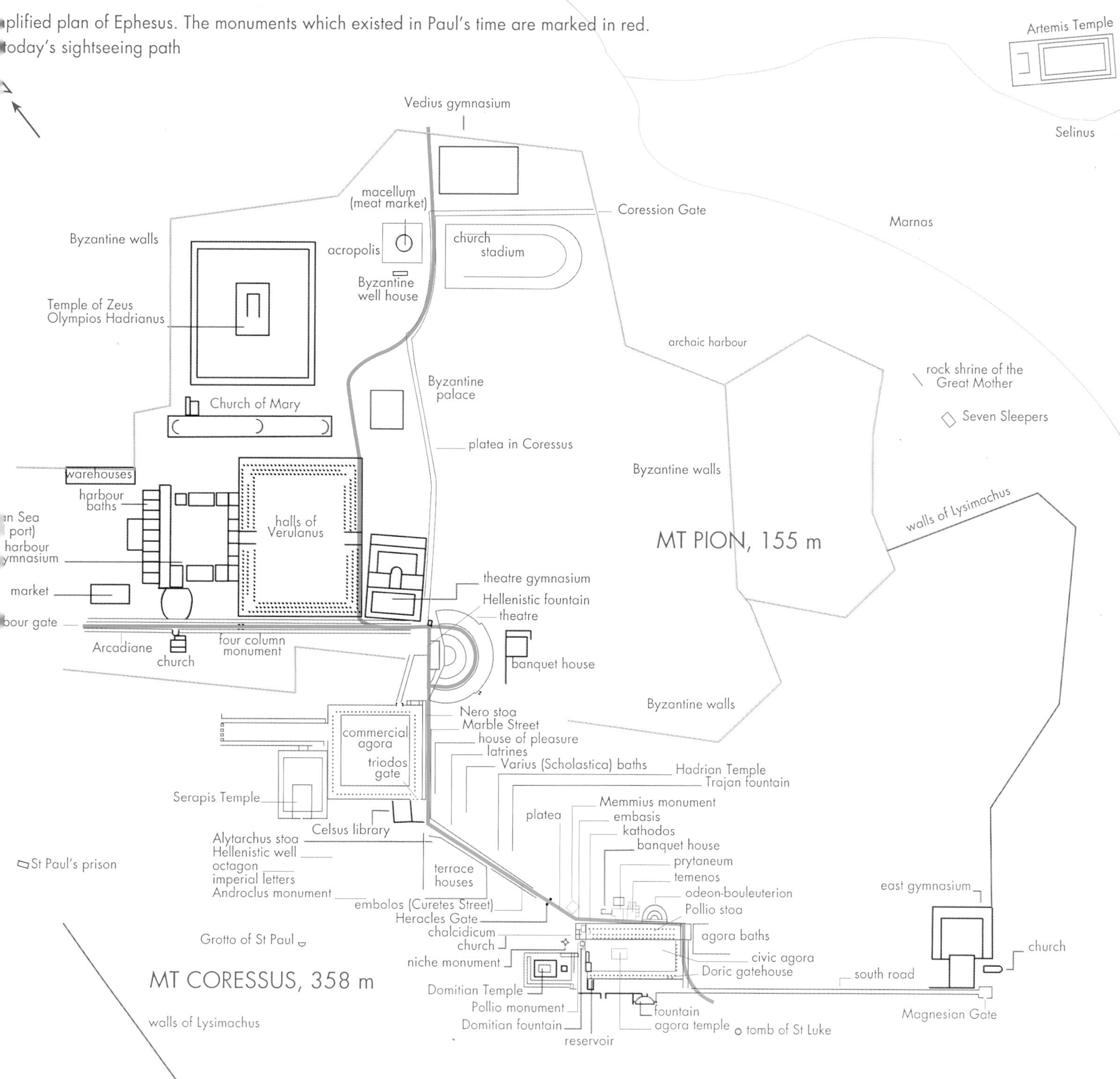

plified plan of Ephesus. The monuments which existed in Paul's time are marked in red.
oday's sightseeing path

Reconstruction of the Mausoleum of Lysimachus at Belevi, some 10 km to the northeast of Ephesus (Fossel).

Mausoleum of Lysimachus. The burial mound of the King is on the hill behind. It was second only to that of Mausolus (377-353 BCE) of Halicarnassus who has given us the very word.

the later Jewish literature. It seems that these Jewish communities survived into Paul's time because ancient literature informs us about the Roman edicts which confirm their ancient privileges such as the freedom of sending money to the Jerusalem Temple, and exemption from military service. The Jews from Asia at 'the so-called Synagogue of Freedmen' in Jerusalem (Acts 6.9) shows the close contact that they maintained with the mother city. When Luke mentions the existence of Jews from Asia along with those from Phrygia he probably uses the word to refer to the coastal strip of the province because much of Phrygia was included in the province of Asia. Thus at the time of Paul's journeys all of these settlements had well-established Jewish communities of smaller or larger sizes and their knowledge by Paul may have been among the reasons why he preferred travelling by land to sea. Although dating after Paul's time, most of these cities have produced archaeological material which shows the existence of Jews.

Acts 19.1 informs us that Paul 'travelled through the interior of the country' and arrived at Ephesus. This is usually regarded as implying that Paul did not travel on the straight Roman highway but took another route. In the Lycus valley there was a second, less popular road which led to Ephesus by way of Laodicea on Lycus, following the Cogamus valley and passing Philadelphia (Alaşehir) and Sardis. This was the route by which Ignatius would be taken to Rome some fifty years later.

For his help at the battle of Ipsus (301 BCE), which had ended with the defeat and death of Antigonus Monophthalmus by Seleucus I, Alexander's former general Lysimachus, who had originally taken over Thrace, received western Anatolia and founded the present-day Ephesus.

The site of the previous city was close to the Artemis Temple but because of the silting of the Cayster was already cut off from the Aegean. Lysimachus, realizing that a deep port was indispensable for a new city, moved its inhabitants to this new location with a sheltered harbour and named it Arsinoe, after his wife. Strabo says that in order to move the Ephesians to the new city the King blocked up the drainage channels during a heavy rainfall and flooded it. Although ancient literature is silent on the matter of the reluctance to move to the new site the reason was probably the existence of an archaic cemetery as early as the sixth century BCE which has been brought to light by recent excavations from below the civic (upper) agora. With the death of Lysimachus at the battle of Corupedium fought in 281 BCE on the flats between the Hermus and eastern foothills of Mount Sipylus

Aqueduct of Pollio built on the Marnas River which still flows under its eastern (right) arch. 4-14 CE. Its two other arches served as a monumental gate through which the main Roman road ran. Above these arches, and repeated on both sides, is a bilingual inscription. Latin above Greek it informs us that the aqueduct was built by C Sextilius Pollio and his wife Ofillia Bassa and his stepson C Ofillius Procolus, using their own sources, for Augustus, Tiberius, and the citizen body of Ephesus.

near Manisa, the region and Ephesus became Seleucid possessions. Its new owner, Antiochus III seems to have made no change in the administration except for installing a garrison. During the Seleucid period Ephesus, as their most important port in the west, was visited by the Seleucid Kings frequently, and prospered. When the Seleucids had to leave the north of the Taurus to Rome after the battle of Magnesia (190 BCE) Ephesus with the rest of the region became Pergamene property.

The Ephesus where Paul would be living for about three years was a Hellenistic-Roman metropolis. Ancient literature refers to the city of the time as the 'largest trading-centre in Asia this side of the Tarsus'. It was the last King of Pergamum Attalus III who, lacking a legitimate heir, had bequeathed his kingdom to the Roman people upon his death in 133 BCE and thus perhaps quickened the inevitable penetration of Rome to Anatolia. After a three-year war between Rome and Aristonicus, the illegitimate son of Eumenes II, with his army of peasants and slaves, in 129 BCE, the province of Asia was established. It is not known when Ephesus replaced Pergamum as the centre of the province and became the seat of the Roman governor, a proconsul who was of senatorial order chosen by lot and for one year; after Africa it was the second and only other province of this kind.

Although some of the buildings of Paul's time disappeared or were built over in the following centuries, today Ephesus is the only city which maintains the character of a Pauline metropolis. Like the rest of the visitors who arrived from the east, treading on the western end of the main route which would be later known as the Common Road (*koine hodos*), or the Southern Highway, Paul would have walked through Pollio's aqueduct which was built not long before his visit and entered the city by the Magnesian Gate, named after Magnesia on Meander, the nearest city in the east. This was a triple-entrance with a courtyard and with towers on two sides, and three marble lions, the symbolic guardians of the city. What has survived to the present mostly dates from the second half of the first century BCE. The surviving ruts show that two passages on the southern side were reserved for wheeled-traffic. The crosses on the jambs of the central entrance may have been added by early Christians. The walls built by Lysimachus began at this gate and after following the gradually rising slope on both sides, climbed toward the top of Mount Pion (Panayır Dağı) on the eastern and Mount Coressus (Bülbül Dağı) on the southern side. The Magnesian Gate was also the spot by which the processions of Artemis, which began at her temple, entered the city after crossing the brooks of Selinus (Şirince Çayı) and of Marnas (Dervent Dere). A colonnaded street, now known as the south road began at this gate and

Magnesian Gate. Ephesus.

A stretch of today's south road by the civic (upper) agora. Ephesus.

continued straight as far as the eastern gate of the civic (upper) agora. Here a Doric gate-house perhaps built in the second-first centuries BCE gave access to a two-aisled colonnade.

The civic agora was in the form of a rectangle of some 160 x 58 m and its history went back to the foundation of the city by Lysimachus. Its name in antiquity is not known. Taking its final form in the reign of Augustus, by Paul's time it had become the centre of the political and religious life of Ephesus. The most important buildings related to the administration and major sanctuaries stood in or around it. Unlike typical agoras it was not encircled by a colonnade. Centrally located to the west of its courtyard there was a temple. It was built in the third quarter of the first century BCE and may have been dedicated to the divine Julius and Dea Roma, the goddess of Rome. In 29 BCE, Augustus had given permission to the resident Romans at Ephesus — and those in Nicaea (İznik) — to dedicate sacred precincts to his adoptive father, the deified Caesar and to the personification of Rome.

The most imposing building of Paul's time was a three-aisled royal stoa built by C Sextilius Pollio and his wife Ofillia Bassa in 11 CE, on the northern side. The building was dedicated to Artemis, Augustus, Tiberius and the citizen body (*demos*) of Ephesus. Today, shortly after entering the ruins, one walks through the edifice's central aisle which was flanked by 67 fluted Ionic columns with bull-head capitals, on each side. The rows of columns originally belonged to the second storey of the building. Behind the stoa stood the odeon-bouleuterion (music hall-council house), the precursor of the present one which was built about a hundred years after Paul's visit.

Next to this in the direction of the city stood a sacred enclosure (temenos) with columns on the three sides. It was dedicated to Artemis and Augustus.

This was followed by the prytaneum (a building for meetings and meals of the chief councils) which was built by Augustus. The building was sacred to the goddess Hestia of the hearth and housed the everlasting flame symbolizing the city's eternity, kept burning by the Curetes. Its entrance was through a façade which bore eight Doric columns. On the surviving ones the names of the 'curetes' or cult personnel and other religious inscriptions survive. The three marble Artemis statues displayed at Ephesus Museum, Selçuk, all dating after Paul's time were found buried under the floor of this building. The fact that they were not sent to the lime kilns but buried even without being vandalized show the weight that the goddess carried for the Ephesians even after Christianity took root in the city.

Prytaneum. Ephesus. First-second centuries CE. The two standing columns are made from the drums of different columns and inscribed with the names of Curetes who were originally priests responsible for some sacrifices and banquets related with Artemis, and were moved here a few decades before

Paul's arrival. The Ephesians held that Leto gave birth to Artemis and Apollo in the sacred grove of Ortygia near their city. Curetes were the demigods who scared away Hera by brandishing their armor and thus prevented her from hearing the children's cry and harming the twins.

A short street called the *kathodos* ('way downwards') led to the *platea* ('broad street') whose entrance — called the *embasis* in antiquity — was flanked by a pair of bases decorated with identical reliefs of Hermes and Apollo's tripod. Today this area is known as the Domitian square, after the temple built on its southern side in 92-93 CE. The large exedra (chalcidicum) of Pollio's stoa which has survived at the end of the building, was added in the reign of Nero (54-68 CE) and later turned into a church.

Behind this, and close to the western wall of the civic agora there are the remains of a memorial tomb. The grant of a funeral monument within the city walls shows that its owner was a very important benefactor. The fragmentary bilingual inscription (Latin to the left, Greek to the right) names Pollio's stepson Ofillius Procolus as the dedicator. Most of it was, however, later incorporated in Domitian's fountain which was built next to it. This fountain had a high arch and a triangular pediment, and water flowed into its pool from a semi-circular wall on the side of the agora. The statues of Odysseus and the Cyclops Polyphemus, and some others related to the same episode which are on display at Ephesus Museum, Selçuk, were parts of the reused material decorating this fountain.

The owner of the originally tower-like monument on the opposite of the Domitian square side was Gaius Memmius. The surviving figures — in high relief — are though to have represented him, his father (Faustus Gaius Memmius), and his grandfather, the Roman dictator Sulla, as well as personifications of virtues. It was built in the late first century BCE, and the fragmentary architrave on its eastern side bears an inscription which in Latin informs us that it was dedicated by Gaius Memmius, son of Gaius, grandson of Cornelius Sulla, the saviour. Originally, this was repeated in Greek. After defeating the forces of King Mithradates VI of Pontus in Greece, Sulla crossed to Anatolia and in 84 BCE after establishing peace with Mithradates exacted twenty thousand talents, an exorbitant sum for the time, as the cost of war from the cities of the province including Ephesus because its inhabitants, even if provoked by the King of Pontus, had rebelled against Rome and eagerly participated in the great massacre of the Romans and Italians in the city. To this he added the unpaid revenues of the last five years. The cities of the province which were already in debt had to again turn to Roman bankers for loans. In the Augustan era a fountain with three basins was added to one side of the monument.

The road which is today known as the Curetes Street, seems to have been, in antiquity, called the *embolos* ('street') or the *platea*. Until Lysimachus built

Ephesus it was the bed of the brook which flowed into the Aegean between the Mount Coressus and Mount Pion. The Curetes Street followed the natural depression between the two mountains and until the excavations began toward the end of the nineteenth century, was completely buried in the debris washed down from the slopes, a fact which ultimately protected much of what one can see today from going to the lime kiln. This thoroughfare began at the square of Domitian and ran as far as the Gate of Coressus at the other end of Ephesus. At Paul's time the procession of the festival of Artemis followed this street to the end, from where, crossing the plain it ended at her temple where it began.

This large street was flanked with colonnades even in Paul's time. The recesses behind the colonnades were used as shops and workshops or foodstalls and drinking parlours. The statues which were lined up on bases on the sides of the street belonged to personages whom Ephesians wanted to honour in this manner for their munificence. In time some of such statues would be replaced by those belonging to other personages and once in a while for expedience the opposite face of the same base would be used for the new epigram. The side streets, which are distinguished on both sides of the Curetes Street led to the houses located on the mountain slopes. At Paul's time on the slope of Mount Pion stood a round two-storeyed monument built during the early Roman period.

Research has shown that the first blocks of apartments, which are today called the terrace houses, were begun to have been built some fifty years before Paul's arrival. The surviving ones show that here each house consisted of an interior courtyard surrounded with columns around which the rooms were placed. The floors were covered with mosaic pavements and the walls with paintings. It seems that most of the slopes of the two mountains which flanked the main street were covered, even if not as spectacular as the surviving ones, with similar houses. The houses were individually owned. Although there is no information about the identity of the people who occupied these houses, it is known that at the time just the social elite, mostly Romans or Roman citizens whose major income was based on patrimony which would include other buildings, farms with wine and oil presses, livestock, cash and luxurious objects, could afford such places. Sometimes their freedmen or slaves ran enterprises: selling and buying or leasing for their masters. The rest of the population lived in flats which were made of perishable materials such as bricks or wood and have not survived.

Seated statue of Livia, wife of Augustus which stood in Pollio's stoa in the upper (civic) agora. Ephesus Museum. Selçuk. The cross on the forehead was put there against idols.

The ruins of a number of tomb and honorific monuments which stood along the Curetes Street at the time of Paul have survived. Although its building may have originally been different, the well in front of the terrace houses (below the point where the mosaic-paved floor of the 400-CE stoa of Alytarchus ended) had been in use since the Hellenistic period. Today it is below the end of the stoa, partly incorporated in the terrace houses. One of the spouts in the form of a lion's head, with round holes for water, has survived on its wall.

At Paul's time, on the left side of the Curetes Street just before it turned to the right, where today it takes the name Marble Street, there were two monuments. One of them was the octagon, today named so after its shape. This tomb, which revealed the bones of a young girl, belonged to Cleopatra's sister Arsinoe. She had proclaimed herself Queen of Egypt but after the defeat of the Egyptian army (47 BCE), was taken to Rome by Julius Caesar as a prisoner. Ancient literature informs us that the reaction of the Roman audience during the triumphal parade to a young girl in chains saved her from execution and she was allowed to seek asylum in the Artemis Temple at Ephesus where she was respected and treated well. When Cleopatra and Antony met at Tarsus (41 BCE), the latter conceded to give orders for her murder and thus saved Cleopatra from her single rival. The location and architecture of the tomb show that Arsinoe was very popular at Ephesus. The edifice began with a base of three steps. Above this stood the funeral chamber which was decorated with a frieze of garlanded bulls' heads in relief on its upper surface, and surrounded with eight Corinthian columns with capitals. It was topped by a pyramidal roof made of steps that ended with a spherical finial. Today the surviving pieces of the tomb are almost hidden by the marble texts of the response written (371/72 CE) to the governors of Ephesus by the co-Emperors Valentinian II, Valens and Gratian which stand on its steps.

Curse formula from *triodos* gate. In Greek it reads 'whoso relieves himself here shall suffer the wrath of Hecate' the common gatekeeper of Greek cities. Below this is a

graffito of an ethrog, a menorah and a shofar, mementoes of the Jewish existence at Ephesus perhaps dating from a later period than the above inscription.

In the depression behind the basin with enclosure panels featuring crosses or lozenges, which date from about the sixth century, there was a fountain and above it a statue of Androclus, the legendary founder of Ephesus built toward the end of the second century BCE.

To the left of today's library square, in Paul's time there was a colossal altar, probably related to the worship of Artemis and behind this a peristyle house. The most impressive building of the square was the south gate of the commercial (lower) agora. This gate, in antiquity, was known as the *triodos* ('three-way'). The inscription in Greek above its central passage is repeated in a more detailed manner above the side passages and informs us that Mazaeus and Mithradates, freedmen of the imperial house, had the gate built in 4/3 BCE in honor of Augustus and his wife Livia, his daughter Julia and her (deceased) husband Marcus Agrippa. The rest of the inscriptions are related to the civic life of Ephesus and consruction activities in the district, and date from after Paul's time. The gate houses with the graves of Mazaeus and Mithradates, which flanked the entrance, have not survived. To the right of the library square are the remains of a fountain and the steps which climbed to the two entrances of the stoa of Nero.

The present-day commercial (lower) agora, although its floor has in time been raised some 3 m, occupies its original ground of Lysimachus' time. An inscription discovered here names it as the *tetragonos* (having four sides) agora. Ephesus in having two separate markets, one for political and educational purposes, and another for commercial activities confirms the advice of Aristotle in *Politics*. Sometime around the time Paul was born it was enlarged to its present measures of about 112 x 112 m and surrounded with two-aisled, about 12 m wide colonnades on all sides. In addition to the *triodos* it

Triodos ('three-way') gate of the lower (commercial) agora. Ephesus.

had an entrance at the corner near the theatre square, and a third one on the side of the harbour. Behind the colonnades there were about a hundred rooms serving numerous commercial purposes. The city does not seem to have suffered the big earthquake of 17 CE which damaged the rest of western Anatolia. In 23 CE a second big earthquake hit the region including Ephesus. About a decade before Paul's visit the association of Roman merchants had set a statue of Claudius in the agora courtyard. If there was one place which the apostle may have frequented during his long stay here this was the commercial (lower) agora. It was here that he and his colleagues would find customers for whom they would manufacture tents, and hear news about what was going around in the world, the West and the East. Here, hundreds of inscribed steles, (in Greek or Latin, or bilingual) informed the visitors about the ancient and recent cultural and political developments in the city. The agora was also the starting point of strikes or riots; and the silversmiths' riots may have begun at one of the stalls here.

At the corner of agora the Curetes Street took a straight course as far as the theatre square. The ruts in the surface of this road, now known as the Marble Street, show that it was open to wheeled traffic. On the side toward the agora stood a 150 m long two-aisled structure with its inner aisle supported by the shops of the agora. Archaeologists, after an inscription found here, have named this long construction the stoa of Nero. In addition to the latter, the edifice was dedicated to the Emperor's mother Agrippina, the Ephesian Artemis and the citizen body of Ephesus. Its entrances were on the building's short sides. On the opposite side of the street there was a columned portico. The slope above this was probably covered with houses.

The main streets of Ephesus met at the theatre square. Some of the most important buildings were also clustered around this square. The theatre occupied the low slope below the saddle between the two low peaks of Mount Pion and commanded a view of the port. Recent research on some blocks from the stage building has shown that the history of the theatre went back to the third century BCE, the Seleucid era. At Paul's time it was a smaller structure with a lower stage building. The extensive rebuilding programme which would include new rows of seats for spectators and a stage building had already taken a start but would not finished until the following century. The spectators' seats commanded a view of the harbour, the city walls and the large tower, which would later be named St Paul's prison, on the isolated hill, beyond the Coressus.

Above the theatre stood a group of ruins which have not been yet completely excavated. This spot with its visual command of the entrance of the harbour seems to have been used from the Hellenistic era well into the Byzantine period.

Although it saw many changes, the final one being in the reign of Arcadius (395-408 CE) after whom it was named, the Arcadiane, the 528 m street which extended from the theatre square to the harbour had existed since the foundation of Ephesus. Its width is 11 m and each sidewalk was 5 m deep. When he sailed into the harbour of Ephesus, accompanied by Priscilla and Aquila, Paul after disembarking at the docks like all travellers would have walked into the city by the antecedent of this street. The port was the western terminal of the ancient trade and communication route from the East and full of vessels of all nationalities from different corners of the Mediterranean and the Aegean throughout the year. Most of the massive ruins which can be seen today date from after Paul's time.

Except for the stadium almost all of the buildings which are situated to the north of Arcadiane owe their existence to the construction programmes which took place after the apostle's time. The main road continued straight by the

Late Hellenistic fountain. About 100 BCE. Theatre square. Ephesus. The fountain house was later incorporated into the stage building. It served the pedestrians and the theatre audience. Originally, water fell into a basin behind the two Ionic columns from the three lion-head gargoyles. The room whose plain columns have survived in the front was added after Paul's time. The inscription on the column to the right indicates that the water was brought from the River Marnas.

theatre toward the Gate of Coressus which was the exit from Ephesus. At Paul's time the road was called the *platea* in Coressus. The Hellenistic stadium, which originally consisted of seats cut on the slope of Mount Pion, was about to take its present-day size and form during the time of Paul's stay in Ephesus. Although it has not yet been excavated it was the most impressive building, which gives the visitor an idea about the size of the city of Paul's time.

When he arrived in Ephesus his friends of the previous mission, Priscilla and Aquila, met and informed the apostle about the work of Apollos and that he was gone to Achaia. At Ephesus Paul found some disciples of John the Baptist. According to Acts their number was twelve and when Paul 'laid hands on them,' just as the twelve on the day of Pentecost the Holy Spirit came on them and they spoke 'in tongues' and prophesied.

Paul returned to the synagogue where he had preached during his previous short visit of one or two years earlier. Ephesus, as being the largest city in western Anatolia with a thriving commercial life, was supposed to have had a large Jewish population whose origins may have gone back to the early history of the city. Ancient literature informs us that during the later history of the city the relations between the Greeks and Jews may have been strained. The Greeks believed that the Jewish minority, who did not believe in the Greek gods, had no right to enjoy their privileges, so-called ancestral rights.

Walls of Lysimachus (290 BCE) on Mount Coressus. They are about 3 m thick and made of large ashlar blocks on both sides and filled with mortared rubble and soil and regarded among the most formidable fortifications that have survived from the Hellenistic period.

The complaint was usually disregarded. In 14 BCE Marcus Agrippa when he was staying at Mithymna on Lesbos together with Herod the Great wrote to the city council of Ephesus and ordered them not to touch the money that the Jews collected for the Jerusalem Temple and not to force the Jews to appear in court on the sabbath. It is surprising that to date, among the thousands of epigraphic materials, except for a fragment with the words *archisynagogoi* and *presbyteroi* and a few lamps with menorahs nothing has been found relating to the existence of Jews.

Paul's teaching in the synagogue seems to have lasted three months, a period much longer than the period that he was allowed at any other known synagogue of his missions. As elsewhere many of the Jews rejected his teachings, and as was the case with Paul's previous stop in the city Acts does not mention the existence of either Gentile proselytes or godfearers at the synagogue here.

For the next two years Paul preached the Gospel in the hall of Tyrannus who may have been a rhetorician and rented his hall to other lecturers when he did not use it. The name is frequently encountered in the Ephesian epigraphy ie among the Curetes mentioned on the surviving columns of the prytaneum. Giving lectures was at the time popular and a very profitable occupation. Here, to the pagan Ephesians the apostle would have appeared as one of the itinerant philosophers, who travelled from one city to another sharing his knowledge and ideas with the listeners and trying to make disciples. Like Paul, such philosophers also tried to establish their communities in each city and keep them in control by sending them letters. During Paul's long stay in Ephesus 'all the inhabitants of the province of Asia heard the word of the Lord, Jews and Greeks alike' from his mouth, despite his break with the Ephesian synagogue. Some of these may have met and heard Paul as he carried on his tentmaking profession here. The western text informs us that the apostle used the hall 'from the fifth to the tenth hour', from about 11 am to 4 pm. The hall may have been available only between these hours. As did other artisans in the city, Paul probably began his daily tentmaking before sunrise and continued until closing time, in summer about 11 am, when he would have been free to devote himself to the missionary work until about 4 pm when most of the artisans began to work again. Or he may even have used his shop for evangelistic purposes because one would easily talk and establish friendships during tentmaking. The working hours in the Mediterranean depended mostly on the mood of the tradesmen in addition to the climate. The implements of a tentmaker were no more than sickle, awl, needles and waxed thread. The customer supplied the leather or canvas material himself. Tents were indispensable for many purposes during the market days or festivals with many sacrifices where the guests were seated under these and probably a tentmaker was never short of business. In his address to the Ephesian elders (Acts 20.34) as with the Thessalonians, Paul, in order not be compared with the Greco-Roman sophists of the time who were paid for their teaching, reminded them that his hands served both his needs and his companions.

Acts says in Ephesus God accomplished mighty things through Paul. One of these was the apostle's dealings with the exorcists. Despite the fact that Paul's miraculous powers were already well known, compared to the previous occasions, the event at Ephesus is regarded by some scholars just as a popular story. The fame of Ephesus in charm and magic exceeded that of the other cities in the Empire. Its cosmopolitan rich atmosphere attracted soothsayers, purveyors of charms, magicians or other people of similar tasks from the distant corners. The 'seven sons of Sceva, a Jewish high priest' (otherwise unknown) thought that Paul's words were a magic incantation and used them for casting out demons. Unless it was a false claim, his title was used mistakenly by Luke. It has been suggested that his name may be a Greek rendering of Latin 'scaeva' which means 'left-handed' and, naturally enough, is encountered in epitaphs belonging to gladiators. The appearance of the word 'exorcism' in Acts 19.13 is regarded as the earliest use of the term in both Christian and Greco-Roman literature. Their attempts did not succeed, and they themselves were overpowered by the evil spirit they sought to control. As a result of this incident, some Ephesian practitioners of magic collected and burned their books, said to have been worth 'fifty thousand silver pieces'. Since a silver piece was about a good day's pay, a drachma, this would mean about 140-years' wage of a worker. The burning of books of magic by rulers is mentioned in ancient literature. However, here it is the owners of the books who by their own free will did it and thus disclaimed their connection with past magic. Paul's fame reached the extent that the handkerchiefs or aprons which touched his skin were credited with miraculous healing power and carried to the sick.

During the time of Paul's missionary works Christian congregations of smaller or larger sizes are thought to have existed in Colossae (Col 1.1), Laodicea (Col 4.13), Hierapolis (Col 4.13), Apamea and in other places such as Miletus, Smyrna, Pergamum, Thyatira, Sardis and Philadelphia. Whether Paul visited all of these cities is not known. Groups of believers from the country around Ephesus may have come to listen to his preaching and invite him to their cities for short stays. He had probably visited and met fellow Christians at some of these cities as he travelled from Pisidian Antioch to Ephesus. In his letter to Philemon of Colossae (22) Paul asks for a guest room for himself. During his long stay in Ephesus Paul was probably in close contact with the churches of smaller or bigger size he had founded on his previous journeys. Visitors and letters he received kept him informed about the developments in each of them. This was a time when people regarded letters more seriously and Paul in order to make up for his bodily absence wrote and sent letters to the churches he founded. The news he received from Corinth was disturbing. The city was just across from Ephesus on the other side of the Aegean and there must have been a heavy sea traffic between the ports which kept the apostle up to date with the developments there.

Paul's letters to the Corinthians constitute his most extended correspondence. Scholars dwelling on some of Paul's remarks in the surviving letters believe that, in addition, the apostle wrote a few more letters to the same church and that some parts of these may have been incorporated in the surviving ones.

Capital piece decorated with three menorahs from a synagogue. Archaeological Museum. Corinth.

(opposite) Commemorative silver coin (*cistophorus*) minted at Ephesus. Ephesus Museum. Selçuk. On the obverse it bears the portraits of Claudius and Agrippina. The reverse shows the Ephesian Diana (Artemis). It was minted for the marriage of the couple and Agrippina's elevation to Augusta in 50 CE.

Paul says that in their answer to his letter the Corinthians wrote to him and requested his answers to some questions, such as relationships in marital life and the behaviour of women, the physical resurrection of the dead, etc. Some Corinthians were also split into factions according to the apostle they favoured: Paul, Apollos, Kephas (Peter) and perhaps others of whom we have no knowledge. Some Gentile Corinthians who seem to have constituted socially an elite group claiming that they had knowledge that idols did not exist, continued eating sacrificial meat even after becoming Christians and were thus offending their more simple-minded brothers who believed in idols. In a similar manner some Christians seem to have failed to understand the meaning of a communal meal and turned it into a Roman symposium. According to the Roman custom of the time the guests were seated at different tables and rooms in accordance with their status. The amount or quality of the food and wine served to them was also different. Thus while some of the believers went hungry some got drunk, as at a symposium.

In addition to the above-mentioned problems a group of Corinthians, probably the same group of higher status than the rest, had reached a negative opinion about Paul's apostleship. It seems that Paul had offended them by refusing their offer of help and instead had worked for wages. Paul's refusal of their help was found insulting. They accused Paul of being inconsistent because they knew that he had accepted the help sent by the Macedonian churches. They ridiculed Paul's working with his hands. They began thinking that Paul was not trustworthy due to the fact that he had not returned after he left Corinth and kept on changing plans, finding reasons not to return. The negative opinion of this group had been fired by some apostles who seem to have arrived in Corinth after Paul's departure. Recommending themselves, these compared Paul's unimpressive physique and unskilled rhetoric with their superior stance. Accepting the offer of the Corinthians who were antagonistic to Paul they won their sympathy. These apostles to whom Paul sarcastically refers as 'superapostles' challenged Paul's authority.

Thus Paul wrote to the church of Corinth answering their questions at length. He told them that he wanted to spend the winter with them and continue to Judea with the collection. Timothy took the letter to its destination by way of Macedonia but returned after achieving nothing. From Paul's second letter we learn that he made an urgent trip to Corinth. Although it is not mentioned, he probably sailed directly to Cenchrea and returned by the

same way. A direct voyage should not have taken long because we are informed that after sailing from Ephesus in 84 BCE the Roman dictator Sulla reached Piraeus on the third day. From Paul's second letter we learn that this was a very distressing visit. Failing to achieve his objective, insulted and humiliated before the Corinthians, perhaps by the other apostles, he returned to Ephesus defeated, his authority badly shaken. He could not accept defeat but he did not want to make 'another painful' visit and his only alternative was to write another letter to the Corinthians which he says Titus took across the Aegean.

Although Acts is silent about it, the apostle might have been imprisoned during his stay in Ephesus. In his letters to the churches at Corinth and Philippi he repeatedly refers to his sufferings. In his letter to the Romans, which he wrote from Corinth the apostle says that Aquila and Priscilla 'risked their necks' for him (16.4) and in 16.7 he mentions 'Andronicus and Junia' as his fellow prisoners. Again sometime later writing to the church at Corinth Paul repeats the persecutions he suffered here: 'We do not want you to be unaware, brothers, of the affliction that came to us in the province of Asia; we were utterly weighed down beyond our strength, so that we despaired even of life. Indeed, we had accepted within ourselves the sentence of death' (2 Cor 1.8-9). If this bondage took place in Ephesus, the charge which led to his imprisonment is not known. The imprisonment may have also affected Paul's plans to visit Corinth. It has been suggested that the Ephesian Jews may have built up a case against the apostle to detach themselves from him, charging him with diverting sums of money which had been collected from the churches he knew, as a relief fund for the mother church at Jerusalem, some of which he may have been carrying with him and that normally would have been sent to its destination. In 2 Cor 12.16 Paul admits that the so-called superapostles who showed up at Corinth claimed that he 'was crafty and got the better of' them by deceit, and was skimming off gifts, that is to line his own pockets. The Ephesian Jews may have approached the Roman governor, and persuaded him to imprison Paul. If he was imprisoned it is not known when and how he was released. It has been suggested that such events may have been the reason why Paul met the elders of Ephesus in Miletus rather than visiting the city. Some scholars hold that Paul's letter to the Philippians was also written during his Ephesian imprisonment.

Writing to the church at Corinth in 1 Cor 15.32 Paul refers to his fighting with beasts at Ephesus. In the Roman world one would have faced wild animals by becoming a professional beast fighter in the arena which was out of question in Paul's case or when one was to be exposed to them in the arena something which would have been avoided by Paul's Roman citizenship. It is believed that, when he wrote the words, the apostle imagined himself as a fighter of this kind struggling not in flesh but spiritually against the wickedness he encountered at Ephesus. Such entertainment was at the top of the public festivities in the city of Paul's time and he may have witnessed them in the theatre or the stadium. In 1 Cor 4.9 writing from Ephesus he says 'God has exhibited us apostles as the last of all, like people sentenced to death [in the arena], since we have become a spectacle to the world, to angels and human beings alike' he compared them with combatants in the arena. The apocryphal *Acts of Paul* dwells on the apostle's imprisonment in the city. Here, the Ephesians became angry at Paul's speech and imprisoned him until he would be thrown to the lions. Eubula and Artemilla, wives of eminent Ephesian men, visited Paul in the prison at night 'desiring the grace of divine washing'. The apostle took them to the Aegean shore and baptized them. The naming of the Hellenistic watch-tower and barracks which was once the closest to the sea as 'Paul's prison' may have been inspired by this event. The conversion of two prominent women caused more persecutions. Paul was put into the stadium and a huge lion, already baptized by the apostle in another story, was let loose on him. But the beast lay down at his feet. The other animals which followed the lion also did not touch the apostle who stood like a statue in prayer. Then a hailstorm poured down killing the other wild animals, and saving the lion which escaped to the mountains. The hailstorm also killed some men and sheared off the governor's ear. Seeing what happened he accepted Christianity and was baptized. The tradition of his exposure to the wild animals may have been derived from Paul's words in 1 Cor 15.32 that he 'fought with beasts' or in 2 Tm 4.17 that he 'was rescued from the lion's mouth'.

Beast fighting in the arena. Tralles Museum. The *bestiarii* were gladiators who fought against wild beasts.

In 1 Cor 16.8-9 Paul says that he wanted to stay in Ephesus until Pentecost 'because a door has opened for me wide and productive for work'. Some scholars think that the wide-opened door which Paul mentions was occasioned by the annual festival of Artemis and it provided a splendid opportunity to do missionary work, for during the feasts the city was crowded with people from all over Anatolia, the islands and the other side of the Aegean. Artemis' cult was worshipped in the Levant, Cyprus and in Europe as far away as the Iberic peninsula: the span between Caesarea Maritime and Massilia (Marseille). She was a truly syncretistic goddess and had for centuries attracted devotees. At Ephesus the Anatolian Great Mother had been identified with their own goddess Artemis by the Greek settlers a thousand or so years earlier. The two major festivals of Artemis were in March-April and May-June and held annually.

The sanctuary of Artemis occupied the same flat piece of land throughout its history; a piece of land frequently flooded by the Cayster. Excavations have shown that the first temple was built in the second half of the eighth century BCE and consisted of a cult room open to the west in an enclosure of wooden columns. The small findings which were discovered in the lower levels below this structure indicate that the spot may have been regarded as a sanctuary since the Mycenean era. In front of the temple building there was an altar. The marble column fragments (British Museum) inscribed with his name show that Croesus of Lydia (560-546 BCE) was the major contributor to the construction. The new building had a larger cult room and was surrounded by a double row of columns — altogether 106 in number. Again its new altar stood to the west. The colossal temple, which in the Hellenistic times would become famous as one of the Seven Wonders of the World on account of its beauty and vast size, was built above this small temple.

Shrine of the Great Mother (Mihraplık, 'place of niches') at the eastern base of Mount Pion, once on the shore of the Aegean. Fifth century BCE to through the Hellenistic period. The holes may have served for placing offerings.

Until Croesus built the temple the Greek colonists had a shrine on the eastern skirt of Mount Pion where the worship of their goddess Athena may have been syncretized with that of the Great Mother or Cybele. Croesus is said to have moved these settlers from their homes here to the city which had by that time had grown near the Artemis Temple. With restorations and alterations the buildings of Croesus survived for two hundred years until 356 BCE, when they were put to fire by one Herostratus, who is said to have wanted to immortalize his name with the event.

Though the Greek Artemis (Roman Diana), goddess of chastity, the hunt and associated with animals, would seem to bear little resemblance to a fecund earth mother deity she was a nature goddess (Mountain Mother) and often in her representations flanked by animals. The statues of Ephesian Artemis are perhaps the most visible evidence of the syncretistic tendency of ancient religions and of the tolerance, courtesy extended to the deities of others, from whom elements, or the entire deity, might be adopted. With the influence of Greek art, by Paul's time, her figure had lost its large buttocks and big breasts, the symbols of fertility, and was on the way to assuming the slender shape of a Greek goddess. The most prominent feature of her image were the ovals covering her upper body on the waist. These are thought to have represented the testicles of bulls sacrificed for her during cultic ceremonies and nailed to a wooden statue of the goddess.

The construction of the Hellenistic Temple of Artemis may have begun shortly after 334 BCE, when the city opened its gates to Alexander's army. It has been claimed that Alexander wanted to build the burnt edifice himself. The Ephesians, however, saying that it was not befitting to a god to build a temple for another god, built it themselves. The building erected in its place was set on a higher platform against flooding and had a third row of columns at the front. The cult statue stood in her shrine, in a long, narrow hall according to Pliny the Elder surrounded by 127 columns, forming a forest of marble. It is not known how much of this building reached Paul's time but like the rest of the sanctuaries its management suffered the civil wars and economic crisis which took place before the Roman imperial era. The repair work carried out under Augustus was not sufficient and the actual restoration would wait for Titus (78-81 CE). Augustus had allowed the temple to retain the lands which it had controlled in the past and redefined its right of asylum precinct to a standard radius of one *stadium* (185 m). One of the novelties, which had taken place with the introduction of the Roman rule, was the placing of an altar dedicated to Augustus in the sacred ground surrounding the temple building. In the course of time altars for other Roman Emperors would be added to this. At Paul's time it was still the richest institution in Ephesus and loaned money to the citizens with low interest rates. Its vaults were open to those who wanted to deposit money or other riches. In 399 BCE, after their safe return from the East at Cerasus (Giresun) Xenophon and the generals, selling the spoil set aside one tenth of the money for the Apollo of Delphi and Artemis of Ephesus. In addition to gifts and offerings the temple had its own estates, livestock, fisheries and similar sources of income.

Temple of Artemis. Selçuk. Looking toward the Ayasuluk hill. The standing column is made of drums belonging to different columns. It is 14 m high, 4 m shorter than its original.

The temple of Paul's time would be destroyed in 263 by Goths. After the acceptance of Christianity as the religion of the Empire in the fourth century, what was left of it began to be dismantled and in the succeeding century a church was built on its ruins. Some of its marble served as building material for the Church of St John on the nearby hill of Ayasuluk and the Church of Mary and bishop's palace next to it at Ephesus.

As Demetrius of the silversmiths' guild claimed in Acts 19.24 Artemis, worshipped throughout the province of Asia, was supported by the number

Statue of Artemis from Ephesus. Second century CE. Ephesus Museum. Selçuk.

of pilgrims who attended her festival. Writing at the end of the first century Philostratus says that the temple was 'open to all who would sacrifice, or offer prayers, or sing hymns; to suppliants, to Hellenes, barbarians, free persons, to slaves'. She brought great wealth to the city, not only through the sale of votives and various offerings, but because of the large numbers of people who poured into Ephesus for her various celebrations and festivals. These people had to be fed, lodged, entertained and generally looked after and there was extra work and extra money for everyone, be they jewellers, money-changers, bakers, tentmakers, fishmongers, shoemakers, musicians, prostitutes or doctors. Festivals then, as now, were big business, producing revenue for the city that held them.

Paul's influence aroused the enmity of the guild of silversmiths who made miniature shrines, statuettes and various offerings for dedication to Artemis. Some of them showed the goddess flanked by stags or other animals. These objects dedicated to Artemis were carried in public processions throughout the city, and then placed in her temple, a parade of some 90 minutes.

For the silversmiths the humiliation that Paul's preaching caused their business was perhaps more damaging than the actual drop in their sale of souvenirs. The number of Christians who stopped buying offerings for Artemis could not have been high. Some fifty years later the situation may have changed because when he wrote to Trajan possibly from Amasia in Pontus, Pliny says 'it is not only the towns, but villages and rural districts too which are infected through contact with this wretched cult [Christianity]' and that it was not possible to find anybody to buy the flesh of sacrificed victims.

Instigated by one Demetrius a riot broke out. Paul's preaching obviously was threatening their trade. After Demetrius had called together the members of the guild and spoken to them about the economic consequences of Paul's teaching, they angrily rushed forth into the street shouting that their religion was in danger. Ephesus was a temple-keeper (Greek *neokoros*), a status which implied the existence of, with all the officials assigned for her rituals, a divine tie between the city and the goddess, perhaps earlier than the extension of the term to the temples of the imperial cult. Thus on a matter like the protection of her cult the Ephesians were very sensitive. The people who worshipped her cult were the best customers of the Ephesian silversmiths whose guild may have comprised other artisan groups working in metal. Their excitement caught the attention of other people, most of whom were ignorant of what was going on. The crowd failed to find Paul because his

Theatre. Looking toward the Arcadiane and the silted port. Ephesus. In the distance to the left the hill is topped by St Paul's prison.

asiarch friends had warned him 'not to venture into the theatre'. On their way to the theatre they seized the apostle's Macedonian companions, Gaius and Aristarchus.

The scene of the riot was the Hellenistic theatre which was somewhat smaller than today's but was being enlarged sometime in the reign of Claudius, perhaps at the time of Paul's stay. Here the Jews put forward another Jew named Alexander to address the mob, to explain that they had nothing to do with Paul and his friends. The Jews knew that because of the privileges granted to them by the successive Roman Emperors they were not popular with the Greek residents of Ephesus and the latter looked for the slightest chance to show them as instigators of unrest in the eyes of the Roman governor. The Jews may have also feared that the protesting crowd might turn against them for their own hostility to images. Acts says that the crowd refused to hear Alexander's defence and for about two hours shouted 'Great is Artemis of the Ephesians!'.

The 'town clerk' or secretary finally managed to calm the crowd. This was not a Roman official but the most important member of the city council. Among his various administrative responsibilities was avoiding disturbances of any kind in the city. The assembly which had gathered here was not a 'lawful' one. The last thing that the town clerk wanted to happen was possibly the involvement of the Roman authorities in a dispute about Artemis. Some ten years earlier Claudius had decreed a number of measures against the economic corruption of the temple. This had already diminished the income of the institution. The riot may have provided the Romans with a reason to interfere once again. He told them that the supremacy of Artemis was not in peril, that the men they had dragged to the theatre had neither robbed the temple nor blasphemed her, and everybody knew that her statue had fallen from the sky. Thus when Paul preached that 'gods made by hands are not gods at all' (Acts 19.26) this was not questioning the origin of their goddess — for the fact was that at that time in her temple Artemis may have been represented by a wooden image or a monolith thought to have been a meteorite, both believed to have fallen originally from heaven: as was the case with the Palladium of Troy about a millenium before such images were afforded apotropaic qualities. Some two centuries before Paul's time the Romans heard that unless they possessed the image of the Great Mother (Cybele) at Pessinus in Phrygia they could not defeat Hannibal and thus carried it, perhaps a black meteorite, to their capital. He also pointed out that for any complaints and disputes the courts were available and the real danger was not the loss of trade but rather 'being charged with rioting', for which the Roman authorities might punish the whole city. Epigraphic evidence supplied by the excavations at Ephesus has shown the existence of guilds of silversmiths, perfume-makers, wool-workers and others. Dating sometime after Paul's era we hear of disorders created by labourers such as bakers in nearby Magnesia on Meander (Menderes Manisası), construction workers in Pergamum and Miletus or linen-workers in Tarsus. Romans were always very suspicious of all kinds of organizations and their outlook is best shown by Trajan's letter to Pliny in which the latter requested the creation of a voluntary fire brigade in Nicomedia (İzmit) which had recently suffered a big fire: 'If people assemble for a common purpose, whatever name we give them and for whatever reason, they soon turn into a political club'. Paul wished to go among the crowd to defend himself, but was prevented from doing so by the disciples and 'some of the asiarchs also, who were friends of his'.

The exact position of the asiarchs, 'the title is first used by Strabo' and later by Acts, in the politico-religious organization of Anatolia can not be described. From the episode in Acts and the epigraphic material brought to light by

Stele dedicated to the family of Polemo by the guild of leather-workers. Cibyra (Gölhisar) on the border of the provinces of Lycia and Asia. Turn of the first century CE. In Greek it mentions the names of four members of the family who held one or the other or both of the posts of asiarch,

lyciarch and high priest between the end of the first century BCE and first century CE. Scholars have suggested that Paul's Ephesus stay during the third journey falls into the asiarchy of Tiberius Claudius Hiero in about the 55s CE.

excavations we understand that there could be more than one at a given time. Although the title does not seem to have given them any official standing the evidence shows that they were certainly in charge of the festivals and games. One of the titles the reigning asiarch sometimes, but not always, bore was 'high priest of Asia'. Just as the town clerk's speech sounds as if it is defending the Christian message, so also is the reference to the asiarchs, the representatives of the official Roman cult as friends of the apostle. Thus, Paul's troubles were just the result of popular hostility, against which he was protected by friendly Roman officials. After the riot, the Roman officials may have compelled Paul to leave the city.

Paul had already decided to go to Corinth again, and through Macedonia where he wanted to collect the fund that was waiting to be taken to Jerusalem. Acts informs us that 'after encouraging' his disciples at Ephesus 'he bade them farewell and set out on his journey'. The complete details of this journey are not known. 2 Cor 2.12 mentions a trip to Alexandria Troas where he expected to meet Titus. He had been unable to preach there when he stopped during his previous journey and now wanted to make it up. He worried about the answer to the so-called 'severe letter' he had sent by Titus. Eager to leave Ephesus as soon as possible at this stage of events the apostle, instead of trying to find a vessel bound for Alexandria Troas, probably began walking in the direction of Smyrna.

The road he may have taken was one of the earliest in the region built by Manius Aquillius, the first Roman governor of Asia in 129-126 BCE. After Smyrna it continued by way of the ancient coastal cities of Cyme and Elea and ended at Pergamum. From here, crossing the mountains in the direction of Antandros, it went to Gargara and Assos or Neandria, probably most of them with Jewish communities. All of these places may have heard of Paul and some of the inhabitants even known him personally. Or, as Epaphras had done in the Lycus valley, some of Paul's disciples may have preached the Gospel.

The last time Ephesus is mentioned in connection with Paul is in the Pastoral Letters. In 1 Tm 1.3 Paul writing from somewhere in Macedonia says that he instructed Timothy to stay at Ephesus to continue working there and that he intends to join him (4.13). He also asks Timothy 'Stop drinking only water, but have a little wine for the sake of your stomach and your frequent illness' (1 Tm 5.23). A later tradition holds that Timothy was martyred on the *embolos*

(Curetes Street) in the reign of Nerva (96-98 CE) for criticizing the Dionysian feast and buried on Mount Pion.

In Alexandria Troas Paul waited for a while for Titus to join him here. When the latter did not show up, anxious to receive the news Paul sailed to Macedonia. He may have found Titus at Philippi and received the good news of the repentance of the church of Corinth.

When Paul later says that he preached 'from Jerusalem all the way around to Illyricum' (Rom 15.19) he may have had in his mind his activities during this journey. Illyricum proper was some 100 km north of Dyrrachium. The part known by the Romans as *Illyris Graeca* comprised western Macedonia and extended as far south as Epirus. When 'he travelled throughout those regions' providing 'many words of encouragement' he may have been in or near Illyricum preaching the Gospel. By then the Roman province of Macedonia was established and Illyria had become a part of it.

From Macedonia Paul travelled south into Greece, 'where he stayed for three months'. Acts does not give any details but it was again at Corinth that the apostle stayed because, in addition to seeing the results of his struggle,

Roman road and the bridge which was once over the Tuzla Çayı, perhaps the Satnioeis of the *Iliad*.

he wanted to collect the fund that the Corinthian church had raised for the mother church at Jerusalem. It was during this Corinthian stay that the apostle wrote to the church in Rome.

Paul's letter to the Romans is the longest and regarded the most important of Paul's extant correspondence. It is also the earliest document which mentions the existence of 'Christ-faith' in Rome. The fact that the apostle took such care in writing the letter indicates that already there was an important Christian community which consisted of Jews and Gentiles in Rome. Paul told them that he had long wished to visit 'God's beloved in Rome', but he had been prevented from doing so. Now, however, as soon as he has taken the collection from his missionary churches in Macedonia and Achaia to Jerusalem, he planned to go to Spain and to stop at Rome on the way (Rom 15.23-9).

Ancient road descending to the harbour of Assos.

Acts 20.3 informs us that just as the apostle was about to leave directly for Syria by ship — either from Cenchrea or Piraeus — the Jews in Greece had prepared an ambush against him. Paul may have planned to embark on a ship carrying Jewish pilgrims to Jerusalem for Passover but a shipload of hostile Jews would not have found a better opportunity to get rid of him than during the voyage when he had no chance to escape. He may not have wanted to take the risks of a long sea journey because of the fact that he would be carrying all the money collected for the poor at the Jerusalem church. Paul's party was split into two. While several of Paul's companions sailed to Alexandria Troas, Paul, accompanied by some of them, travelled to Philippi by land. Leaving Athens he would have had to travel to Thebes and Lebadia (Levadhia). Lake Copais on whose shore the latter was located is now a large plain. The road continued by way of Chaironia (Kapraina) where in 87 BCE Sulla had defeated King Mithradates VI of Pontus to Lamia, and through Dhomokos (Thaumacoi) and Pharsalus (Farsala), where Julius Caesar won the victory against Pompey in 48 BCE, to Larissa from where one would reach the coast by way of the Tempe Pass. Paul's party may have reached the Via Egnatia at Allante and continued to Philippi by way of Thessalonica and Amphipolis. Luke may have joined him at Philippi. After arriving at Philippi the apostle and his friends would travel to Neapolis and sail to Alexandria Troas to meet their friends. At Philippi the party seem to have waited until the Jewish 'feast of Unleavened Bread' was over. Acts 20.6 informs us this sea voyage, which had taken about two days during his second journey, from the opposite coast, took five days. The ship may have made stops at more islands or been delayed by bad weather. Here they joined some of their friends who had already arrived and all together they stayed in Alexandria Troas for a week. The length of their stay was perhaps determined by the availability of favourable winds.

It was on this last visit to Alexandria Troas that the famous episode involving the young man called Eutychus occurred. On the evening of the first day of the week Paul, his friends and some other Christians met in one of the houses at Alexandria Troas 'to break bread'. It is not known if the expression is used just in its ordinary meaning as the opening of a Jewish meal or for the Lord's Supper. The first day of the week may have been Saturday or Sunday according to the Jewish or Roman reckoning, respectively. During this gathering Paul began a very long lecture and 'talked on and on'; and the young Eutychus who was listening seated on a window-sill of the third floor fell all the way down, onto the ground. He had fallen asleep, maybe not only because of the long lecture but also too much wine or the stuffy air caused by the resin torches or lamps in the room. Everybody thought that Eutychus was dead; but Paul throwing himself on the young boy's body told the others that there was nothing to worry about and the boy was fine. Paul

Port of Assos. Across the Aegean is Lesbos (Midilli).

resumed his discourse. From what survives at Alexandria Troas it is impossible to construct the civil architecture of the time, but from what Acts tells, a building of three storeys with rooms encircling a central inner courtyard, typical for the time, is imagined.

Paul's stay at Alexandria Troas was probably caused by the absence of an earlier ship leaving in the direction of the Mediterranean. Finally a vessel going to Miletus was found, probably again carrying Jewish pilgrims who travelled to Jerusalem for Pentecost which was now about thirty days ahead.

During this part of the journey the apostle and his friends were separated for a day or so. While the rest of his party embarked the ship Paul 'was going overland' to Assos. The reason is not known. The apostle's companions may have decided that the hand of the plotting Jews in Greece might have reached here and they did not want to put Paul on a ship whose passengers they did not know. Or Paul may have wanted to be by himself for a while to clear his mind. By then he had heard plenty of things about Rome from Priscilla and Aquila, the Christians there, and the idea of taking his ministry to Rome, his final goal, heart of the Gentile world, and beyond, to Spain had been on his mind for a long time. He was now about sixty, 'an old man' as he would later refer to himself, an age only a very low percentage of the population, according to the study of surviving funerary inscriptions some five percent, reached at that time. He may have wanted to make best use of his time in Troas since sailing down the Aegean, especially to double Cape Lectum, was much slower than riding because of opposing currents and

Northern harbour of Mytilene. At the time of Paul the small acropolis at the tip of the peninsula to the right was an island.

Roman period ruins at the northern harbour of Mytilene.

winds. He may have worried about the challenge that was waiting for him at Jerusalem. In Rom 15.31 he asks for prayers that he 'may be delivered from the disobedience in Judea' and that his collection for the Jerusalem church may be acceptable. After concluding his preaching at daybreak Paul 'departed'. He left for Assos, the closest city with a harbour. Because of the fact that the distance between the two cities was not less than 40 km and may have taken more than a day on foot, the apostle may have ridden or used a carriage. The road to Assos left the city by the Neandria Gate and after descending to the junction where today the cold and hot springs (Kaplıcalar) exist turned toward the sea and followed the coast. After crossing the Satnioeis (Tuzla Çayı) it turned in the direction of Assos, avoiding Cape Lectum (Baba Burnu) and ran by way of Smintheium (Gülpınar).[1] The latter was a shrine dedicated to Apollo and famous for its Hellenistic temple built in the second century BCE. The temple housed a statue of Apollo Smintheus, crushing a mouse with his foot and its reliefs were related to the Trojan War.

Set on a steep sloping hill, with spectacular views across the bay to Lesbos, Assos (Behramköy) was a beautiful and ancient city founded in the seventh century BCE by immigrants from the nearby island of Lesbos. It was now long past its great days, when in the fourth century BCE, the eunuch Hermias of Atarneus (near Dikili), a former student of Plato in Athens, ruled here and whose friend Aristotle, lived here for three years from 347 BCE on and married Pythia, the ruler's niece. Assos is the birth place of the former boxer and later Stoic philosopher Cleanthes, who later moved to Athens and studied under Zeno and who is known as the first person who suggested a heliocentric view of the cosmos. Most of the ruins which have reached the present belong to the city which stood here at the time of Paul's journeys. The city had also recently seen some rebuilding in the reign of Tiberius (14-37). The white porous marble that the region supplied was used for coffins and due to the hastening of decay by the seeping of moisture took the name *sarcophagus* (literally 'flesh-eating'). Upon arrival at Assos, without going up the acropolis he may have walked down to the small harbour.

The expression 'we took him aboard' in Acts 20.14 gives the impression that some kind of arrangement was made. It is probable that Paul found a

[1] At the beginning of the *Iliad*, Apollo, who was worshipped in the region as 'Smintheos' ('mouse god') sends a pest to the lines of the Achaians, which he does not stop until he is appeased.

Southern harbour of Mytilene.

caique to take him when he spotted the ship carrying his friends, and thus the vessel saved the time that sailing in and out of the harbour of Assos would take.

In addition to Luke the apostle's party included Sopater from Beroea, Aristarchus and Secundus from Thessalonica, Gaius from Derbe,[2] Timothy, Tychicus and Trophimus from Asia (Ephesus) carrying the money collected as gift for the poor Christians at Jerusalem. Despite the absence of representatives from Corinth and Philippi the visit of Gentile Christians to Jerusalem from such distant churches would manifest the solidarity of the Gospel of Paul for both Jewish and non-Jewish Christians. Paul, after all the rumours about his pilfering church money, may have thought it better if each delegate carried the money of his own church. This was many years' collection and more than one person was needed for its both protection and transportation. It is possible that for convenience of transportation the collection may have been turned into gold.

Before reaching Miletus their boat made stops at Mytilene on the island of Lesbos, and Samos. The first island they stopped at and spent the night was famous for its woman poet Sappho who lived there in about 600 BCE. The acropolis of the early city was on the small island separated from the mainland by a narrow channel. Beginning in the Hellenistic period the settlement spread to the other side of the channel and at the time of Paul Mytilene was a flourishing Roman city with its major harbour in the north.

[2] Some texts have Doberus which makes the city in Macedonia.

Next day they took anchor and sailed as far as a point opposite Chios. It is known that in antiquity some vessels by dropping passengers and cargo at such nearby spots saved the time of sailing in and out of the Bay of Smyrna. The next port was Samos which then occupied the site of ancient Pythagoras (Pithagorio) and faced the peninsula. This island was an extension of Mount Mycale (Samsun Dağı, 1,200 m) and its rich history was inseparable from that of western Anatolia. Theodoros of Samos was one of the architects of the Artemis Temple of Ephesus in the sixth century BCE. Herodotus tells us that then Samos was ruled by the famous tyrant Polycrates until he was lured to Magnesia on Meander (Menderes Manisası) and killed by the Persian satrap Oroetes. The island was also famous as the home of the rhapsodists known as the Homerids, who kept the oral tradition living as late as the fourth century BCE. Greek folklore holds that the island was the birthplace of Hera and where she spent the wedding night, which lasted three hundred years, with Zeus. It was also the birth place of both the famous mathematician Pythagoras (late sixth century BCE) and Epicurus (342-271 BCE). Paul is said to have encountered the followers of the latter at the Athens' agora during his previous journey.

After spending a night on Samos, the ship carrying Paul and his friends crossed to Anatolia and spent a night at a point named Trogyllium, mentioned only in the AV (Acts 20.15). The name is thought to have been inserted in

Christian inscription influenced by the Septuagint on the western wall of the theatre. Miletus. Third century CE or earlier. Below seven symbols, of which five survive, and their magical names of seven vowels in each cartouche an unnamed archangel is addressed with the same formula: 'archangel, protect the city of Miletus and those who live in it.' Each planet is represented by a mysterious symbol. The bottom line is an adjuration. The inscription is thought to have been added when the theatre served as a citadel.

Mount Mycale (Samsun Dağı). View before entering into the strait between Turkey and Samos from the south. The piece of land to the left belongs to the latter.

the text by someone familiar with the area for local colour. It is an inlet situated at the southern tip of the cape formed by the Mycale which was once called Mount Arinnanda by the Hittites. The islets are named Sandolin (Sandal Adası), Philion (Su Adası) and Argennon (Tavşan Adası). Research around the bay has not brought to light any ruin of the Pauline era. When Mursili II (1321-1295 BCE) captured Apasa (Ephesus) some of the city's population had sheltered here. The King's Annals describe the mountain as being 'very steep and extends out into the sea. It is also very high, difficult of access, and rocky, and it is impossible for horses to advance up it'. The Hittites besieged the mountain and the enemy had to surrender because of hunger and thirst. Later visitors have named the only bay on this coast 'Paul's anchorage'. Eighteenth-century travellers say that the mountain was infested with tigers and other wild beasts even in their time.

In antiquity Miletus enjoyed several harbours and it is not possible to know which one Paul's ship entered. In fact its number of sheltered harbours was one of the reasons why it had been a popular place of settlement in the early ages. The peninsula had seen Minoan and Mycenean settlers and the city had been passed back and forth between the latter and the Hittites who called it Milawata/Millawanda. In the middle of the eleventh century BCE it was settled by Ionians, probably from Athens, and in time became the most prosperous Ionian *polis*. Although the ninety colonies that the ancient literature attributes to Miletus is thought too high, the Milesians may have founded as many as half of this number. It was not just the number of its colonies but names like Thales, Anaximenes, Anaximander, Hecateios or Hippodamus that made the city famous in the intellectual world of antiquity. Following the

Ionian revolt (499-494 BCE) which was initiated by Miletus the Persians besieged and took the city and sacking it moved the survivors to the Persian gulf. Miletus was relieved from the Persian rule in 334 BCE by Alexander the Great and was ruled successively by the Seleucids and the Attalids of Pergamum until it became a part of the Roman Empire in 129 BCE. Ancient literature informs us that when Caesar was caught by the Cilician pirates of nearby Pharmacusa (Farmako Adası) he provided the ransom from Miletus, and having been released, securing some ships from the city, destroyed the pirates' lair and later crucified most of them in Pergamum. By Paul's time the easternmost harbour on the side of the Gulf of Latmus (Bafa) was already silted up. Silting had also reached the so-called lion harbour whose connection with the Aegean was then probably no more than a narrow channel. The other two harbours were on the opposite side of the peninsula and were open to the sea. One of these, the theatre harbour which faced to the west and was situated away from the mouth of the Meander, is known to

Remains of the harbour monument at the lion harbour of Miletus. 63 BCE. It was named after the two lion statues which stood at its entrance. This harbour may have been the one which Strabo refers as being 'closed' by a chain. The monument was dedicated for the victory of Pompey over the Mediterranean and Aegean pirates. One of the tritons which decorated it has partly survived.

Inscription in the spectators' seats at the theatre. Miletus. Second-third centuries CE. In Greek it reads: 'Place of the Jews who were also called godfearers' (or pious) (*topos Eioudeon ton kai Theosebeion*). The last word *theosebeion* which may also be translated as 'worshippers of God' or 'devout' is, in addition to Acts, used by other ancient literature and also encountered in epigraphy after the third century CE and could be used for Jews as well as proselytes or Gentiles attached to the synagogue. The poor Greek of the inscription has caused extensive discussions. It is sometimes translated as 'Place of the Jews and Jewish sympathizers, and the godfearers'.

have been active in the Roman period. When Paul's coaster sailed into the harbour the city stood on a promontory. Today, it lies some 7 km from the sea, because of the activity of the Meander River, moving and depositing silt which was already becoming a major problem then. The river was then on the opposite side of the gulf, but now partly encircles the site in a large loop round the north. Most of what Paul would have seen at Miletus, ie the council house, the gymnasium and the stadium were built by the city's Seleucid rulers. What survives today, however, was mostly built by Marcus Aurelius (161-80 CE) and his wife Faustina and other Antonine rulers, after Paul.

The origin of the Christian congregation in Miletus is not known. While Paul may have visited the city previously during his long Ephesus stay and proclaimed the Gospel, the Milesians may have also attended his preaching in Ephesus and been converted. The existence of a Jewish congregation in the city, although it dates after Paul's time, is attested to by an inscription on one of the steps of the theatre. From Josephus we learn that at the time of Julius Caesar Milesian Jews told the proconsul in Tralles that, in spite of the latter's previous instructions, the Jews were being attacked by Gentiles in the city and forbidden to observe their sabbaths and follow their other rites. The Roman proconsul replied in favour of them.

The wording in Acts 20.16 that 'Paul had decided to sail past Ephesus in order not to lose time in the province of Asia' have led some to think that Paul had chartered a vessel. But it seems that like the other passengers on board Paul had to follow the schedule of the ship-master. The riot which

Harbour. Cos.

compelled Paul to depart all of a sudden from Ephesus was still in Paul's mind and he may not have wanted to get entangled with either Jews or Gentiles unfriendly to Jews. Obviously his departure from Ephesus was not as quiet as told by Luke. Miletus was closer to the Mediterranean and enjoyed better communications with central Anatolia and consequently was the most popular harbour for changing ships sailing in this direction and thus the choice of the captain instead of Ephesus. Paul may have wanted not to lose the occasion created by unforseen changes in his sailing schedule. He may have stayed here about a week because it would take some time for his messenger to reach Ephesus. The north-south land communication in western Anatolia was interrupted by mountain ranges running east-west toward the sea, and in Paul's time one had to climb over the Mycale peninsula or take the longer but smoother route through Magnesia on Meander to take a message from Miletus to Ephesus. Thus he sent to Ephesus and called to him the elders of the church. It is not known where Paul summoned his audience. This meeting is regarded one of the most touching episodes in Acts. He reminded his listeners of the opposition of the Jews in Ephesus which had caused him tears and trials. Now he was on his way to Jerusalem expecting more affliction, which he saw as a culmination of his ministry. He was deeply concerned about heretics and schismatics in Ephesus, and he admonished the elders to remain alert, commending them to God. The elders wept that they would not see the apostle again. After he decided that his mission here was over, putting the church in their care he was escorted to the harbour and embarked on a ship and continued his voyage to Jerusalem.

Paul's remark that he 'left Trophimus sick at Miletus' in 2 Tm 4.20 informs us about a another visit of the apostle to the city, after he was released from his first imprisonment in Rome.

Acts (21.1) briefly informs us that the vessel 'set sail, made a straight run for Cos, and on the next day for Rhodes and from there to Patara'. These were just stopovers for almost all vessels which sailed from the Aegean to the south. Cos, just some 30 km from Halicarnassus on Anatolian soil, was the last Greek outpost in the east. In antiquity the island boasted one of the three most important sanctuaries of the healer god Asclepius (the other two being at Epidauros and Pergamum). The trees of the sacred grove had been cut down in 32 BCE to supply wood for making war ships for the fleet Antony assembled at Ephesus before his defeat at Actium. A few years before Paul stopped here Claudius was poisoned (on the initiation of his wife Agrippina Minor, mother of Nero) by his physician Xenophon who was a native of the island. It was owing to this physician that Claudius had remitted the island's taxes in perpetuity. Thus the act of this obscure doctor had led to the emergence of Nero, who would be the instrument of Paul's martyrdom. The island was famous as the home of Hippocrates, the 'Father of Medicine' who has left to the modern world, in addition to his medical treatises, the medical oath named after himself. The stop at this island may have been more exciting for Luke than the rest. Horace says the remedy of worst hangovers is Coan wine and recommends it to be used with fried shrimps. At the time of Paul the island was also a major silk producer whose market was soon to be usurped by imported Chinese silk.

Byzantine church in the agora. Cos.

Next day they sailed and passing Cape Triopium where Cnidus is situated and spotting the islands of Tylos and Nisyros to the southwest and Symi in the opposite direction arrived at Rhodes, the capital of the island of the same name. Founded toward the end of the fifth century BCE at the crossroad of the east and west the island had a well-known maritime history. It was famous for the Colossus which was the work of the sculptor Chares of Lindos. In antiquity the statue was regarded as one of the Seven Wonders of the World. The fame of the Colossus led some people in the Middle Ages to think that the Colossians to whom Paul had written were the inhabitants of Rhodes. At the time of Paul's visit the Colossus was already in pieces lying buried where it had crashed in an earthquake in about 227 BCE.[3] This was a gigantic bronze statue of Helios. It was some 40 m high and 250 tons, standing on the mole or the hill overlooking the harbour where the Castello stands today. A Rhodian tradition places it where St Paul's Gate is now. The statue commemorated the defeat of the siege of Demetrius Poliorcetes who failed to capture the city, his nickname 'Poliorcetes' standing for 'Besieger of Cities'. This bronze statue showed the god naked and wearing a gold crown of rays with his arms stretched out in front. It is said that it could be seen from a distance of some 100 km.

After the battle of Pydna because of its support of Macedonia, the island was treated with suspicion and punished by Rome by the establishment of a free port at Delos. During the following period Rhodes would either be

[3] The last time that the remains of the statue was heard of were in 667 CE when a Jewish merchant from Emesa (Homs) bought it from the Umayyad Caliph Muawiyah. He had it sliced into strips and removed it to the mainland. The bronze was loaded on nine hundred camels and sent across the desert where it disappeared.

St Paul's harbour. Lindos. Rhodes. The church to the right is named after the apostle.

punished or rewarded according to its behaviour during Rome's wars. In the century before Paul's it had become a popular shelter for the Roman aristocracy banished from the capital. At the time that Paul's ship entered into the port of Rhodes the island had been deprived of its nominal independence (since 44 CE) because in a demonstration some Roman citizens, perhaps money-lenders, had been impaled. The island's later inhabitants held that the apostle stayed here and preached and converted many, and the tradition chose Prochorus, one of the seven deacons (Acts 6.5) as the first bishop of the island. Another tradition claims that Paul and his friends got off the vessel at Lindos, which was one of the most important cities on the island, in the small harbour situated at the foot of the acropolis where pilgrims since ancient times had been worshipping Athena Lindia. The small bay is named St Paul's harbour.

The Anatolian part of Paul's return trip which began at Assos came to an end at the Lycian port of Patara (Gelemiş). Here the apostle and his companions had to find another vessel, obviously a larger one which could sail the high seas, bound to Tyre on the Phoenician coast (Acts 21.1-2).

Lycia was a small and strategically unimportant province and left free by Rome until 43 CE. It consisted of mountains between the Indus (Dalaman)

Delikkemer ('aqueduct with holes'). A section of the system which brought water to Patara at Paul's time. The inscription above the opening to the right informs us that it was repaired in 69 CE by Vespasian.

River on one side and Cape Chelidonium on the other, with little cultivable land, and except for the timber supplied by its cedar, pine or juniper forests its resources were limited and thus not worth Rome's effort of turning it into a province. This protected it from the attention of greedy Roman bankers until the time of Claudius who on the pretext of punishing the Lycians for the death of some Roman citizens during internal strife, added Lycia to Pamphylia, making them a single province. Patara on the southwest Lycian coast was one of the principal cities of the region. Its original Lycian name was 'Pttara', later mistakenly thought to have derived from the Latin *patera,* a sort of cup. The settlement obviously owed its existence to a narrow but long natural harbour at the mouth of the River Xanthus (Eşen Çayı) which is now flowing to the northwest of the ruins. The city was also famous for its oracle of Apollo, where it was believed the god spent the winter, having been in Delos for the summer. Apollo was the most popular god in Lycia where he was worshipped as 'Lykeios' ('wolf god', Greek *Lykos*, 'wolf') and had given the region its name. In the *Iliad* some of the Lycians fight on the side of the Trojans under Sarpedon and Glaucus. Most of what is visible at the site today had not been constructed when Paul changed ships here and dates mainly from the late first and the second centuries. One of the monuments that Paul might have seen on his very brief visit was the precursor of the theatre which lay on a hillside to the southeast by the dunes and across the bay. Recent excavations have revealed the remains of a light tower, which was dedicated to Claudius, stood at the entrance of the harbour. It is the earliest of its kind discovered to date.

Sometime after Paul stopped here Patara became one of the Roman grain supply stations and in the reign of Hadrian (117-38), who is known to have visited the city, a large granary was built on the western side of the quay. The giant rock-cut cistern situated on top of the mountain above the theatre, whose history must have dated to the pre-Pauline period, is clear evidence of the scarcity of a sweet water supply in this dry and hot region. The miracles of St Nicholas, who was born in Patara and would later become famous as the Bishop of Myra in the fourth century, which are related to the discovery and purification of wells, were not incidental and show the value that the local people afforded to water.

Leaving Patara Paul's ship began a long voyage of some 600 km to Tyre. This could be done in front of the westerly winds without making a stop. The fact that the ship did not follow the Anatolian coast but sailed by the south of Cyprus show that it was a large vessel. As they sailed by the island Paul may have wondered what had become of the false prophet Bar-Jesus, and Sergius Paulus, his first non-Jewish convert known by name and if he had remained true to his conversion. The information that in Tyre Paul and his party 'sought out the disciples' may have been mistaken since Paul had passed through the city during his trips between Antioch and Jerusalem and should have known some of the Christians here. Before he left the city his Christian friends implored him that, whatever he did, Paul should not go to Jerusalem. Paul's objective however was to deliver the money collected for the poor at Jerusalem and thus show how much the Gentile Christians living so far away cared for their brothers at the mother church. From Tyre the ship sailed a short distance, some 50 km, and called in for a day at Ptolemais/Acco. Although Acts does not say anything the city may have been visited by the apostle again before he travelled between Antioch and Jerusalem. Ptolemais, originally founded by Ptolemy II, Philadelphus ('brother-loving') of Egypt, was made a Roman colony and settled with veterans from the Syrian legions by Claudius following the troubles between Jews and Samaritans. It is not clear if they travelled from Ptolemais to Caesarea by sea or land.

Here Paul stayed at the house of Philip the evangelist and his four prophetess daughters. Agabus — the same man who had predicted the famine years ago — came down to the city, and having been warned by the Holy Spirit implored him not to go to Jerusalem. Arriving in Jerusalem Paul and his companians spent the night at the house of Mnason, a Cypriot convert. The distance between Caesarea and Jerusalem is some 100 km and the western text places Mnason's home at an unnamed village on the route between the two cities, perhaps a reduction because of the need for an overnight place on the way.

At Jerusalem Paul's first act was to see James and the elders of the church and to hand over the money that had been collected from the smaller or larger churches in his missionary field for the general relief fund. This collection and its delivery carried a special meaning for Paul, for he may not have been sure of its acceptance by the Jerusalem church. Such an act, on the part of the latter, would symbolize the acceptance of Paul's work and the unity of Jewish and Gentile Christians. He had not forgotten that at the Jerusalem Council he was told 'to be mindful of the poor' (Gal 2.10). Acts does not mention if it was accepted or rejected. Those whom Paul met were delighted at the success that had accompanied Paul, the extraordinary missionary who had been to so many places that they would never see, and who had managed to found so many churches so far afield. Paul was told that some of the Jewish Christians were informed that Paul was 'teaching all the Jews who live among the Gentiles to abandon Moses' and 'not to circumcise their children or to observe their customary practices'. Jerusalem now was full of pilgrims who had come for Pentecost and would soon hear of Paul's arrival. They suggested that he could show the population his observance of the law by paying the purification expenses of four poor men. They may have suggested that Paul use the collection for such a good cause. This may have also enabled them to disclaim any contact with it. They may have even suggested that they were willing to accept the collection on condition that Paul did as he was told. Although Acts is silent about it some scholars believe that this suggestion seems to have been accepted by Paul because providing four poor men with the requirements of a Nazirite's vow was an expensive act. In Paul's case the vow involved the sort of purification ceremony which included the shaving of heads and offering sacrifices by those who came from foreign lands. It lasted one week. Paul did as he was told but his act was misinterpreted.

One of the two pieces of identical stones which survived from the destruction of the Jerusalem Temple by Titus in 70 CE. İstanbul Archaeological Museums. The inscription in Greek reads: 'No intruder is allowed in the

courtyard and within the wall surrounding the temple. Those who enter will invite death for themselves'. The second inscription is fragmentary and in the Rockefeller Museum, Jerusalem.

Before the ceremonies would be completed some pilgrims from the province of Asia, most likely coming from Ephesus, saw Paul and, in addition to the usual accusation that he taught against the law, said that he had taken his Gentile friends into the area reserved only for Jews at the Temple. Here as one passed from the court reserved for the Gentiles into the one open to the Jews, there were notices in Greek and in Latin informing the non-Jews about the capital punishment the tresspassers would suffer. Paul would certainly know about this, and the accusation did not stick. Otherwise, it might have ended with his and Trophimus' lynching. The accusation was supplemented with claims of Paul's attack on Judaism and its institutions. This was, however, outside the concern of Roman officials.

The events which took place beginning at Pentecost of 57 CE and during the following two years or so after Paul's arrival in Jerusalem, his false accusation, his arrest and stages of his trials are beyond the scope of this volume. Today the second-century-CE remains of the so-called Pontius Pilate's praetorium, where once the trial of Jesus was held, on the Via Dolorosa, is believed to occupy the spot of these events.

Acts informs us that Paul was kept prisoner for two nights in the compound of the Roman force next to the Temple. This would have been the fortress built at the northwestern corner of the Temple by Herod the Great and named 'Antonia' after Mark Antony. When Paul was moved to Caesarea, four hundred of the total escort of 470 soldiers went as far as Antipatris (Ras el-Ain) which was some 50 km from Jerusalem. While some scholars try to justify the high number by emphasizing the Jewish uprisings in the region some believe that Luke tried to increase the importance of the prisoner Paul. This city was founded (rebuilt and renamed) by Herod around 9 BCE and named after his father Antipatros. This road, which also crossed Lydda (Tel Aviv's suburb of Lod) was the most common route between Jerusalem and the capital, and probably used by Paul on different occasions.

Caesarea was first established by the Phoenicians in the fourth century BCE and had survived as an anchorage with a tower which was probably built by one of the Stratons who ruled Sidon in the fourth century BCE.[4] It

[4] The sarcophagus called the 'Mourning Women' in the İstanbul Archaeological Museums from Sidon (Saida) is thought to have belonged to a Straton.

seems to have survived as an obscure settlement under the rule of the Ptolemies or the Seleucids. Here Herod the Great (37-4 BCE) built a brand new port city and named it Caesarea after his benefactor (Caesar) Augustus (27 BCE-14 CE) sometime during the last decade of his reign. Later it would be known as 'Maritima' ('by the Sea'; Sdot Yam) with the adjective to distinguish it from Caesarea Philippi, which was built inland to the north of Lake Tiberias by Herod's son Philippus. Even if Josephus' saying that the size of Herod's port 'was not less than the Piraeus' was exaggerated it was the only one in which ships could shelter in a distance of about 80 km along the Mediterranean shore. Josephus informs us of the immense work done to create the harbour moles of which the southern one can still be distinguished. The city was surrounded by a wall and Josephus mentions the existence of a theatre and amphiteatre and the forum with the Temple of Augustus and the Goddess Roma. The latter rose on a high podium and dominated the harbour probably on some of the vaulted structures which have been brought to light by excavations in this area. An aqueduct supported on 10-km of stone arches carried water from a spring on Mount Carmel. The city owed its future development to its port. The remains of the theatre of Herod, partly rebuilt, stand to the south of the city. Excavations have brought to light remains which date to the Herodian buildings. Among them there is a building with a large pool of freshwater as its nucleus. It has been speculated that these may have belonged to the palace of Herod and some of the premises of 'Herod's praetorium' (headquarters-building) where according to Acts 23.35 Paul was held in custody for two years. The word is used to refer to the official residence of the Roman provincial governor. The Roman governor of the time Marcus Antonius Felix (54-59) listened to Paul's case and decided to keep him in custoday. He was guarded by a centurion, something reserved for prisoners of high status, and it is possible that he lived in light custody so that he could be visited freely. It has been speculated that he may have written some of his letters, possibly those known as 'prison letters', addressed to the Ephesians, Colossians and Philippians and Philemon during his imprisonment there. Christianity may have first been introduced to the city by those who fled from Jerusalem after Stephen's death. Acts informs us that Philip settled here after travelling in the region. The city is also the place where the conversion of Cornelius by Peter took place.

Felix was a freedman of Claudius, also brother of Pallas who was the emperor's advisor, and had served in Syria and Judea for two years before he took up his new post. Claudius' act of giving such a post, which was usually held by members of the equestrian order, was the first of its kind and a scandal. In addition to the information supplied in Acts 24.26 Josephus informs us that Felix was known to have accepted bribes. In 59 when Felix was recalled to Rome, for an inquiry about a riot that broke out in Caesarea between the Jewish and Greek inhabitants, the handling of Paul's case was left to the new procurator Porcius Festus (59-62). Acts informs us that when Festus asked him if he was willing to go and stand trial in Jerusalem Paul refused for he knew the result of such a trial. It has been speculated that King Agrippa's words to Festus, 'This man could have been set free if he had not appealed to Caesar' (Acts 26.32) may not reflect the situation truthfully. Paul took the ultimate step and as a Roman citizen asserted his right to appeal to the court of the Emperor which was granted. This action did certainly not guarantee more favourable treatment. Nero would be likely to pass over his case leaving it to the praetorian prefects who presided over most of the civil actions. But he would at least be far away from those who had sworn not to eat or drink until he was done away with. Despite Paul's appeal, Festus could have tried the case and passed his sentence on Paul. He, however, preferred to grant the apostle's request and get rid of this notorious Jew with Roman citizen status.

Relief with prisoners and their guard from Miletus. Second-third centuries CE. İstanbul Archaeological Museums. A group of condemned probably being led to the circus by their custodian. The prisoners are clad in loincloths and bound by a rope around their necks from their shackles.

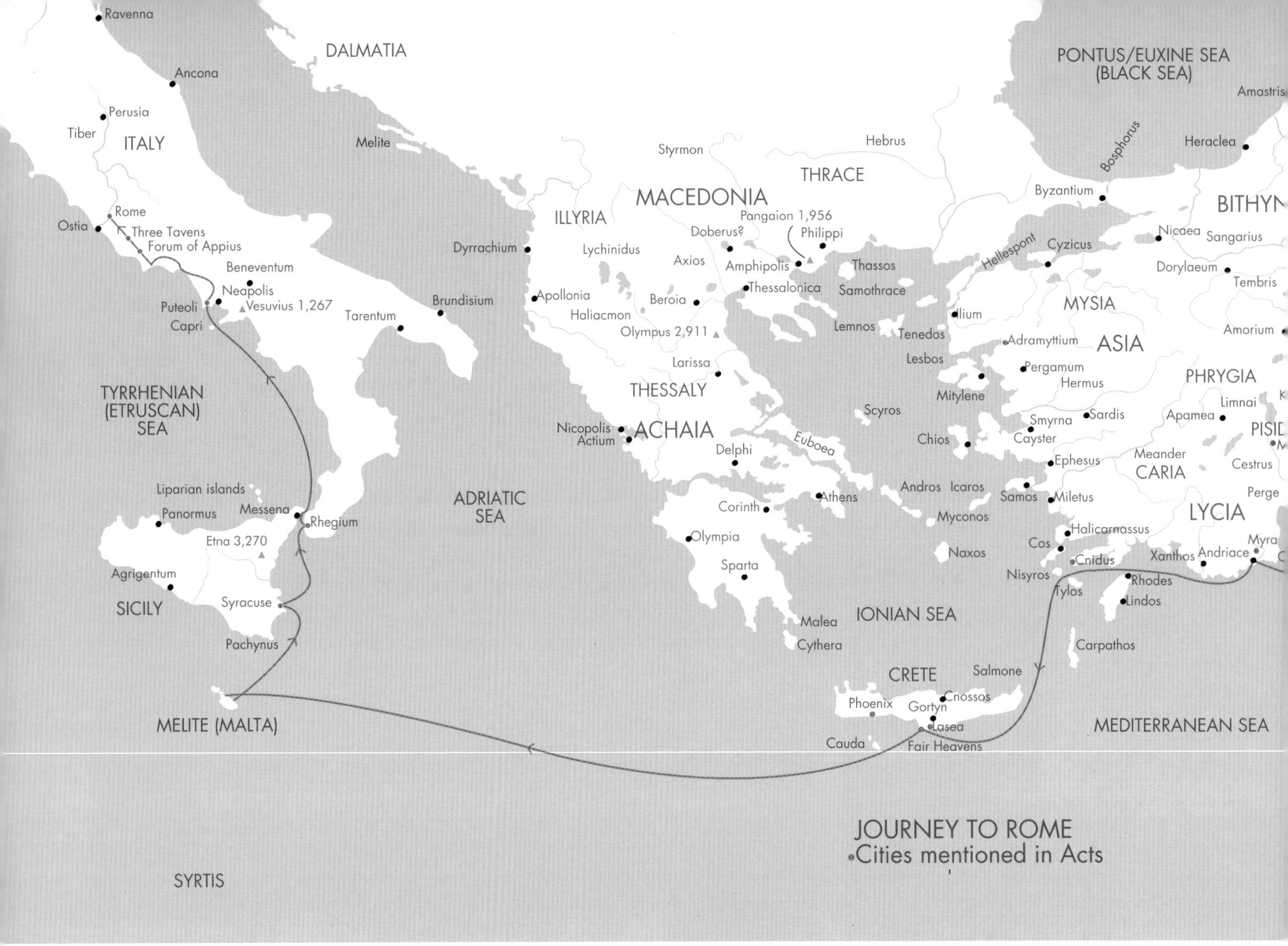

JOURNEY TO ROME

•Cities mentioned in Acts

Ravenna
DALMATIA
Ancona
Perusia
Tiber
ITALY
Melite
Rome
Ostia
Three Tavens
Forum of Appius
Beneventum
Neapolis
Puteoli
Vesuvius 1,267
Capri
Tarentum
Brundisium
Dyrrachium
Apollonia
TYRRHENIAN (ETRUSCAN) SEA
Liparian islands
Panormus
Messena
Rhegium
Etna 3,270
Agrigentum
SICILY
Syracuse
Pachynus
MELITE (MALTA)
SYRTIS
ADRIATIC SEA
ILLYRIA
MACEDONIA
Styrmon
Hebrus
THRACE
Pangaion 1,956
Philippi
Doberus?
Lychinidus
Axios
Amphipolis
Thassos
Thessalonica
Samothrace
Beroia
Haliacmon
Olympus 2,911
Lemnos
Tenedos
Larissa
THESSALY
Nicopolis
Actium
ACHAIA
Delphi
Euboea
Scyros
Athens
Corinth
Olympia
Sparta
Malea
Cythera
IONIAN SEA
Andros
Icaros
Myconos
Naxos
CRETE
Phoenix
Gortyn
Cnossos
Salmone
Lasea
Fair Heavens
Cauda
MEDITERRANEAN SEA
PONTUS/EUXINE SEA (BLACK SEA)
Amastris
Bosphorus
Heraclea
Byzantium
BITHYN
Nicaea
Sangarius
Hellespont
Cyzicus
Dorylaeum
Tembris
Ilium
MYSIA
Amorium
Adramyttium
ASIA
Pergamum
Hermus
Lesbos
Mitylene
PHRYGIA
Limnai
Apamea
Smyrna
Sardis
Cayster
Chios
PISID
Ephesus
Meander
CARIA
Cestrus
Samos
Miletus
Perge
LYCIA
Halicarnassus
Cos
Cnidus
Nisyros
Tylos
Rhodes
Lindos
Xanthos
Andriace
Myra
Carpathos

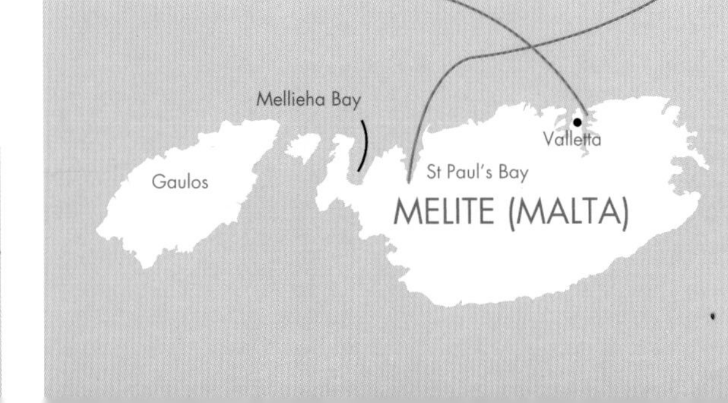

Ph
Cauda

JOURNEY TO ROME

Caesarea — Sidon — Myra — Cnidus — Fair Heavens — Malta — Syracuse — Rhegium — Puteoli — Forum of Appius — Three Taverns — Rome

In the autumn of possibly 59, Paul and a group of other prisoners, probably unlike Paul who were not Roman citizens 'on appeal' but condemned to death, on their way to Rome's arenas, were put on a coaster at the port of Caesarea. Paul was accompanied by Luke and Aristarchus, 'a Macedonian from Thessalonica'. The latter was one of the delegates who had accompanied the apostle on his return from the previous journey carrying Jerusalem his city's gift. The only way that they could be allowed to travel with Paul was that they passed as his slaves unless they bought their tickets as passengers. Paul's case and his long imprisonment must have been known by the officer and he was allowed to have servants with him. The vessel was from Adramyttium,[1] a small prosperous town on the western coast of Anatolia opposite Lesbos, perhaps sailing back home.

It was late in the season, probably already late fall, the end of the navigation period for the high seas and the centurion[2] Julius from Cohort Augusta, who was in charge of the prisoners, was unable to find a vessel which would have taken them directly to one of the ports of Italy, a trip which would, in summer months, have taken about two months. It has been speculated that in Acts Cohort (I) Augusta, which was a contingent of the Roman legion based in Syria during this period, might have been included to increase the prominence of the prisoner Paul. The frequent appearance of centurions in Acts gives Paul's story a military atmosphere like the crucifixion of Jesus, at which there was a centurion standing. The season was so late that the centurion may have even regarded himself lucky in finding a vessel bound for the Anatolian coast where he intended to find another vessel bound for

[1] Situated on the coast to the southeast of present-day Edremit. The city is rarely mentioned in ancient history. It was said to have been founded by the Lydians and was the government post of Croesus (561-546 BCE) of the fabulous wealth until he succeeded his father Alyattes. Later during the Peloponnesian War in 422 BCE it was settled by the exiles expelled from Delos by Athens.

[2] A post similar to that of non-commissioned officers (NCOs). He could continue serving in the army after the expiry of his period of enlistment. A Roman legion consisted of 10 Cohorts of usually 480 men, and each cohort into six centuries of 80 men.

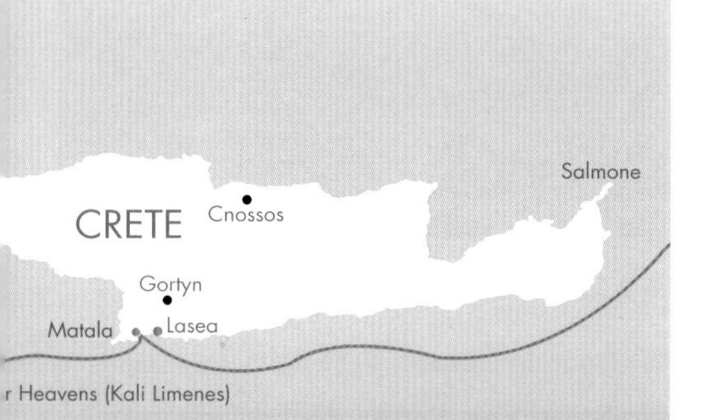

Rome. He may have also planned, after Adramyttium, to continue to Alexandria Troas and crossing to Neapolis travel by way of the Via Egnatia and the Via Appia across to the Adriatic. This was the route that Ignatius is thought to have followed when taken to Rome sometime at the beginning of the following century.

After a brief stop at Sidon, where Paul was allowed by his custodian 'to visit his friends who took care of him' the vessel set sail, its captain making use of the currents which run to the north along the coastline of Syria and Anatolia and round the lee of Cyprus 'because of the headwinds, and crossing the open sea off the coast of Cilicia and Pamphylia' (Acts 27.2-5). This long sea voyage must have been very melancholic for the apostle. The silhouette of the coast toward Antioch and Taurus brought him memories of his childhood, friends and relatives. Beyond the worn-out peaks of the Taurus were Derbe, Lystra, Iconium and another Antioch and probably many other places not named in Acts where his early converts still lived and preserved Paul's memory, some continuing his work. Thus, rounding Cyprus by the north with the help of the current and winds blowing off the Anatolian coast they sailed westward and leaving Cape Chelidonium (Yardımcı Burnu) behind, made a stop at Myra before continuing on toward the Aegean. At the time that Paul's vessel sailed into Andriace, Myra's port, the region after going through the Persian and later the Ptolemaic hegemonies had been in 43 CE annexed to the Roman Empire by Claudius. The western text (Acts 27.5) informs us the voyage to Myra had taken fifteen days, a length of time which may infer delay at one or

Cape Chelidonium (Yardımcı Burnu) and the Chelidonian isles (Beş Adalar).

Roman sarcophagus in Andriace, the silted port of Myra looking south. Last quarter of the second century CE. In the background are the ruins of the warehouses which were lined along the wharf.

more ports because of inclement weather. Isolated from the interior by mountains reaching 3,000 m the region did not have any other natural resource than its timber but owing to its location on the major routes of the maritime trade it was in close contact with the rest of the world. 1 Mc 15.23 mentions Lycia among the places to which the Roman consul sent letters in the middle of the second century BCE to inform the region about the imperial protection granted to the Jews. Although the existence of such letters is doubted, there were probably Jewish communities of varying sizes in most of such ancient and commercial urban centres of Lycia.

Short stays in the ports of Lycia were not something particular to the vessel which was carrying Paul. Since antiquity it had become a custom for the maritime traffic coming from the eastern Mediterranean to shelter at one of the well-protected Lycian ports to replenish the wine and water stock on board and wait for favourable winds. These ports offered shelter to a crowded sea traffic leaving for all directions, the Aegean, the Mediterranean or the Black Sea, throughout the navigation season and also gave captains a chance to do some extra business on the way.

Myra, situated by the Myros (Demre) River, was an important city of Lycia in the classical and Hellenistic eras. The city's name is thought to have come from the Greek word for myrrh. Strabo describes Myra being on a high crest, that is the precipitous hill which now rises behind the theatre. The inhabited city was on the level ground at the foot of the hill. In the apocryphal *Acts of Paul*, the apostle comes to Myra where he cures several locals. Later Thecla joins him here.

The city's harbour was at the mouth of the River Andracus a few kilometres away. Like Patara this would become an important port under the Romans for supplying grain to the troops campaigning in the east, and the granary which was dedicated to Trajan and Hadrian is the largest of its kind in Anatolia. The cistern built below the courtyard of the market place is also probably the largest in Anatolia and gives an idea of the large number of vessels to which it must have supplied sweet water in the hot season when the rivers dried up.

Even though it was late in the season there must have been other vessels anchored along the dock, some probably already having decided to spend the winter here. Among these ships the centurion Julius came across a freight vessel carrying wheat to Italy. This was probably one of those which regularly carried grain between Egypt and Italy and the captain during its last voyage stopped at Myra because of opposing winds. The season was already late for such merchant ships and this was perhaps a private vessel which had already done a round-trip grain voyage and was trying to squeeze a risky second one into the short sailing season left. Some time ago Claudius had given special privileges to ship-owners who could carry a minimum of 70 tons of wheat. The cost of sea transportation for merchandise was about one fifth of the cost by land and Egypt was the most important grain source for Rome. Suetonius informs us that the Emperor 'employed to ship grain [to Rome] even in the winter season. For he guaranteed the merchant shippers profits by assuming himself any losses someone might suffer on account of storms, and he instituted great rewards for those who built merchant ships'. The half-walnut-shell shape of a usual grain freighter made it known in Greek as *gaulos*, 'bathtub'. It generally bore a single sail carried on a single mast, and had to be towed in and out of harbour. Since the loading and unloading of its cargo took several weeks, a vessel could usually make a single round-trip in a sailing season. To sail the high seas these grain freighters were the best because in addition to offering room and safety they did not make calls at many ports. While a trip from Italy to Egypt took maximum two weeks under the northwesterlies the return was against strong winds, mostly northeasterlies. On their return journeys such vessels would sail toward the southern coast of Anatolia and after Rhodes continue by the north of Crete in the direction of Syracuse and further. Since they had to sail upwind, frequently, when chased by opposing winds, they sheltered in Lycian harbours. However, since they were built for carrying cargo the facilities were limited. Apart from a few cabins used by the skipper or important passengers such as the owner of the cargo or his agent there was no room but the deck. The ship's supply consisted only of water. The travellers had to have their own food, bedding, wine, etc.

The centurion probably bore a *diplomum,* a pass which gave him priority to use any facility he required with or without payment until he took his prisoners to Rome. Such passes were issued in the reigning emperor's name by the governor of a province, outlining the route that the pass was valid for and carried a date of expiry. The death of the emperor led to the cancellation of the pass as well. The ship carrying Paul, rounding Rhodes by its north, sailed toward Cnidus to make a final stop before sailing across the Ionian (Aegean) Sea. The city was one of those mentioned in the circular letter written by the Romans for the support of the Jews (1 Mc 15.23). However, they failed to shelter there because of the inclement weather and continued sailing between Nisyros and Tylos. The captain probably hoped to run straight across the southern Aegean to the island of Cythera. However, the rig of the period depended almost entirely upon one square sail and his ship would make so much leeway that, instead of reaching Cythera off the Peloponnese

Harbours of Cnidus. The trade that the city carried out with the vessels was the major income of Cnidus. The inhabitants also supplied the ships with some basic necessities such as wine, almonds, dry figs, onions and so on. The city was famous for its Temple of Aphrodite and the goddess' statue made by Praxiteles (active 350-330 BCE). It was lost shortly after it was produced. Roman copies of it have survived to the present in numerous museums.

to round Cape Malea, he would find himself on the rugged northern coast of Crete where harbours into which he could shelter were scarce.

Nevertheless, following the relatively safe waters and rounding Cape Salmone (Sammium) the captain sailed to Crete's southern coast. In remote antiquity the island was ruled by Minos, the son of Zeus whom he begot by ravishing Europa whom he had kidnapped disguised as a bull from Phoenicia. Here Minos' wife Phasiphae would fall in love with the white bull of Poseidon and after meeting the animal disguised in a wooden cow that Daedalus made for her she would beget the Minotaur, a monster with a bull's head and a human body. But this was all left in the past. The island had lost its power after the economic and social feuds in the third century BCE and became a lair of pirates until it became a Roman property in 67 BCE. At the time of Paul, together with Cyrenaica in North Africa, it was organized as one province with Gortyn for its capital.

Christianity may have first been introduced to the island by the Cretan Jews who were, according to Acts 2.1.1, among the pilgrims in Jerusalem during Pentecost. Paul's letter to Titus is usually believed to have been composed after his death and toward the end of the century. In the letter we are told of the rivalry on the island between the Christian bishops and the Jewish-Christians who preached the narrow type of Christianity. Paul blames the inhabitants, repeating the words of one of their own sages: 'Cretans have always been liars, vicious beasts, and lazy gluttons'; a quotation which is known to have belonged to the sixth-century-BCE poet Epimenides. Paul's words at the begining of his letter 'I left you in Crete so that you might see what remains to be done and appoint presbyters in every town, as I directed you' infers another visit to the island. Tradition regards St Titus as the first Bishop of Crete.

The southern coast of Crete had its own dangers. Even after entering the lee of Cape Salmone (Sammium) navigation was not easy. About half way along the inhospitable coastline they sheltered at a place called Fair Heavens (Kali Limenes), near which was the city of Lasea, one of the two ports of Gortyn. This was a small bay, a little east of Cape Matala. Here they waited for some time for the improvement of the weather which, however, became worse.

The ship would have to winter in this 'unfavourably situated' harbour; it had no protection but a few islets lined in front of the bay against the wind. The captain, pilot and the crew, and certainly the centurion, who was in command of the ship as the army officer, decided to leave the port at the first opportunity. When the wind turned to a southerly, listening to the advice of the captain and the owner of the ship it was decided not to miss the opportunity and weighing anchor they

St Paul's Chapel at the foot of the Ori range near Phoenix. Crete.

sailed. At a point some 50 km across the gulf beyond Cape Matala on the other side of the Gulf of Messara the Ori range makes a short low extension which creates two harbours. The name of Phineka, which is on the west side may have been the Phoenix mentioned in Acts. Today it is shallow and open to winds. It is thought that at the time it was a large and deep bay and has been changed in time by earthquakes. It was, however, risky because if the wind changed to an east-northeasterly there was nothing a pilot could do. The captain had no choice but set his ship at the best angle to the wind and let himself be driven, something which happened to Paul's vessel. After they rounded Cape Matala and entered into the large Gulf of Messara the ship seems to have been caught in the one of the worst northeastern winds, called *euroclydon* ('northeaster') in Acts.

The ship ran before the wind by the little island of Cauda (Gavdos) which is the southernmost point of Europe. It rises to a height of some 350 m and gives little shelter to ships. They were able to get the dinghy under control and took it aboard, thus preventing it from foundering. They also passed ropes under the keel, and then up and around the vessel, for if the cargo of grain got wet it would start to swell and spring the ship's timbers. Then the tackle was thrown overboard. They were afraid that the wind would hurl them to the shoal of Syrtis some 400 km away on the Libyan coast. Strabo informs us that here in many places the deep waters 'contain shallows, and the result is, at the ebb and the flow of tides, that sailors sometimes fall into the shallows and stick there, and that the safe escape of a boat is rare'. As she rounded Cape Malea the Odyssey had found herself in a similar situation and Homer says after being chased by winds for nine days she was thrown as far as the country of the Lotus-eaters on the Libyan coast, somewhat farther than Syrtis.

The storm continued: 'Neither the sun nor the stars were visible for many days'. Aware of the danger of the bulk cargo, they were compelled to dump some of it. The third day they added some of the ship's gear to the things they had thrown out to lighten it. Although the order of the steps that the ship's crew took may not have exactly followed the account in Acts, scholars reflect that the details fit operations which should be done under such conditions. The ship by then had drifted somewhere to the central area of the Adriatic Sea; exhausted and lacking food they had lost all hope of survival.

It was round about midnight on the fourteenth day of the strong cold northeast wind which had driven them across the Mediterranean from Crete

Fair Heavens (Kali Limenes). Crete.

St Paul's Chapel above the Fair Heavens (Kali Limenes). Crete. To the left below the big cross is the cave where, traditionally, Paul is said to have stayed.

that the lookouts on the bows heard the sound of breakers ahead. Soundings were taken and the water was rapidly shallowing. The crew sensed by their sailors' instincts that land was not far away. As the ship was blown on the dark winter night toward the rocks, 'they dropped four anchors from the stern' to keep the vessel where it was until day broke. The sailors now attempted to abandon ship and began lowering the dinghy. Paul saw what they were up to and pointed out to Julius that, if the sailors went, the ship was certainly doomed. Without these professional hands they would be helpless. Thus the flight of the crew was avoided. They cut the ropes securing the boat to the anchors and let it wash ashore. An experienced traveller, Paul guessed that they would have to swim ashore and urged everyone to eat some bread. Paul saying 'Today is the fourteenth day that you have been waiting, going hungry and eating nothing' (Acts 27.33) must be read metaphorically for none of them would have survived this long without eating. Following Paul's advice they ate something and set to work alongside the sailors to throw the rest of the wheat cargo into the sea. When dawn broke and visibility improved they saw that they were near an unknown shore, so they cut the anchors, let go the two big steering paddles and headed for the beach.

Acts says that the bows hit a sandbank and got stuck. As the ship was breaking up, the soldiers decided that it would be better to kill the prisoners under their charge than give them the opportunity of escaping. This was natural enough, for to lose a prisoner meant forfeiting one's life. Julius intervened for Paul and ordered the soldiers not to harm any prisoners. Those passengers who could swim he ordered to jump overboard and make for the shore first, the rest would follow on planks or pieces of broken timber. There was no loss of life, and all reached the shore safely as Paul had predicted.

They learned that the island in Greek was called Malta (*Melite Africana*) by its inhabitants. The word in Greek meant 'honey' for the island was famous for the quality of the honey which its black bees made. The island was some 30 km long by 15 km wide, and a part of a submerged ridge that once connected Europe with Africa. It had been settled by colonists from Tyre around 800 BCE. Some of the people possibly spoke a version of demotic Greek but most of them spoke a Semitic tongue called Punic[3] by the Romans, whose origins went back to the Phoenician inhabitants of the island. It is possible that some of the words they spoke could be understood by a person who spoke Hebrew or Aramaic, and to the surprise of both his friends and

[3] 'Puni', the Latin name for the Carthaginians.

Western harbour (Phineka) of Phoenix. Looking down from Cape Mouros. Crete.

Church of St Titus. Gortyn. Crete. Its origins may go back to the fourth century CE.

the locals Paul may have achieved some communication with them even if only by some isolated words. The 'natives' of Acts are called in Greek *barbaroi,* ('barbarians'). The term meant a person of unintelligible speech, a person who went 'bar-bar-bar' (Greek *barbarophonoi*, 'barbarous talking') and was not civilized enough to speak Greek. The island had become a part of Rome in 218 BCE during the Second Punic War. Under Roman rule the Maltese were allowed a measure of autonomy.

The friendly islanders welcomed them. Here Paul ventured to help the locals who had already lit a fire by gathering brushwood. As he was putting a bundle of it on fire 'a viper, escaping from the heat, fastened on his hand' (Acts 28.3). When the Maltese saw the snake hanging from his hand they assumed that he must be a murderer, a man whom their deities had allowed to escape from the sea, but would not allow to escape from justice. Paul merely shook it off into the fire. The locals expected him to die but, when he carried on quite normally, they decided that he must be a god. The snake possibly was not poisonous. The island is known to have three species of non-venomous snakes. The legend has it that it was Paul, to this day, that removed venom from all the snakes there.[4]

Publius was 'the chief of the island' (*protos*), the first or chief magistrate there. Acts does not mention that he was converted but he is traditionally credited with having been the first bishop or elder of the church in Malta. The principal cause of Paul's success was that he managed to heal Publius' father, who had fever and dysentery, by the traditional laying on of his hands — an act which was interpreted as supplementing baptism by the giving of the Holy Spirit. The man probably suffered the so-called 'Malta fever' caused by infected goat-milk. Julius, Paul and his attendants stayed three days in the house of the chief magistrate and then left, probably to rent a room in the capital city. It is very unlikely, contrary to local tradition, that Paul was imprisoned in a cave or dungeon. Julius by now had come to trust his prisoner completely and, in any case, it was Paul who of his own will was taking his case to the Emperor in Rome. He must have been informed by Festus before departing from Caesarea that his prisoner 'could have been set free if he had not appealed to Caesar'. The small island was a kind of prison because the sailing season had long been closed and no ships would be available.

Acts records that after the sensational recovery of Publius' father numerous islanders 'came to Paul and were cured'. Luke's medical knowledge may have come into some of such healings for he says 'they paid us great honour and when we eventually set sail they brought us the provisions we needed'. It has been suggested that Luke's brief account of the winter in Malta may have been the result of his failure to understand the language.

Among the three churches commemorating the incident, St Paul of the Sea, St Paul of the Wreck and St Paul Welcomed, the last one was built on the site of an ancient Roman house which was, for a while, thought to have belonged to the important Roman official mentioned in Acts. Furthermore, graffiti depicting a bearded man with the inscription 'Paul' below, in Greek letters, as well as what appears to be a shipwreck scene, would seem to confirm what the Maltese themselves have long believed. Archaeology, however, has shown that the site was occupied before and after the first century CE but not at the time of Paul's journeys.

The traditional site of the wreck, today's St Paul's Bay, does not fit into the very clear description in Acts that the ship came into a place 'where two seas met' (AV Acts 27.41) because the two seas meet further northwest at the

[4] Just as St Patrick is credited with having done the same some four centuries later. Like the Maltese, Cretans also claim that Paul saved them from 'wild beast and noxious animals' which include vipers.

strait between the mainland and the small island of Gozo. It has also been speculated that the geography of the Bay of Mellieha beyond that of St Paul fits better to the description in Acts. In addition to the remains of Roman wrecks found here the bay was once a strait thus more suitable to be a place of 'seas'.

Another island of the same name, *Melite* (Mljet), situated in the Adriatic not far from Dubrovnik has also its own tradition as the place of Paul's shipwreck. The earliest and only known tradition about this second Malta in relation to the incident comes from *De administrando imperio* of the Byzantine Emperor Constantine VII, Porphyrogenitus (913-59 CE) where, speaking about Dalmatia, he says 'also another island, Meleta or Malozeatae. It was here that a viper fixed itself on the finger of St Paul, who burnt it in the fire'. This tradition, about which nothing was heard for centuries, was revived by a local abbot in the eighteenth century and has been kept living since by the islanders at several sites on the island.

St Paul's Bay. Malta. View from the Church of St Paul Welcomed.

Acts concludes the account of the stay on Malta with the words: 'Three months later we set sail on a ship that had wintered at the island. It was an Alexandrian ship with the Dioscuri as its figurehead'. This vessel may have tried what Paul's ship did but luckily had been able to shelter at the island. It was one of those grain-carrying vessels and had probably been lying in that great limestone cleft in Malta's eastern side which is now known as the Grand Harbour. Although it is difficult to make suggestions about where Paul and his companions lived on Malta, their departure point must have been the island's capital Valletta, which had a sheltered bay with a few well-protected harbours where such a large grain-carrying vessel could spend the winter. The prow of the ship they embarked on was decorated with the Dioscuri, Castor and Pollux, sons of Zeus, to whom he awarded immortality by placing their images in the sky as the constellation now known as Gemini ('twins'). Poseidon had made them saviour of ship-wrecked sailors, and granted them power to send favourable winds and Paul's ship seems to have sailed whenever they began to blow. It has been speculated that the Sts Cosmas and Damian are their Christian form. They probably left before the official opening of the sailing season — in early February in 60. The captain must have wanted to catch the grain market as early as possible to get a high price just after the winter, and before the other big grain-carriers began to move up from Alexandria, and left as soon as the southerly winds began.

Sicily, his next landfall, lay only about 100 km to the north. They passed Cape Pachynus (Passero), the southernmost promontory of the island. The favourable wind seems to have failed them because Acts mentions a three day stop at Syracuse. Once the greatest port in the central Mediterranean, Syracuse was at this time no more than just another big commercial port in the communication network of the Empire. It was originally a Corinthian colony founded on the island of Ortygia, separated from the mainland by a narrow channel over which there was a bridge at Paul's time connecting it to the city, Neapolis. It had two harbours, the great harbour and little harbour. Paul's ship having failed to sail north probably sheltered in the first one. At Paul's time much of the Hellenistic city protected by the walls of the Euryalos castle existed. The theatre, which was cut from the living rock of the mountain in the late fourth and early third centuries BCE by Athenian prisoners, commanded the view of a great harbour.

From Syracuse they headed on up north, passing under the giant bulk of Mount Etna (3,270 m) which at this time of the year would have been covered with snow. People believed that Zeus buried the titan Typhon under the mountain and the monster belched its fire and smoke from time to time through Etna's cone. Suetonius says that Caligula on a visit to Sicily, woken up at Messena 'suddenly fled in the middle of the night, terrified by the smoke and noise which came from the crater of Etna' and cancelling his travel plans returned Rome. At the time of Paul it had already become a touristic attraction and on the top of the mountain to placate its wrath people still burned incense. The ship called in at Rhegium (Reggio di Calabria), the port on the toe of Italy. Some of the travellers may have wanted to disembark here, but it seems more likely that the current which pours through the Messena strait was against them. This strait connects the Adriatic and Tyrrhenian (Etruscan) Seas.

They got a favourable southerly again and were on their way up the coast of Italy, perhaps sailing between Capri and the mainland. They were now in the Bay of Neapolis (Naples) with the great mountainous peak of Vesuvius (1,267 m) on their starboard hand. Later in 63, it would begin to stir and eventually suddenly erupt in 79 CE bringing an end to Herculaneum and Pompeii.

The region that Puteoli, the arrival port of Paul's vessel, was located in Campania. The city which lay to the west on the north shore of the Bay of Neapolis has been identified with the ancient port of Pozzuoli. The history of this busy port went back to the eighth century BCE and began with a small colony by nearby Cumae at Dicearchia ('just government'), the present-day Rione Terra, the tip of the long promontary. The settlement enjoyed a natural harbour perfect for handling large ships and after the mid-second century BCE became the principal port of arrival for the Alexandrian grain trade. From Seneca we learn that whenever the grain ships were sighted on the horizon people rushed to the port to watch them. This flourishing period lasted well into the second century CE when its function was gradually usurped by Ostia at the mouth of the Tiber. Strabo says that the settlement took its name from the wells (Latin *putei*) or from the foul smell (Latin *puteo*, 'stink') because of the sulphur and hot waters of the district.

Puteoli at the time of Paul's arrival still served as the main port of Italy for trade coming from the Mediterranean. The epigraphic material brought to light by excavations has shown that the leading families of the city such as the Calpurnii had trade connections with Anatolia and the Levant from which there were trading groups living here and who had brought along their own deities and cults. Cicero mentions a Marcus Cluvius of Puteoli who had an agent at Ephesus and lent money to the Carian cities of Mylasa, Alabanda, Heraclea, Bargylia and Caunus. When Paul's ship anchored here the sailing season had, probably, not yet begun and it lacked its summer activity when thousands of tradesmen or merchant agents traded in wine, olive oil, slaves, grain and other supplies of more luxurious nature.

Great harbour of Syracuse. Sicily. In the foreground is the spring Arethusa which as Strabo says 'empties immediately into the sea'.

Here Paul was permitted by his escorting officer to stay for a week with the small Christian community he found. Julius would probably be busy with arranging transportation for his prisoners for Rome. He may also have thought that his soldiers deserved a break after such a long voyage. He knew in any case that Paul would not desert. The distance between Puteoli and the capital was some 250 km. The road first went to Capua, at the time the second city of Italy after Rome, to join the Via Appia coming from Brundisium (Brindisi).The latter received almost all of the traffic arriving in Italy by way of the Via Egnatia across the Adriatic. Capua also had one of the earliest gladiator schools where the revolt of Spartacus had begun. After touching the coast at Minturna, Formia and Anxur (Terracina) the Via Appia ran as far as Rome in a straight course through the Pomptine marshes. Heavy loads were carried through a canal by mule-drawn barges from Terracina as far as the Forum Appii, where the canal ended. A similar barge may have been used for the transportation of the prisoners since some Christians from Rome waited for the apostle at the Forum of Appius (Forum

Appii and the Three Taverns (Tres Tabernae). The settlement was established by Appius Claudius, the builder of the Appian Way, and was about some 60 km from Rome. In the apocryphal *Acts of Peter* the captain after reaching Puteoli says to Peter 'tarry and refresh yourself, and so shalt thou set forth: for from hence to Rome upon a pavement of flint I fear lest thou be hurt by the shaking'. Nothing is known about the Three Taverns (Tres Tabernae), mentioned as the second station in Acts some 40 km before Rome. The road of Paul's time, passing by the Temple of Mars, entered the capital by the Porta Capena and descended by the Palatine toward the forum.

The first arrival of Jews in Rome is not known. 1 Maccabees informs us that they were there about the mid-second century BCE. Ancient literature informs us that in 139 BCE a number of Jews were expelled from Rome for their proselytizing activities directed toward the Romans. A more reliable date about their existence here is 63 BCE when Pompey brought them as prisoners of war following his conquest of Judea. Josephus' words that when a Jewish delegation came from Palestine in 61 BCE 8,000 of the Jews of Rome accompanied them when Julius Caesar met them is regarded with suspicion. These slaves were later supplemented by those brought following various Roman and Jewish conflicts. Some of these slaves are thought in time to have gained their freedom by manumission and become Roman

Harbour of Pozzuoli (Puteoli).

citizens. According to Josephus in 19 CE Tiberius is said to have deported 4,000 able-bodied Jews to Sardinia and expelled the rest from the capital for being members of a 'superstitious faith'.

Research has shown the Jewish communities were settled in the suburbs of Rome mostly at Transtiberinum, on the western bank of the Tiber and excavations have brought to light the ruins of a first-century-BCE synagogue at Rome's port city Ostia. Epigraphical evidence shows that there were also other synagogue buildings in Rome named after benefactors such as Herod, Marcus Agrippa or Augustus. Some scholars estimate the number of the Jewish population in Rome at the time of Paul as 20,000, and their largest settlement was in Transtiberinum (Trastevere), across the Tiber and the district along the via Appia outside Porta Capena.

The beginning of Christianity in Rome is obscure. The remark in Acts 2.10 that there were Jewish 'travellers from Rome' in Jerusalem during Pentecost, probably in the year 30, is regarded by scholars to refer to Roman citizens not to visitors from Jewish Rome. According to Acts 12.17 at the time of the persecutions of Herod Agrippa in 43 CE, the year before his death, Peter left Jerusalem and went 'to another place'. Christian tradition regards the expression as an allusion to Rome and consequently regards Peter as the founder of the Roman church. 'Christ-faith' may have first been introduced by Jewish pilgrims coming from Jerusalem to both Jews and Gentiles. Even if, as is mentioned in Acts 18.2, 'all the Jews' and even some Gentile Christians

The market place (*macellum*) near the port. Pozzuoli (Puteoli). It is also known as the Temple of Serapis after a statue of the deity that was found here. The god was a patron of seamen and merchants and his statue may have been dedicated by an enclave of Egyptian merchants whose existence in the city went back to the second century BCE.

A stretch of the Via Appia. Rome. The road was begun as early as 312 BCE by Appius Claudius Caecus after whom it was named, to reach Capua, the largest city of Campania faster, and in time was extended as far as Brundisium on the eastern coast of Italy. It is the oldest of the Roman roads known and first one to be named after a person. The width of the path, which is still in use, varies from about 5 to 6 metres. After defeating Spartacus in 71 BCE the Roman triumvir Marcus Crassus crucified some 6,000 prisoners along this road.

who were proselytes and lived like Jews, were expelled from Rome by Claudius in 49, this must have left some Gentile Christians in the city. When the Jewish Christians who were expelled by Claudius returned after Nero in 54 CE rescinded Claudius' edict, they found a church which was predominantly Gentile. Even if they had gathered in the synagogues until the edict of Claudius, by this date they had begun to establish their own assemblies in house churches and the relation between these and the Jewish Christians who now came back must have been strained. In Rom 15.1-13 this separation is reflected when Paul asks the Jews and Gentiles in the city to welcome each other, just as Christ welcomed and accepted them. Paul's words in Rom 1.13 that he 'often planned' to visit the city, and in 15.22 that he was 'so often prevented from coming' and in 15.23 that he has 'desired to come' for many years show that a visit to the capital had been on his mind for a long time. It has been speculated that he planned to visit the city during his second journey but was prevented from doing so upon hearing of the edict of Claudius when he was in Macedonia.

In Rome Paul seems to have lived in his own quarters, under house arrest chained or handcuffed in part of a tenement rented and paid for by himself

Pyramid of Cestius by St Paul's Gate. First century BCE. Rome. This 40-m high marble-covered pyramid, built beside the ancient Via Ostiensis leading from Rome to Ostia, showed Rome's growing interest in her new province of Egypt. It was erected as a funerary monument to the praetor Cestius. Eusebius in his *The History of the Church*,

written about 311 CE, records the tradition: 'It is related that in his [Nero's] time Paul was beheaded in Rome itself' he then quotes an earlier writing as associating this with 'the Ostian way'. If this tradition is not wrong Paul would have passed by this pyramid on the way to execution.

and his supporters. Scholars have pointed out that at about that time the monthly rent of an upper floor apartment (cheaper than the lower ones) was about two months pay of a common worker and Paul's financial sources have been questioned. Still, it is believed that somebody like Paul, even in the service of his Gospel, would not have used the collection if it had been refused by the Jerusalem church. It was probably in the vicinity of a barracks, for day and night there was a soldier on duty, chained to him. Paul called on the Jewish elders who did not have any information about him and wanted to hear his message that 'was denounced everywhere'. At the end even though only 'some were convinced by what he said' there was no opposition to him. The church in Rome would have certainly known about Paul's missionary activities and Paul's letter to the Romans shows that his picture there was not a popular one. Acts concludes with the words 'He remained for two full years in his lodgings. He received all who came to him and with complete assurance and without hindrance he proclaimed the kingdom of God and taught about the Lord Jesus Christ'. Some of his letters, to the Philippians, Philemon, Colossians, and Ephesians (if by Paul) may have also been written during this imprisonment.

Paul would to the last have been able to insist on the rights of a Roman citizen. As a Roman citizen, he was not subject to any sort of humiliation and he would normally have been beheaded, as a later tradition claims. Even if Paul's death did not take place immediately after the two-year captivity mentioned in Acts it seems highly unlikely that he survived Nero's persecution of the Christians which followed after the great fire of Rome in 64. Historians agree that the fire started accidentally. As the city was composed largely of wooden tenements it would have spread swiftly from house to house if a wind was blowing. Nero looked around for a scapegoat, and found an easy one in the most unpopular sect in Rome — the Christians. The Jews with their arrogance, their extraordinary god, and their strange eating and social habits were bad enough — but even Jews hated the Christians. By this time the Romans were able to distinguish the Jews from the Jewish or Gentile Christians.

Some of the monuments whose meager ruins have survived here to the present day existed when Paul was in Rome. One of them was the Basilica Julia, dedicated by Julius Caesar in 46 BCE. This was the main hall of justice; and Paul may have been condemned to death here. On one side of the Palatine hill stood the Mamertine Prison (Carcer Mamertinus) used for state prisoners. A room made out of one of the vaults beneath the Church of San

Synagogue. Ostia. The core of the building shows brickwork, common to the buildings of Ostia in the latter part of the first century CE. The standing four columns belonged to the inner entrance, with the Torah shrine of the later period to one side of the main hall. This ruin is the only known diaspora synagogue which has been claimed as having been built originally for this purpose, not adapted from another building.

Giuseppe dé Falegnami has traditionally come to be known as the place where Paul was imprisoned. Among the famous political prisoners who ended their lives hereabouts were Vercingetorix, the commander of Gallic rebellion (d 46 BCE). Sejanus, the infamous minister of Tiberius (d 31 CE), and Simon ben ('son of') Gioras (d 70 CE), the defender of Jerusalem during the First Jewish War.

There are several traditions about the site in which Paul's martyrdom took place and his burial. The priest Gaius, writing at the end of the second century in his defence against the heresy of the Phrygian Montanist Proclus says 'But I can point out the monuments [burials] of the victorious apostles [Peter and Paul]. If you will go as far as the Vatican or the Ostian Way, you will find the monuments of those who founded this church'. Proclus was leader of the Phrygian Montanists[5] who believed that the world was soon

[5] A heretic movement of this period which originated with one Montanus and the prophetesses Priscilla and Maximilla in Phrygia about 165 and lasted until the mid-sixth century CE. They proclaimed that he was the one promised in John's Gospel (14.26; 16.7) and the heavenly Jerusalem would soon descend on Pepuza (Kara Yakup, 'Black Jacob' village near Karahallı, Uşak).

coming to an end, and to support the legitimacy of his claim that his beliefs were founded on ancient church tradition he pointed to the tombs of Philip and his daughters in Hierapolis (Pamukkale) and others. In answer, Gaius was able to show in Rome the memorials of Paul and Peter to validate his claim. In the course of time the other traditions were superseded and the two churches came to be accepted as the burial spots of Paul and Peter. The first church over the traditional tomb of Paul would be built by Constantine the Great about 324. This was also one of the first churches in Rome, later called St Paul Outside the Walls (San Paolo fuori le Mura). Two marble slabs bearing the inscriptions PAULO APOSTOLO MART ('To Paul, apostle and martyr') were brought to light during the building of the present-day church and are believed by some to date to the time of Constantine. In the course of time Peter alone would come to be regarded as the founder of the church in Rome and its First Pope. Under the present altar and the *Confessio Petri* in St Peter's are the remains of the memorial built by Constantine over the traditional tomb of Peter. Some regard the fact that both graves are located in pagan necropoleis may point to the authenticity of the tradition because of the fact that later tradition would not have chosen such places.

Entrance to the traditional prison of Paul and Peter under the Church of San Giuseppe de' Falegnami. Rome.

Church of St Paul Outside the Walls. Rome.

FOURTH JOURNEY

Later tradition informs us that Paul was tried at the imperial court and was acquitted. According to the letter that Clement, Bishop of Rome, wrote to the Corinthians (First Clement 5.1-7) perhaps around the end of the first century, Paul 'passed out of this world' after he reached 'the furthest limits of the West', that is to the Pillars of Heracles (Strait of Gibraltar). This implies that having been released, Paul journeyed to Spain. In Rom 15.24,28 the apostle expresses his plans to go to Spain. In Spain, however, there is no surviving tradition about Paul's visit.

The Pastoral Letters also suggest that Paul was released from prison and made other journeys. In 2 Tm 4.16-18 Paul says 'At my first defense no one appeared on my behalf, but everyone deserted me. May it not be held against them! But the Lord stood by me and gave me strength, so that through me the proclamation might be completed and all the Gentiles might hear it. And I was rescued from the lion's mouth'. Once released the apostle may have resumed his missionary activities. His companions were Timothy and Titus. In I Tm 1.3 Paul mentions leaving Timothy in Ephesus and himself going to Macedonia from where he sends the letter.

According to the letter to Titus, Paul seems to have left Titus in Crete (Ti 1.5) and Timothy at Ephesus on his way to Macedonia. As he intended to return to Ephesus Paul was arrested again, probably at Troas (2 Tm 4.13). Under Roman custody Paul seems to have stopped at Miletus, leaving Trophimus sick there (2 Tm 4.20). In his letter to Titus (3.12) he also mentions the city of Nicopolis ('city of victory') saying that he has decided to spend the winter there but it is not known if he went. The site, which was near the place the battle was fought, was founded by Augustus to commemorate his defeat of Anthony and Cleopatra in the sea battle off Actium in 31 BCE. Some scholars depending on the information in the Pastorals claim that Paul spent a summer at Ephesus and another one in Crete and Greece.

Paul was again in chains in Rome and contact with him proved highly risky. Everyone from Asia deserted him. In this case tradition places Paul's death in Rome during Nero's persecution of Christians around 67.

Colossae

Colossae (Honaz) was founded on two hills side by side by the River Lycus. By the first century CE the city was no longer the large and prosperous city it had been in the fifth century BCE, when the Persian King Xerxes stopped here after Celaenae (Apamea/Dinar) on his way to the conquest of Greece, according to Herodotus. Some eighty years later, in 401 BCE, Cyrus the Younger travelled through the region in the opposite direction to dethrone his brother. When the wars between Alexander's generals came to an end at about the end of the fourth century BCE the region became a part of the Seleucid Kingdom. The latter did not miss the strategic location of Colossae on the north-south and east-west military routes, and refounded it.

Scholars have noticed ambiguities about the origin of the apostle's letter to the Colossians. It was written when Paul was in prison. In Rome, Paul was not in prison. It was written at the same time as another prison letter, to the Ephesians (if written by Paul) which could not have been written from Ephesus. In addition to Tychicus, who took the letter to its address, the mentioning of Timothy, Aristarchus and Luke fits better to his captivity at Rome. It has been

Mound of Colossae. Looking toward Mount Honaz (2,500 m).

speculated that the letter may have been written by Timothy who is introduced as the co-author at its beginning. It is believed that the city was destroyed by the earthquake which destroyed Laodicea in 60 CE according to the *Annals* of Tacitus. The fact that this important event is not mentioned in Paul's letter has led commentators to suggest that the letter must have been written before the event, thus at the beginning of Paul's captivity.

Although it is not clear if Paul passed through the region as he travelled 'through the Phrygian and Galatian territory' (Acts 16.6) on his way to Bithynia on his second journey, there is a good chance that he walked through the Lycus (Aksu) valley on the third journey. Acts 18.23 speaks of his travelling 'through Galatian country and Phrygia,' and 19.1 of his going 'through the interior of the country for reaching Ephesus'. This should very probably be interpreted as a route by way of Apamea (Dinar), Colossae (Honaz) and Laodicea on Lycus (Goncalı) in the direction of Philadelphia and Sardis. Although his words 'and for those in Laodicea and all who have not seen me face to face' (Col 2.1) make it clear that the Colossians had not seen him in the flesh, he may have passed through their cities on one of the journeys or visited during his long stay in Ephesus on the third journey. In his letter to Philemon of Colossae (22) the apostle asks for a guest room to be prepared for him.

Epaphras, the leader of the church in Colossae, came to where Paul was imprisoned and informed the apostle of the situation in his parish. It was Epaphras 'our beloved slave' (Col 1.7) who took Christianity to the city and neighbouring Laodicea and Hierapolis in the Lycus valley. He reported that the Colossians were attracted by some more sophisticated cults than that which was preached by the apostle.

In addition to the fact that Paul regarded all the believers in his churches as sharing a universal fellowship, his statement in his letter to the Colossians 'for you [Colossae] and for those in Laodicea and those in Hierapolis' (4.13) shows that he regarded the congregations in the Lycus valley as belonging to a single church and saying 'when this letter is read before you, have it read also in the church of the Laodiceans and you yourselves read the one from Laodicea' (4.16) associated these with each other.

From Paul's letter we learn that the Colossians had cultivated their own angel cult which was based on some Hellenistic and Jewish elements founded on some kind of mystic ascetism.

Hierapolis

The city is thought to have been refounded on the site of an ancient religious centre as its name means 'city of the sanctuary'. Its founder may have been the Seleucid King Antiochus I or II. It is not known if some of the Jewish families whom Antiochus III is said to have moved to Lydia and Phrygia from the east were settled here. To date the earliest epigraphic material about the existence of Jews in Hierapolis is not earlier than the late second century. It is very probable that they were in the city at Paul's time or earlier. In Col 4.13 Paul informs us that Epaphras 'works very hard' for the Christians Colossae and also at Laodicea and Hierapolis and that it was Epaphras who took the new faith to the region (1.7). Traditions which claim the evangelization of the region by Philip are confusing is that it is not clear if he was one of the twelve apostles or Philip the evangelist of Acts 21.9.

Reused sarcophagus lid bearing a menorah and inscription in Greek, which reads 'Belonging to the Jews', at the top of the door of a Roman tomb. Northern necropolis of Hierapolis (Pamukkale). The tomb seems to have belonged to the first century CE. The lid was placed on top at a later period by a Jewish family who used it for itself.

Laodicea

Laodicea on Lycus (Goncalı) is thought to have been founded by the Seleucid King Antiochus II, Theos (261-246 BCE) and named after his wife Laodice. Since he is known to have divorced Laodice in 253, the city may have been founded before this date. The name of the River Lycus (Aksu) near which it was founded was attached to the name of the city to distinguish it from the other settlements of the same name. The Lycus was a tributary of the Meander whose water has been a major source of the region's agricultural wealth. As usual the spot chosen for the new city was on the most important trade and military route from the Aegean coast to the interior of Anatolia and Syria.

The early population of the city probably consisted of the natives of the area, Hellenized Greeks and veteran soldiers in the army of Antiochus II. The origins of the Jewish community in the city may have dated back to the end of the third century BCE when Antiochus III moved some Jewish families from Mesopotamia and settled them in western Anatolia. After the battle of Magnesia (190 BCE) which the Seleucids lost against Rome, the region, including this city, was given to Eumenes II of Pergamum for his help in the battle. In 133 BCE in accordance with the will of Attalus III, the last king of Pergamum, Laodicea was incorporated in the Roman Empire together with the rest of western Anatolia.

Pipeline (double) which brought water to Laodicea from the east.

Columned street and monumental fountain which was later turned into a church. Laodicea.

The population of the city must have included a Jewish community during the Roman period for Josephus informs us that in 62 BCE the Roman governor Lucius Valerius Flaccus confiscated the annual sum of gold (more than 200 pounds in weight) that the Laodicean Jews had collected to be sent to the Jerusalem Temple. After a few years the local people wrote to the proconsul of Asia Gaius Rabirius that in accordance with his command they would allow the Jews to follow their customs and regard them as friends. The city was also the centre of the thriving wool industry in the region. In his letters Cicero relates how badly the region was exploited both by the local officials and the previous Roman governors.

Although Laodicea received the generosity of the Roman Emperors less than the rival coastal cities, it was founded on the network of trade routes and close to fresh water sources and flourished easily. Unfortunately, it was also founded on the major earthquake belt and natural disasters interrupted its progress and growth frequently. Strabo refers to these earthquakes by saying that the region is 'full of holes'. From Tacitus we learn that the city suffered a big one in 60 CE while Paul was in captivity in Rome.

Although the city being on the main Roman road from Lycaonia to Ephesus, was on Paul's way during the third journey, Acts does not mention it. In Col 4.13 Paul tells us that the city was evangelized by Epaphras and that they should read the letter that he had written to Laodicea (4.16).

Theatre. Laodicea. Looking toward Hierapolis (Pamukkale, 'cotton citadel') in the background to the left.

Grotto of St Paul with the wall paintings of apostle and Thecla. Sixth century. Ephesus. Courtesy of Österreichisches Archäologisches Institut.

Story of Paul and Thecla

If it may be summarized very briefly, for Paul celibacy was an ideal Christian condition because it did not prescribe any worldly obligation which might prevent one from devotion to the Lord. This message and the absurdity of marriage in the light of the expected kingdom of God was taken further in the course of time and became a source of popularity of legends of virgins in Anatolia.

The legend of Thecla begins with Paul's flight from Antioch to Iconium and his preaching there. His praise of the virgin life and resurrection attracted a certain girl named Thecla, who sat and eavesdropped on Paul at the open window of her house, because her mother did not let her go and listen to the apostle. Thecla's mother, alarmed about the devotion of her daughter to the preaching of Paul, took the news to her fiancé Thamyris; 'for three days and three nights Thecla did not arise from the window, neither to eat nor to drink...this man upset the whole city of the Iconians...for all the women and the young men go in to him'. When Thamyris' efforts to prevent the young girl from listening to the apostle gave no result, the men of Iconium caught Paul and brought him to the office of the governor where he was accused of corrupting young girls, teaching them to stay virgins and not to marry, thus disregarding the traditional customs. The governor ordered Paul to be thrown into prison so that he could listen to him later at leisure.

When Thecla learned what had happened, she left her home in secret and bribing the doorman and the jailer entered the prison and 'went in to Paul and sat by his feet and heard the wonderful works of God...as she kissed his chains'.

The following morning, however, when she was found in the prison, the governor ordered Paul to be scourged and thrown out of the city. Thecla was also brought to trial and condemned to be burned in the theatre so that this might teach a lesson to all the women who had listened to and believed in the apostle. When the pile of wood and straw on which she was placed bound to the stake was lighted, a sudden rainshower put out the pyre and Thecla was saved. Changing into male attire she searched for Paul and found him in a new tomb outside the city[1] where he was hiding with

[1] The text reads on the way 'from Iconium to Daphne' which is near Antioch on Orontes.

Icon of Thecla. Twentieth century. Barnabas Museum. North Cyprus.

Onesiphorus and his family. Thecla vowed to cut her hair short and follow the apostle wherever he went. Paul saying 'The time is ill-favoured and thou art comely' refused her wish. Thecla, nevertheless, followed him to Antioch.[2]

In Antioch a Syrian nobleman named Alexander saw Thecla and falling in love with her on the spot tried to buy her from Paul with money and gifts. When the man tried to take her physically she resisted, tearing the man's cloak and taking his crown with the figure of Caesar (the priestly crown of the imperial cult) from his head.

Thecla was taken before the governor and charged with sacrilege and condemned to wild beasts. Another text adds that it was Alexander who gave the spectacle. Epigraphic material from the region dating from the last quarter of the first century CE mentions the existence of a wooden amphitheatre for animal fights and gladiatorial combats in Pisidian Antioch, and the games held here may have inspired the writer of the story of Thecla at this point. Several attempts to carry out the verdict failed. She was thrown to lions and bears but saved by a lioness which 'licked her feet' and was slain after saving her from the other animals. Then saying 'In the name of Jesus Christ do I baptize myself on the last day' she jumped into the great pit of water full of seals and the wild beasts were struck dead by a flash of lightning that did not harm her. Thus Thecla was also baptized and whether married or not was now bound to live a celibate life, the act symbolizing her decision to stay celibate and her covenant with Christ that ruled out sexual intercourse forever. Her naked body was shielded by a curtain of fire. When the last beast let into the theatre did not touch her she was bound by the feet between the bulls and hot irons were put under the animals' bellies, but the flame burned the ropes and she was saved. Meanwhile one of the spectators, Queen Tryphaena ('lady magnificence') who had lost her daughter a short while earlier and who had given Thecla shelter in her house, fainted and Alexander thought that she had died. Worrying that the Emperor might punish the city and that her death would be bad for his city, Thecla was forgiven. Queen Tryphaena is a historical personage. She is thought to have already been a very old age during the time of Paul's journeys. At the time of Paul's travels, from 41 CE a part of Rough Cilicia was given to her son Polemo II by Claudius and this may have been the reason why her name is associated with the episode.

[2] The texts say only 'Antioch' and whether it means Pisidian Antioch or Antioch on Orontes is disputed. The appearance of the Syrian infers the latter.

Remains of the apse (westernmost quarter) of the church built above the grotto of Thecla. Meryemlik. Silifke (Seleucia on Calycadnus).

At the end of the episode Thecla dressed as a boy searches for Paul and finds him at Myra in Lycia. Thecla told the apostle her sufferings for Christ's sake and received her baptism: 'I have received the washing [the vow of lifelong celibacy], O Paul; for he that has worked together with thee in the Gospel has worked with me also unto my baptizing'. Paul offered her the commission of teaching the Gospel. Later, Thecla returned to Iconium but did not stay there. She went to Seleucia on Calycadnus (Silifke) where she retired to a cave on Mount Calamon and lived to the age of ninety. When she was threatened by men, who were jealous of her healing powers, for she was by then running a nunnery which threatened the business of local healers, she was saved by the rock of her cave opening to receive her. Although she died peacefully in her cave she was regarded as the first Christian woman martyr. Her sanctuary became a popular place of pilgrimage. A tradition adds that she went underground to Rome which accounts for the presence of her body there.

Christian tradition regards a cave at Silifke's Meryemlik ('place of Mary') district as the place where Thecla disappeared into the rock. In the fourth century the cave was probably enlarged and given the shape of an underground basilica. The reused building material shows that there was a Roman building here probably belonging to a pagan shrine. During the second half of the fifth century a church, one of the largest in Cilicia, was built over the cave.Only a section of its apse has survived to the present. Pilgrimage to this cave church was revered throughout Byzantine history and at one time its walls were probably decorated with mosaics.

The story of Thecla, the most famous virgin martyr of early Christianity, is narrated in the apocryphal *Acts of Paul* which is thought to have been recorded by a presbyter in Anatolia toward the end of the second century. According to Tertullian its author was deposed from the church for writing this document which created a false view of Paul and the role of women in the church, such that in the Pastoral Letters Paul permits 'no woman to teach (1 Tm 2.12)' and condemns those who 'forbid marriage' (1 Tm 4.3). In the story Thecla is discouraged from matrimony and encouraged to become a teacher, tendencies best manifested in the Montanist movement which was then growing in Anatolia. Its popularity has led some scholars to believe that the story may have been based on a real Christian martyr of the same name.

IC XC
NI KA

Abbreviations

Acts	Acts of the Apostles	Gal	Galatians	OT	Old Testament
AV	Authorized Version	Gn	Genesis	p	page
BCE	Before the Common Era (BC)	Is	Isaiah	Ps	Psalms
CE	Common Era (AD, *anno Domini*, 'in the year of the Lord')	Jn	John	Phil	Philippians
		Jon	Jonah	Phlm	Philemon
		1 Kgs	1 Kings	1 Pt	1 Peter
2 Chr	2 Chronicles	2 Kgs	2 Kings	Rom	Romans
cm	centimetre(s)	km	kilometre(s)	1 Sm	1 Samuel
Col	Colossians	Lk	Luke	St	Saint
1 Cor	1 Corinthians	m	metre(s)	1 Thes	1 Thessalonians
2 Cor	2 Corinthians	1 Mc	1 Maccabees	2 Thes	2 Thessalonians
d	death/died	2 Mc	2 Maccabees	Ti	Titus
Dt	Deuteronomy	Mk	Mark	1 Tm	1 Timothy
Eccl	Ecclesiastes	Mt	Matthew	2 Tm	2 Timothy
Ez	Ezekiel	NT	New Testament		

(opposite) One of the hundreds of graffiti which Christians carved to consecrate pagan temples and tombs in Anatolia, especially after Christianity became a free religion in the fourth century. This one is on the wall of a second-century-CE Roman funeral monument and in Greek reads: 'Jesus Christ, Nika ['victory']. Arycanda (Arif Köy). Lycia.

OTHER TITLES

HARDBACK

ANTIOCH MOSAICS a corpus (F. Cimok)

ICONS IN TURKEY (N. Yılmaz)

MOSAICS IN İSTANBUL (F. Cimok)

MOSAICS OF ANTIOCH (F. Cimok)

MOSAICS OF ZEUGMA (M. Önal)

PAINTINGS OF THE DARK CHURCH (H. Yenipınar & S. Şahin)

RELIEFS OF AHTAMAR (T. Harada)

SAINT SOPHIA (F. Cimok)

THE BOOK OF ALEXANDER SARCOPHAGUS (A. Pasinli)

THE BOOK OF RÜSTEM PAŞA TILES (F. Cimok)

THE LYDIANS AND SARDIS (H. Dedeoğlu)

SOFTCOVER

a guide to EDİRNE (G. Goodwin)

a guide to the SEVEN CHURCHES (F. Cimok)

BIBLICAL ANATOLIA (F. Cimok)

HAGIA SOPHIA (F. Cimok)

İSTANBUL ARCHAEOLOGICAL MUSEUMS (A. Pasinli)

NORTH CYPRUS (North Cyprus Museum Friends)

PERGAMUM (F. Cimok)

Saint Saviour in CHORA (F. Cimok)

TROIA (N. Sevinç)

TURKISH COOKING (G. Sancaklı & M. Oliphant)

for more information www.aturizm.com